INTERNATIONAL CONSUMPTION COMPARISONS

A System-Wide Approach

STUDIES IN MATHEMATICAL AND MANAGERIAL ECONOMICS

Editors

HENRI THEIL
HERBERT GLEJSER

VOLUME 30

NORTH-HOLLAND PUBLISHING COMPANY
AMSTERDAM–NEW YORK–OXFORD

INTERNATIONAL CONSUMPTION COMPARISONS
A System-Wide Approach

by

HENRI THEIL
University of Florida

and

FREDERICK E. SUHM
U.S. Army Corps of Engineers

with an Appendix by

JAMES F. MEISNER
University of Chicago

1981

NORTH-HOLLAND PUBLISHING COMPANY
AMSTERDAM–NEW YORK–OXFORD

ISBN 0 444 86 312 5

Publishers:
NORTH-HOLLAND PUBLISHING COMPANY
AMSTERDAM–NEW YORK–OXFORD

Sole distributors for the U.S.A. and Canada:
ELSEVIER/NORTH-HOLLAND INC.
52 VANDERBILT AVENUE
NEW YORK, N.Y. 10017

Library of Congress Cataloging in Publication Data

Theil, Henri.
International consumption comparisons.

(Studies in mathematical and managerial economics ; v. 30)
Bibliography: p.
Includes index.
1. Consumption (Economics)--Mathematical models.
I. Suhm, Frederick H. II. Meisner, James F.
III. Title. IV. Series.
HB801.T49 339.4'7'0724 81-18847
ISBN 0-444-86312-5 AACR2

Printed in The Netherlands

INTRODUCTION TO THE SERIES

This is a series of books concerned with the quantitative approach to problems in the social and administrative sciences. The studies are in particular in the overlapping areas of mathematical economics, econometrics, operational research, and management science. Also, the mathematical and statistical techniques which belong to the apparatus of modern social and administrative sciences have their place in this series. A well-balanced mixture of pure theory and practical applications is envisaged, which ought to be useful for universities and for research workers in business and government.

The Editors hope that the volumes of this series, all of which relate to such a young and vigorous field of research activity, will contribute to the exchange of scientific information at a truly international level.

THE EDITORS

PREFACE

This monograph is in the tradition of the system-wide approach to consumption theory and the analogous approach to econometric modeling in general. The origin of the latter topic is usually associated with Haavelmo's (1943, 1944) critique of the use of least squares in Tinbergen's (1939) League of Nations study. This critique stimulated considerable research activity at the Cowles Commission for Research in Economics of The University of Chicago, which was followed by even more activity at several other centers, and it ultimately led to the large number of econometric macromodels which are presently used to describe the operation of a national economy. Such models typically contain more than one endogenous variable in each equation; this was the main problem to which Haavelmo addressed himself. However, it was not generally recognized until recently that there may also be statistical problems when each equation contains only one endogenous variable. Such problems can be particularly serious when the equation system consists of many equations.

The system-wide approach to consumption theory has a shorter history; its origin is usually associated with Stone's (1954) application of the linear expenditure system to British data. The major research activity in this area started in the mid-1960s. Publications in monograph form include, in chronological order, Solari (1971), Phlips (1974), Powell (1974), Deaton (1975), Theil (1975–76), Lluch et al. (1977), Deaton and Muellbauer (1980a), Barnett (1981), and Deaton (1981). An extension of the system-wide approach to production theory was formulated by Laitinen (1980), while Theil (1980a) provided a survey of the area, covering both consumption and production theory, which puts less emphasis on technical details.

The main topic of this monograph is the application of the system-wide approach to international consumption data published by Kravis et al. (1978). This research started in collaboration with Kenneth W. Clements when he was on the Faculty of The University of Chicago. Clements left Chicago in 1979 to join the Research Department of the Reserve Bank of Australia, and in 1981 he accepted a chair at the University of Western Australia. Clements and Theil (1979) applied Working's (1943) model to a four-good classification; they used this model as a starting point for the construction of a complete demand system in preference-independent form. Subsequently, Suhm (1979a, b, c, d) extended this approach to an eight-good classification, while Clements et al. (1979) and Suhm and Theil (1979) provided further results for this classification.

The papers mentioned in the previous paragraph are based on a two-step procedure, the first step of which consists of estimating income effects while ignoring the relative-price differences of the four (or eight) goods across countries, while the second step consists of estimating the effects of relative prices on demand given the estimated income effects obtained in the first step. It is clearly more attractive to estimate income and relative-price effects simultaneously rather than consecutively, particularly since the data published by Kravis and his colleagues show that there is correlation among income and relative prices across countries. This simultaneous estimation was performed by Theil, Suhm and Meisner (1980), and it led to different estimates of the parameters. In this monograph all earlier results have been updated and extended.

After the first draft of this monograph was completed, it became apparent that more attention should be paid to the problems of testing demand homogeneity and Slutsky symmetry and of symmetry-constrained estimation. These are among the problems alluded to above (see the end of the first paragraph). The work of Klevmarken (1975), Laitinen (1978) and Meisner (1979a) has shown that the application of standard statistical tests to hypotheses such as demand homogeneity and Slutsky symmetry may lead to serious error. Such tests are asymptotic tests, but the accuracy of the asymptotic distribution of the test statistics as an approximation to the true distribution diminishes rapidly as the demand system consists of more equations. One possible way of solving this problem is by means of the maximum entropy distribution proposed by Theil and Laitinen (1980). This approach is pursued in the Appendix to this monograph. The evidence (based on simulation experiments) is rather encouraging, particularly for symmetry-constrained estimation. Recently, the maximum entropy distribution has also been used for several other statistical problems such as the estimation of medians and quartiles, the estimation of covariance matrices from multivariate samples with missing values, and the estimation of systems of simultaneous equations from undersized samples. Therefore, we hope that the Appendix will also be useful for statistically oriented readers whose primary interest is not in consumption theory.

We are indebted to Kenneth W. Clements and to Herbert Glejser (Free University of Brussels and Faculté Universitaire Notre Dame de la Paix at Namur, Belgium), who provided comments on the first version of this monograph; to Delores Conway of The University of Chicago and to Denzil Fiebig, Arie Kapteyn, and Esfandiar Maasoumi of the University of Southern California for the numerous discussions which we had with them on the maximum entropy distribution; and to the National Science Foundation for its support by means of a series of grants.

THE AUTHORS

Chicago, June 1981

CONTENTS

LIST OF TABLES

Chapter 6

Appendix B

Appendix C

Appendix D

Appendix E

Chapter 1

PROLOGUE

The traditional sources of empirical economic information on consumer behavior are family budget data, which offer the opportunity for cross-section analysis, and time series data on per capita consumption. Such data are typically confined to one country, but it has long been recognized that a comparison of consumption across countries would be quite valuable. We refer here to the pioneering work of Houthakker (1957, 1960a, 1961, 1963, 1965) and to the more recent monograph by Lluch et al. (1977).

The major promise and also the major difficulty provided by international comparisons results from the differences in per capita real incomes across countries. Such differences are large, which is promising from the viewpoint of accurately estimating the income effects on demand, but since incomes in different countries are expressed in different currencies, it is difficult to determine how large their differences actually are. An attempt to solve this problem was made by Kravis and his colleagues (1975, 1978) for the U.N. International Comparison Project at the University of Pennsylvania. These authors did not use exchange rates to convert expenditures in national currencies; for a variety of reasons, using exchange rates results in an overestimation of the difference in affluence between rich and poor countries, at least on the average. Rather, they estimated purchasing power parities across countries for detailed consumption categories such as fresh vegetables (see Section 2.1), after which they aggregated these categories in order to obtain price indexes and consumption volumes per capita for broader groups of goods. The volume of total consumption per capita (used as a measure of per capita real income) varies considerably across countries as may be seen from line 9 of Table 2.3 on pp. 8 and 9 below.

A major objective of this monograph is to use these data (including price data) to establish a system of cross-country demand equations. The underlying assumption is that "all countries are the same" in the sense that their per capita consumption of goods and services can be viewed as being generated by essentially the same consumer preferences. If this assumption is acceptable, the only (but major!) differences between countries result from their differences in income and prices, apart possibly from random effects. But this assumption immediately raises the objection that different nations have different cultures. We should expect that Indians spend little on meat and, indeed, the data produced by Kravis et al. confirm that this is so. The appropriate answer is that a cross-country demand system should be constructed, not for a very large number of detailed consumption categories, but only for a modest number of much broader categories. Accordingly, meat is part of a "good" called Food, which includes beverages and tobacco also. As a whole, we shall consider eight such goods, listed in Table 2.2 on p. 7. On the matter of the effect of different cultures on consumption habits, see also Clements and Johnson (1980) for an analysis of disparities of Australian income elasticities by the ethnic origin of the consumers (native Australians and immigrants from four countries or groups of countries).

The order of discussion is as follows. In Chapter 2 we describe the data used in this monograph, including the country-product-dummy (CPD) method which Kravis et al. used for the estimation of purchasing power parities at the level of detailed consumption categories. In Section 2.3 we apply a weighted version of the CPD method to the eight goods mentioned above, mainly in order to establish that there exists a systematic relationship among the independent variables of the demand system: on average, the prices of luxuries increase relative to those of necessities when we move from less affluent to more affluent countries. In particular, food (a necessity) is relatively cheaper than luxuries in the richer countries.

In Chapter 3 we present evidence of the validity of Working's (1943) model at the cross-country level and we enlarge this model by endowing it with a substitution term formulated in terms of Slutsky coefficients. Such an extension enables us to test for demand homogeneity and Slutsky symmetry, but these tests have serious statistical problems when the number of goods (eight in this case) is not small relative to the sample size. In the Appendix an effort is made to restore the standard F tests of homogeneity and symmetry by means of the maximum entropy distribution of the dependent and the independent variables of the demand system.

Given the size of the sample, and accurate estimation of the 8×8 Slutsky matrix is not a feasible project so that simplifying assumptions are necessary. We have estimated the demand system under the condition of preference independence, which means that the consumer's preferences can be represented by a utility function which is additive in the eight goods. This yields a manageable system of demand equations which we estimate by maximum likelihood. In Section 4.1 we compare the income elasticities of this system with those obtained when the differences in relative prices across countries are ignored. There are systematic differences between these two sets of elasticities, which should be ascribed to the relationship among the independent variables that was mentioned above (concerning price differences of luxuries and necessities depending on the affluence of the country).

Although the assumption of preference independence is restrictive, even when applied to broad groups of consumer goods, it does have the merit of greatly simplifying the picture. Chapters 4 to 6 exploit this feature by providing useful summary measures, mainly on a country-by-country basis. In particular, Chapter 5 discusses the quality of consumption measured by the luxury-necessity composition of the consumer's basket. It should come as no surprise that the most affluent countries have a higher quality of consumption index than the less affluent countries, but it is interesting that the quality index of the former countries is reduced relative to the latter by the substitution effect of relative prices. This effect results from the tendency of luxuries to be higher-priced than necessities in the more affluent countries. Chapter 7, finally, discusses possible applications and extensions of the results obtained in this monograph.

Chapter 2

THE DATA

The objective of this chapter is to describe the methodology used by Kravis and his colleagues for the construction of their data, to present the basic data used in this monograph, and to discuss an empirical relation based on these data between relative prices and real per capita income across countries. The description of the methodology of the data construction will be brief and somewhat simplified in minor respects. Details can be found in Kravis et al. (1975, Chap. 5).

2.1. The Country-Product-Dummy Method

Kravis and his colleagues divided national expenditures into more than 150 so-called detailed categories, including 110 categories for consumption expenditure. Each detailed category consists of one or several items. An example is shown in Table 2.1, from Kravis et al. (1975, p. 59), which deals with the 20 items of Fresh vegetables (one of the detailed categories) in 10 countries in 1970. The figures shown are prices per kilogram in national currencies, while – indicates that the relevant data are missing.

Let the objective be to construct purchasing power parities for Fresh vegetables from Table 2.1. The so-called country-product-dummy (CPD) method performs this by means of regressions of the logarithm of the price of each item in each country on two dummy variables, one for the item and one for the country,

$$\log p_{ic} = A_i + B_c + \text{residual} \tag{2.1}$$

where p_{ic} is the price of item i in country c and log (here and elsewhere in this monograph) stands for natural logarithm. The fitting method used by Kravis et al. is a weighted form of least squares, the weight of each country being selected so as to correct for the number of items with missing price data. The B_c's of the 10 countries are shown in the second-last row of Table 2.1, followed by their antilogs in the last line. The B_c's are normalized so that the U.S. value equals 0, and the antilogs are thus normalized so that the U.S. value equals 1. These antilogs are estimated

Table 2.1
Prices per kilogram of fresh vegetables in 10 countries in 1970

	Colombia (Peso)	France (Franc)	Germany[a] (D. Mark)	Hungary (Florint)	India (Rupee)	Italy (Lira)	Japan (Yen)	Kenya (Shilling)	U.K. (Pound)	U.S. (Dollar)	Coefficient A_i
1. Artichokes	–	2.75	3.26	–	–	646	–	–	–	2.22	.56
2. Beets	3.90	–	–	–	–	–	–	–	.07	.42	–.89
3. Brussels sprouts	–	2.35	1.69	–	–	485	–	–	–	1.89	–.23
4. Cabbage	1.41	.98	.55	2.9	.91	157	75.4	.47	.08	.32	–1.02
5. Cauliflower	5.33	1.90	1.13	–	1.27	195	156.6	2.58	.17	.63	–.18
6. Carrots	2.10	.93	.86	3.2	.75	172	115.1	2.58	.07	.39	–.67
7. Celery, pascal	4.49	–	–	–	–	–	–	–	–	.44	–.59
8. Cucumbers	–	–	–	4.7	.87	–	173.3	–	–	.61	–.39
9. Eggplant	–	–	–	–	.72	–	–	–	–	.59	–.63
10. Escarole	–	1.82	.98	–	–	212	–	–	–	–	–.41
11. Green peppers	17.40	2.62	2.32	8.7	–	186	195.4	–	–	1.16	.14
12. Kunde greens	–	–	–	–	.56	–	–	.79	–	.67	–.78
13. Lettuce	4.82	3.23	2.27	9.3	–	239	218.1	.62	–	.53	–.21
14. Mushrooms	–	7.90	5.60	–	–	790	–	–	.54	1.95	1.00
15. Onions, yellow	5.59	1.18	.86	4.8	.67	127[b]	98.6	.77	.13	.35	–.66
16. Radishes	–	–	–	–	.55	–	–	–	–	.88	–.68
17. Red cabbage	–	1.27	.56	–	–	–	–	–	–	.12	–1.20
18. Spinach	4.71	–	–	–	–	–	133.8	–	–	1.24	–.29
19. Tomatoes	5.79	2.55	1.85	6.7	1.21	226	160.9	1.19	.31	.92	–.10
20. Yellow squash	2.29	–	–	1.5	–	–	–	–	–	.66	–1.22
Coefficient B_c	1.96	.92	.57	2.02	.34	5.68	5.32	.57	–1.56	.00	
Antilog	7.11	2.52	1.77	7.53	1.41	291.9	204.5	1.76	.21	1.00	

[a] Federal Republic of Germany (West Germany).
[b] This entry represents a correction of the corresponding figure in Kravis et al. (1975, p. 59).

purchasing power parities of Fresh vegetables, or "prices" of this detailed category in national currencies. The A_i's of (2.1) are the coefficients of the 20 items that constitute Fresh vegetables. They are shown in the last column of Table 2.1, but they will play no further role in this monograph.

2.2. *The Data Used in This Monograph*

When expenditures on all detailed categories (in national currencies) are available and when their prices are obtained as outlined in Section 2.1, the next problem is to aggregate these results so that prices and volumes for broader groups are obtained. Kravis and his colleagues solved this problem using the Geary–Khamis method, which yields volumes in the form of expenditures in "international prices", and they applied a special weighting scheme in order to correct for the fact that the 10 countries listed in Table 2.1 are on average more affluent than the world as a whole. We refer to Kravis et al. (1975, Chap. 5) for further details.

In Kravis et al. (1978) the same procedure was applied to data for 16 countries in 1970 and 1973. The discussion from now on will be confined to these data for 1970, and in particular to eight consumption categories which will be referred to as the eight *goods* in the sequel. Table 2.2 gives a description of these goods, followed by the abbreviations which will be used throughout this monograph.

Table 2.2
Eight consumption goods

Description	Abbreviation
Food, beverages and tobacco	Food
Clothing and footwear	Clothing
Gross rent and fuel	Rent
House furnishings and operations	Furniture
Medical care	Medical care
Transport and communications	Transport
Recreation and education	Recreation
Other consumption expenditures	Other expenditure

The 16 countries are listed at the top of Table 2.3. The figures in the upper half of this table are per capita quantities valued at international prices. The entries in line 9 are the sums of the earlier figures in the same column. These sums measure total per capita consumption; they will be

Table 2.3
Per capita quantities and budget shares of eight goods in 16 countries in 1970

Good	U.S.	Bel-gium	France	Ger-many[a]	U.K.	Nether-lands	Japan
1. Food	714.2	631.9	686.8	512.0	645.2	586.9	452.8
2. Clothing	266.6	164.8	151.5	200.6	171.9	199.5	182.6
3. Rent	549.6	308.2	315.9	307.4	314.3	275.5	159.5
4. Furniture	259.5	255.2	171.0	273.8	126.4	239.1	128.3
5. Medical care	175.6	135.9	212.0	186.7	138.1	170.5	209.1
6. Transport	543.2	163.0	175.5	207.3	215.6	148.5	58.5
7. Recreation	397.6	273.4	200.0	223.6	273.2	226.6	161.4
8. Other	331.9	332.8	242.8	196.6	155.3	191.3	253.0
9. Total[d]	3238.2	2265.2	2155.5	2108.0	2040.0	2037.9	1605.2
1. Food	.1738	.2581	.2649	.2259	.2952	.2568	.3231
2. Clothing	.0734	.0806	.0862	.1015	.0779	.0958	.0913
3. Rent	.1739	.1448	.1294	.1378	.1702	.1126	.1441
4. Furniture	.0737	.1079	.0788	.1180	.0664	.1150	.0872
5. Medical care	.0975	.0629	.0969	.0871	.0597	.0754	.0797
6. Transport	.1367	.0955	.0993	.1100	.1098	.0849	.0394
7. Recreation	.1536	.1249	.1203	.1227	.1381	.1628	.1201
8. Other	.1175	.1254	.1241	.0969	.0826	.0967	.1152

[a] Federal Republic of Germany (West Germany).
[b] Republic of Korea (South Korea).
[c] Expenditures valued at international prices.
[d] The entries of this line differ from those in the first line of Summary Multilateral Table 4.5 of Kravis et al. (1978) because the latter include line number 110 (net expenditure of residents abroad) which is deleted here.
[e] Ratios from Summary Multilateral Table 4.1 of Kravis et al. (1978).

used as real income per capita in the sequel. (Note that the 16 countries are listed in the order of declining real income per capita.) The entries in the lower half of Table 2.3 are the budget shares of each good in each country, i.e., the shares of the eight goods in total consumption expenditure in national currency.

Table 2.4 contains the prices of the eight goods in national currencies, obtained by dividing corresponding entries of the Summary Multilateral Tables 4.1 (expenditures in national currencies) and 4.5 (quantities at international prices) of Kravis et al. (1978). The use of prices in different currencies for different countries presents no problems because we shall

Italy	Hun-gary	Iran	Colom-bia	Malay-sia	Philip-pines	Korea[b]	India	Kenya
Quantities[c]								
591.0	436.7	249.0	254.2	251.9	217.8	208.9	133.6	108.7
132.7	110.3	62.8	48.2	45.3	29.2	40.8	13.7	7.9
227.5	136.5	140.3	34.7	67.2	50.5	26.8	17.9	14.1
87.6	74.6	33.3	48.1	36.1	22.8	13.9	7.9	11.1
136.2	127.7	26.1	30.3	32.5	11.5	22.3	10.8	12.4
142.7	57.5	32.4	75.7	59.8	11.2	23.9	10.7	11.6
155.6	214.5	38.0	62.1	69.6	63.3	52.4	28.7	28.3
110.4	189.2	65.0	63.8	39.7	38.4	27.0	10.7	14.6
1583.7	1347.0	646.9	617.1	602.1	444.7	416.0	234.0	208.7
Budget shares[e]								
.3747	.3557	.4667	.3963	.4096	.5649	.5588	.6665	.4887
.0874	.1157	.0870	.0965	.0496	.0583	.1034	.0686	.0392
.1208	.0763	.1702	.0939	.1150	.1005	.0825	.0740	.1029
.0537	.0823	.0454	.0689	.0558	.0576	.0290	.0291	.0619
.0648	.0581	.0530	.0602	.0388	.0331	.0285	.0254	.0516
.1001	.0585	.0443	.1000	.1449	.0248	.0553	.0511	.0728
.1129	.1110	.0541	.0812	.1132	.0802	.0843	.0504	.1176
.0856	.1423	.0793	.1030	.0732	.0805	.0581	.0348	.0653

need only relative prices in the sequel. The lower part of Table 2.4 contains these prices in index form, obtained by dividing by the price of Food (which is shown in the first row of the table). Note that these price indexes tend to decline when we move from left to right in the table; we shall have more to say about this in Section 2.3.

2.3. A Weighted Version of the Country-Product-Dummy Method

Average Budget Shares as Weights

In (2.1) we considered the CPD method for an item of some detailed category, but it is of interest to apply it also to our eight goods. A comparison of Tables 2.1 and 2.4 shows that the latter application does not require us to bother about the problem of missing price data. Let w_{ic} be

Table 2.4
Prices of eight goods in 15 countries in 1970[a]

Good	U.S. (Dollar)	Belgium (B. Franc)	France (Franc)	Germany (D. Mark)	U.K. (Pound)	Netherlands (Guilder)	Japan (Yen)
						Prices in national currencies	
1. Food	.790	34.65	3.797	2.981	.2898	2.404	265.2
2. Clothing	.894	41.50	5.605	3.418	.2870	2.639	185.9
3. Rent	1.028	39.86	4.034	3.028	.3430	2.246	335.8
4. Furniture	.922	35.88	4.540	2.912	.3324	2.642	252.5
5. Medical care	1.803	39.26	4.500	3.150	.2738	2.428	141.7
6. Transport	.817	49.69	5.573	3.585	.3226	3.141	250.4
7. Recreation	1.255	38.74	5.923	3.708	.3201	3.947	276.4
8. Other	1.150	31.96	5.033	3.331	.3370	2.779	169.2
						Price indexes, Food = 1	
2. Clothing	1.13	1.20	1.48	1.15	.99	1.10	.70
3. Rent	1.30	1.15	1.06	1.02	1.18	.93	1.27
4. Furniture	1.17	1.04	1.20	.98	1.15	1.10	.95
5. Medical care	2.28	1.13	1.19	1.06	.94	1.01	.53
6. Transport	1.03	1.43	1.47	1.20	1.11	1.31	.94
7. Recreation	1.59	1.12	1.56	1.24	1.10	1.64	1.04
8. Other	1.46	.92	1.33	1.12	1.16	1.16	.64

[a] See Section 3.1 for the reason why Kenya is deleted. All columns in the upper part of this table are in three or four digits, but the calculations in this monograph are based on the ratios of corresponding entries in Summary Multilateral Tables 4.1 and 4.5 of Kravis et al. (1978) which permit more precision. See also notes a and b below Table 2.3.

the budget share of good i in country c (see the lower part of Table 2.3). We consider a weighted version of (2.1) of the form

$$n\bar{w}_i \log p_{ic} = \alpha_i + \beta_c + \epsilon_{ic} \tag{2.2}$$

where n is the number of goods ($n = 8$ in our case), ϵ_{ic} is a random disturbance, and

$$\bar{w}_i = \frac{1}{N} \sum_{c=1}^{N} w_{ic} \tag{2.3}$$

is the budget share of good i averaged over all countries, N being the number of countries.

The specification (2.2) has the merit of making homoscedasticity across goods more plausible because prices of goods with small budget shares may be expected to have larger random components than those of goods

Italy (Lira)	Hungary (Florint)	Iran (Rial)	Colombia (Peso)	Malaysia (M. Dollar)	Philippines (Peso)	Korea (Won)	India (Rupee)
471.3	15.30	35.42	7.26	1.279	2.147	160.0	2.810
489.6	19.71	26.17	9.33	.861	1.652	151.5	2.821
394.6	10.50	22.92	12.60	1.346	1.647	184.2	2.329
455.9	20.73	25.74	6.68	1.215	2.092	125.0	2.075
353.6	8.55	38.38	9.26	.939	2.385	76.5	1.326
521.3	19.13	25.85	6.15	1.905	1.834	138.5	2.692
539.4	9.72	26.91	6.09	1.279	1.048	96.3	.989
576.6	14.12	23.07	7.52	1.450	1.736	128.7	1.834
1.04	1.29	.74	1.29	.67	.77	.95	1.00
.84	.69	.65	1.74	1.05	.77	1.15	.83
.97	1.35	.73	.92	.95	.97	.78	.71
.75	.56	1.08	1.28	.73	1.11	.48	.47
1.11	1.25	.73	.85	1.49	.85	.87	.96
1.14	.64	.76	.84	1.00	.49	.60	.35
1.22	.92	.65	1.04	1.13	.81	.80	.65

with large budget shares. The least-squares estimates of α_i and β_c constrained by $\Sigma_c \beta_c = 0$ are

(2.4) $$\hat{\alpha}_i = n\bar{w}_i \log \bar{p}_i$$

(2.5) $$\hat{\beta}_c = \sum_{i=1}^{n} \bar{w}_i \log \frac{p_{ic}}{\bar{p}_i}$$

where $\bar{p}_i$ is the geometric mean price of good i across all countries:

(2.6) $$\log \bar{p}_i = \frac{1}{N} \sum_{c=1}^{N} \log p_{ic}$$

To verify that (2.4) and (2.5) constitute the least-squares solution subject to $\Sigma_c \beta_c = 0$, we write Y_{ic} for the left side of (2.2) and consider the Lagrangean function

$$\frac{1}{2} \sum_{i=1}^{n} \sum_{c=1}^{N} (Y_{ic} - \alpha_i - \beta_c)^2 - \mu \sum_{c=1}^{N} \beta_c$$

where μ is a Lagrangean multiplier. When we differentiate this function with respect to α_i and equate the derivative to zero, we obtain

$$-\sum_{c=1}^{N} (Y_{ic} - \alpha_i - \beta_c) = 0$$

which yields the solution $\alpha_i = (1/N) \Sigma_c Y_{ic}$ because $\Sigma_c \beta_c = 0$. This solution is equivalent to (2.4) in view of (2.6). Next we differentiate the Lagrangean function with respect to β_c and equate the result to zero:

$$-\sum_{i=1}^{n} (Y_{ic} - \alpha_i - \beta_c) - \mu = 0$$

This is equivalent to

$$n\beta_c = \mu + \sum_{i=1}^{n} (Y_{ic} - \alpha_i)$$

which yields $\mu = 0$ after summation over c because $\Sigma_c Y_{ic} = N\alpha_i$ and $\Sigma_c \beta_c = 0$. The solution (2.5) is then easily obtained. The zero value of the Lagrangean multiplier μ is due to the fact that imposing the constraint $\Sigma_c \beta_c = 0$ does not raise the residual sum of squares above the unconstrained minimum. Ultimately, this results from the fact that raising α_i for each i by any number k and lowering β_c for each c by the same k does not affect the right side of (2.2).

See also Clements and Izan (1981) and Clements and Nguyen (1980b) for a model similar to (2.2) in a time series context.

Relative Prices Dependent on Per Capita Real Income

Voltaire and Stack (1980) subtracted α_i from both sides of (2.2), using the estimate (2.4), which yields $n\bar{w}_i \log (p_{ic}/\bar{p}_i)$ on the left, and they extended the specification to

$$n\bar{w}_i \log \frac{p_{ic}}{\bar{p}_i} = \beta_c + \gamma_i \log Q_c + \epsilon'_{ic} \tag{2.7}$$

where Q_c is per capita real income of country c (line 9 of Table 2.3) and ϵ'_{ic} is a random disturbance. The extended specification allows the relative price of good i in each country (relative to the geometric mean price of i) to vary with per capita real income.

When we select the geometric mean of the per capita incomes of the N countries as the income unit,

$$\sum_{c=1}^{N} \log Q_c = 0 \tag{2.8}$$

and estimate β_c and γ_i by least squares constrained by $\Sigma_i \gamma_i = 0$, we obtain the estimate (2.5) of β_c, which is thus unchanged, while the estimate of γ_i takes the form

$$\hat{\gamma}_i = \sum_{c=1}^{N} A_{ic} \log Q_c \Big/ \sum_{c=1}^{N} (\log Q_c)^2 \tag{2.9}$$

where

$$A_{ic} = n\bar{w}_i \log \frac{p_{ic}}{\bar{p}_i} - \hat{\beta}_c \tag{2.10}$$

The verification of this solution is again a matter of differentiating a Lagrangean function. We write this function as

$$\frac{1}{2} \sum_{i=1}^{n} \sum_{c=1}^{N} (Z_{ic} - \beta_c - \gamma_i q_c)^2 - \mu' \sum_{i=1}^{n} \gamma_i$$

where Z_{ic} stands for the left side of (2.7) and q_c for $\log Q_c$, while μ' is the multiplier associated with the constraint $\Sigma_i \gamma_i = 0$. We differentiate the Lagrangean function with respect to β_c and equate the derivative to zero,

$$-\sum_{i=1}^{n} (Z_{ic} - \beta_c - \gamma_i q_c) = 0$$

which yields $\beta_c = (1/n) \Sigma_i Z_{ic}$ because $\Sigma_i \gamma_i = 0$. This solution confirms (2.5). Next we differentiate the Lagrangean function with respect to γ_i and equate the result to zero:

$$-\sum_{c=1}^{N} q_c (Z_{ic} - \beta_c - \gamma_i q_c) - \mu' = 0$$

Summation of both sides over i yields $\mu' = 0$ because $\Sigma_i Z_{ic} = n\beta_c$ and $\Sigma_i \gamma_i = 0$. The solution (2.9) is then directly obtained.

As in the case of the previous subsection, the zero value of the Lagrangean multiplier indicates that the constraint $\Sigma_i \gamma_i = 0$ does not raise the residual sum of squares above the unconstrained minimum: raising γ_i for each i by any number k and subtracting $kq_c = k \log Q_c$ from β_c for each c does not affect the right side of (2.7). Note that the solution (2.9) satisfies $\Sigma_i \hat{\gamma}_i = 0$ because $\Sigma_i A_{ic} = n\hat{\beta}_c - n\hat{\beta}_c = 0$ follows from (2.10) and (2.5). Also note that (2.8) ensures that summation of (2.7) over c yields $0 = 0 + 0 + 0$.

Application to the Eight Goods

Voltaire and Stack computed the estimates (2.5) and (2.9) for the data of Tables 2.3 and 2.4. For reasons to be explained in Section 3.1, they deleted Kenya so that the estimates are confined to the other $N = 15$ countries listed in the top row of Table 2.3. The $\hat{\gamma}_i$'s are shown in Table 2.5. The largest negative value is that of Food and the largest positive value is that of Recreation. Thus, when we move from poor to richer countries, Food becomes cheaper relative to Recreation.

Table 2.5
Estimates of the relative-price model (2.7)

Good	$\hat{\gamma}_i$	Income elasticity[a]
Food	−.63	−.21
Clothing	.03	.04
Rent	−.05	−.05
Furniture	.06	.11
Medical care	.13	.26
Transport	.05	.07
Recreation	.33	.38
Other expenditure	.09	.11

[a] Equal to $\hat{\gamma}_i/n\bar{w}_i$ with $n = 8$.

It follows from (2.7) that $\gamma_i/n\bar{w}_i$ is the income elasticity of the relative price of good i. The estimates of these elasticities are shown in the last column of Table 2.5. It will appear in Chapter 4 that these elasticities are positively correlated with the income elasticities of the demand for the eight goods. This means that luxuries (with income elasticities larger than 1) are on average more expensive relative to necessities (with income elasticities smaller than 1) in richer countries. One possible explanation, which goes back to Balassa (1964), is that international productivity differences tend to be larger in traded goods (such as food) than in non-traded goods (such as services). This means that, on average, the price of the former goods relative to that of the latter is lower in rich countries than in poor countries.

There is no need to consider this and other possible explanations in any detail. For the purpose of this monograph it is sufficient to note that there exists such a relation between the relative prices and the per capita incomes in our sample of 15 countries, and that these are the explanatory variables in the demand system that will be fitted in Chapter 3.

Concluding Remarks

Remark 1. The constraint $\Sigma_i \gamma_i = 0$ implies that the income elasticities of Table 2.5 have a zero weighted mean with the $\overline{w}_i$'s as weights. In Chapter 4 we shall have more to say about such weights in connection with income elasticities of demand.

Remark 2. The relative price in (2.7) involves deflation by the geometric mean price (2.6) which includes the price of good i in country c. But we have the identity

$$\log \frac{p_{ic}}{\overline{p}_i} = \frac{N-1}{N} \log \frac{p_{ic}}{\overline{p}_{ic}}$$

where $\log \overline{p}_{ic} = (N-1)^{-1} \Sigma_{d \neq c} \log p_{id}$. Therefore, $\log (p_{ic}/\overline{p}_i)$ can be written as a fraction $(N-1)/N$ of $\log p_{ic}$ deflated by the geometric mean price of good i in the $N-1$ countries other than country c. So we obtain income elasticities of relative prices in the latter sense by multiplying the entries in the last column of Table 2.5 by $N/(N-1) = 15/14$. This amounts to an increase of about 7 percent.

Remark 3. It follows from (2.5) that $\hat{\beta}_c - \hat{\beta}_d = \Sigma_i \overline{w}_i \log (p_{ic}/p_{id})$, which shows that the $\hat{\beta}_c$'s can be viewed as purchasing power parities in logarithmic form for consumption as a whole. Indeed, the $\hat{\beta}_c$'s obtained by Voltaire and Stack are in rather close agreement with the purchasing power parities in the first line of Summary Multilateral Table 4.3 of Kravis et al. (1978). The comparison is approximate, not only because of the different methodology used, but also because line number 110 (net expenditure of residents abroad) is deleted in this study (see Table 2.3, note d). This deletion ensures that the expenditures on the eight goods add up to total consumption expenditure.

Chapter 3

A SYSTEM OF CROSS-COUNTRY DEMAND EQUATIONS

3.1. Working's Model

Budget Shares and Working's Model

Holbrook Working (1943) analyzed family expenditure data and observed that the share of total expenditure allocated to food (the budget share of food) tends to decline linearly with the logarithm of total expenditure. To express this relation in appropriate symbols, we write n for the number of goods and p_i and q_i for the price and the quantity consumed, respectively, of good i. Then total expenditure equals

$$M = \sum_{i=1}^{n} p_i q_i \tag{3.1}$$

and the budget share of good i is

$$w_i = \frac{p_i q_i}{M} \tag{3.2}$$

which yields 1 when summed over i:

$$\sum_{i=1}^{n} w_i = 1 \tag{3.3}$$

Working's model applied to good i thus amounts to

$$w_i = \alpha_i + \beta_i \log M \tag{3.4}$$

with $\beta_i < 0$ for i = food. It follows from (3.3) that the α_i's and β_i's are subject to the constraints

$$\sum_{i=1}^{n} \alpha_i = 1, \quad \sum_{i=1}^{n} \beta_i = 0 \tag{3.5}$$

Working's Model in a Cross-Country Context

Figure 3.1 provides evidence on the validity of Working's model for the n = 8 goods of Table 2.2. In each of the eight figures, the variable measured vertically is the budget share of one of the eight goods, and the

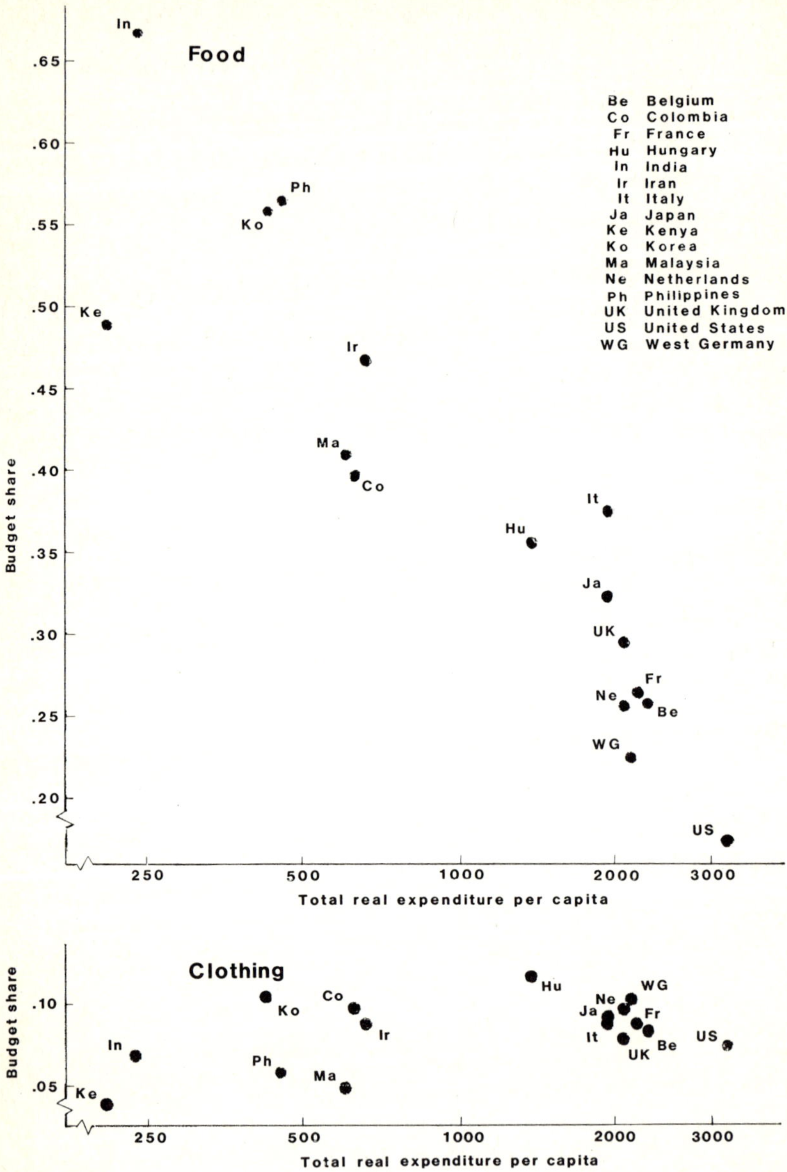
Food
Clothing
Budget share
Total real expenditure per capita
.65
.60
.55
.50
.45
.40
.35
.30
.25
.20
.10
.05
250
500
1000
2000
3000
Be Belgium
Co Colombia
Fr France
Hu Hungary
In India
Ir Iran
It Italy
Ja Japan
Ke Kenya
Ko Korea
Ma Malaysia
Ne Netherlands
Ph Philippines
UK United Kingdom
US United States
WG West Germany
In
Ph
Ko
Ke
Ir
Ma
Co
It
Hu
Ja
UK
Fr
Ne
Be
WG
US

Figure 3.1

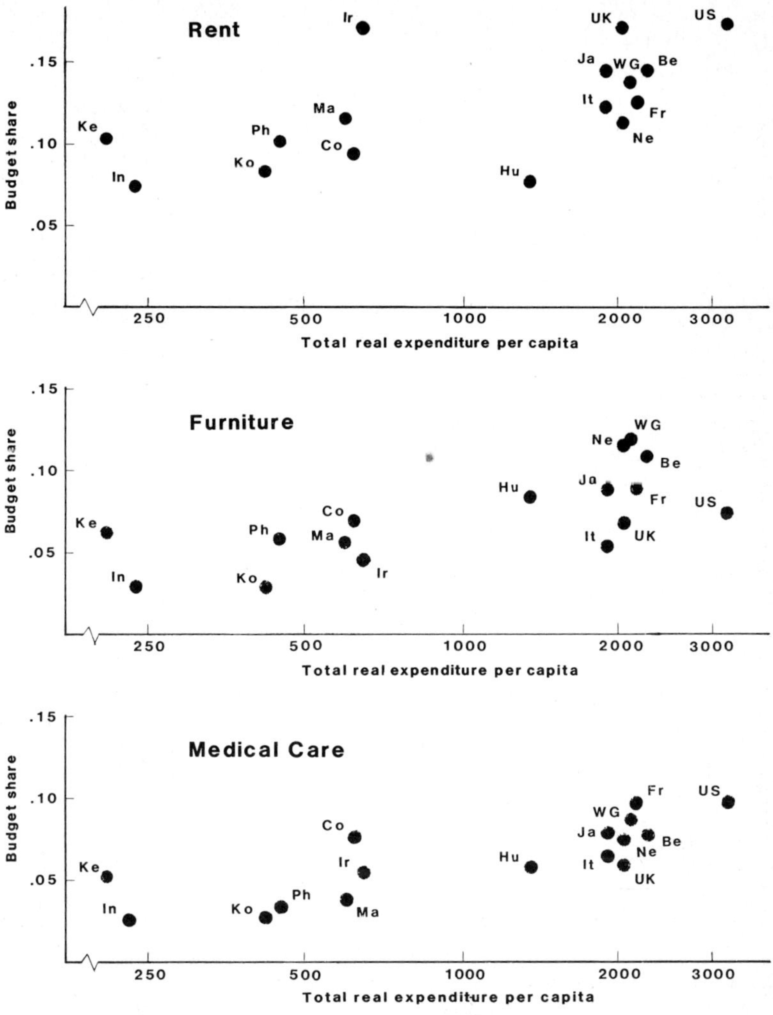

Figure 3.1 (continued)

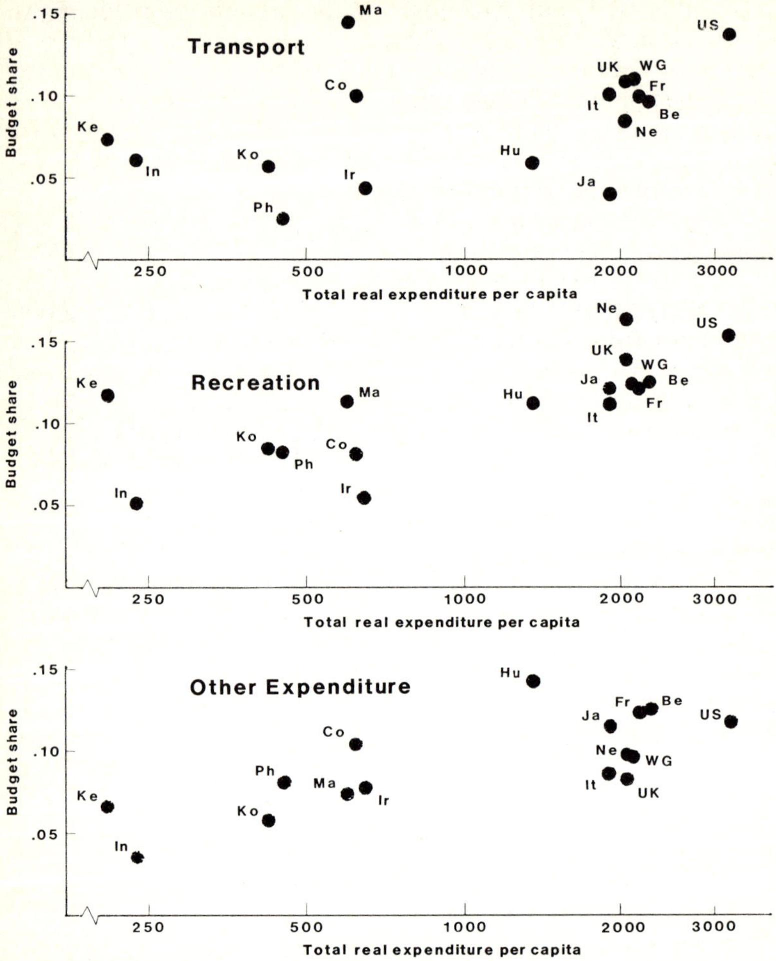

Figure 3.1 (continued)

16 values of this variable are the entries in the relevant row of the lower part of Table 2.3. In each figure, the variable measured horizontally is log Q_c, which replaces log M in (3.4), where Q_c is per capita real income of country c (line 9 of Table 2.3). The scatters indicate that (3.4) provides a rather good fit, particularly for Food for which Working originally

proposed his model, but two qualifications should be made. First, the model cannot hold for a good with $\beta_i < 0$ when total expenditure is sufficiently large because it would yield a negative w_i. This should be evident from the figure for Food when we imagine that a country is included with a per capita income much higher than that of the U.S. However, this qualification appears unimportant for the data considered here and we shall therefore ignore it in the sequel.

The second qualification has to do with the data for Kenya. That country's point in the figure for Food is well below the straight line which we would fit through the 15 other points if Kenya were deleted. This suggests that Kenya should be viewed as an outlier. Of course, this argument by itself is not fully satisfactory, because the scatter diagrams ignore the effects of relative prices (see Section 3.2). However, it seems unlikely that pursuing this route will yield satisfactory results in Kenya's case since other investigators have also encountered difficulties with the Kenyan data. For example, Isenman (1979) observed that the cost comparison of dental services in Kenya and India yields unrealistic results.

Kenya has to some degree a dual economy, which yields considerable difficulties for the construction of per capita data. If we imagine that the food grown by Kenyan tribesmen has been underestimated, the "true" point of Kenya in the figure for Food would be above and to the right of the point shown in that figure and would thus be closer to the straight line fitted through the 15 other points. We shall not attempt to make such corrections and prefer to delete Kenya. Accordingly, the remainder of this monograph is based on the data of Tables 2.3 and 2.4 for the 15 countries other than Kenya.

Marginal Shares

Since Working's model will play a prominent role in the sequel, we shall consider some of its properties here. For this purpose we introduce

$$\theta_i = \frac{\partial (p_i q_i)}{\partial M} = p_i \frac{\partial q_i}{\partial M} \tag{3.6}$$

which is the marginal budget share or, for short, the *marginal share* of good i. This share answers the following question: If total expenditure M increases by one dollar, the prices $p_1, \ldots, p_n$ remaining constant, what is the resulting change in the expenditure on good i? The marginal budget shares add up to 1,

$$\sum_{i=1}^{n} \theta_i = 1 \tag{3.7}$$

which may be verified by differentiating both sides of (3.1) with respect to M. The adding-up property (3.7) should be compared with the corresponding property (3.3) for budget shares, but note that there is a difference between the two sets of shares in that marginal shares may be negative. If $\theta_i < 0$, good i is said to be inferior.

To find the marginal shares of Working's model, we multiply (3.4) by M so that the left side becomes $w_i M = p_i q_i$,

$$p_i q_i = \alpha_i M + \beta_i M \log M$$

which we differentiate with respect to M:

$$\frac{\partial (p_i q_i)}{\partial M} = \alpha_i + \beta_i (1 + \log M)$$

A comparison with (3.4) and (3.6) shows that this can be written as

$$\theta_i = w_i + \beta_i \tag{3.8}$$

or, in words, under Working's model the ith marginal share exceeds the corresponding budget share by β_i which is a constant with respect to total expenditure M. Evidently, good i will be inferior under this model when β_i is negative and larger in absolute value than the budget share.

Budget-Constrained Utility Maximization

Further insight is obtained when we use a utility-maximizing framework. Suppose that the consumer's preferences can be represented by a utility function $u(\boldsymbol{q})$, where $\boldsymbol{q} = [q_i]$ is the n-element column vector of the quantities consumed. Let the consumer's objective be to select the quantities which maximize his utility function subject to (3.1) for given values of $M, p_1, \ldots, p_n$. In the present context we refer to (3.1) as the consumer's budget constraint. If the utility function is appropriately differentiable, we can solve this constrained maximum problem by means of the Lagrangean function

$$u(\boldsymbol{q}) - \lambda \left(\sum_{i=1}^{n} p_i q_i - M \right)$$

where λ is a Lagrangean multiplier. We differentiate the Lagrangean function with respect to q_i and equate the result to zero,

$$\frac{\partial u}{\partial q_i} = \lambda p_i \tag{3.9}$$

which is the familiar proportionality of the marginal utilities and prices with λ as proportionality coefficient.

This λ is commonly known as the *marginal utility of income*. We can visualize this definition by dividing (3.9) by p_i, $\partial u/\partial(p_i q_i) = \lambda$, which shows that if the consumer receives an extra dollar of income and spends it on any of the n goods, his utility level increases by λ units.

The Klein–Rubin Utility Function and the Linear Expenditure System

For example, suppose that the utility function takes the Klein–Rubin (1948) form

$$u(\boldsymbol{q}) = \sum_{i=1}^{n} \theta_i \log(q_i - c_i) \tag{3.10}$$

where $\Sigma_i \theta_i = 1$. Application of (3.9) followed by elimination of λ by means of the budget constraint (3.1) yields a system of demand equations which can be written in the form

$$p_i q_i = p_i c_i + \theta_i \left(M - \sum_{j=1}^{n} p_j c_j\right) \tag{3.11}$$

This is known as the *linear expenditure system*, the expenditure on each good being expressed as a linear function of total expenditure M and the prices $p_1, .., p_n$.

Differentiation of both sides of (3.11) with respect to M yields $\partial(p_i q_i)/\partial M = \theta_i$ in agreement with (3.6). However, note that the θ_i's and c_i's in the Klein–Rubin utility function (3.10) are constants so that the marginal shares of the linear expenditure system are also constant. This is in contrast to the marginal share (3.8) of Working's model which equals the budget share plus β_i. Since budget shares typically vary with total expenditure, so do the marginal shares under Working's model.

Income Elasticities of Demand

A further comparison of Working's model and the linear expenditure system based on income elasticities is even more instructive. Division of (3.6) by (3.2) yields

$$\frac{\theta_i}{w_i} = \frac{\partial q_i}{\partial M}\frac{M}{q_i} \tag{3.12}$$

which shows that the ratio of the marginal to the budget share of good i is equal to the elasticity of the demand for this good with respect to total expenditure M. For simplicity, we shall refer to M as income from now on so that the right side of (3.12) is the income elasticity of good i. It is customary to designate a good as a luxury (necessity) when its income elasticity is larger (smaller) than 1. Inferior goods are special cases of necessities.

It follows from (3.12) that if θ_i is a constant, as is the case under the linear expenditure system, the income elasticity of the demand for each good is inversely proportional to its budget share. When this is applied to the scatter diagram for Food in Figure 3.1 the implication would be that the income elasticity of Food is much higher for the U.S. than for India. But we shall see in Section 4.1 that our estimated income elasticities behave in precisely the opposite way, thus illustrating the inadequacy of the assumption of constant marginal shares.

3.2. Working's Model with a Substitution Term Added

Working's Model at Geometric Mean Prices

Working's model (3.4) describes a budget share in terms of income M, not in terms of the prices $p_1, ..., p_n$ of the n goods. We may view (3.4) as a conditional demand model given that the prices take certain fixed values. This conditional nature was not of great concern for Working (1943) in his analysis of family budget data, because it is reasonable to assume that the relative prices paid by different households in a given country and a given short time period are not too different. But the picture changes when we compare different countries rather than different households within one country. Indeed, the relative prices shown in the lower part of Table 2.4 are not equal at all. This does not mean that (3.4) cannot be applied to these data. It simply means that we have to select n prices at which (3.4) is supposed to be applicable and that we must make appropriate corrections for the fact that the observed budget shares do not correspond to these but to different prices. This procedure requires the introduction of a substitution term which will ultimately enable us to estimate price elasticities.

A natural choice for the price of good i at which (3.4) is postulated to hold is the geometric mean across countries. This geometric mean was defined in (2.6) and is reproduced here:

$$\log \bar{p}_i = \frac{1}{N} \sum_{c=1}^{N} \log p_{ic} \tag{3.13}$$

For the application of Working's model to the data of Tables 2.3 and 2.4, we modify (3.4) to

$$\hat{w}_{ic} = \alpha_i + \beta_i \log Q_c + \epsilon_{ic} \tag{3.14}$$

where Q_c is per capita real income of country c (line 9 of Table 2.3), ϵ_{ic} is a random disturbance, and $\hat{w}_{ic}$ is the budget share of good i at the prices $\bar{p}_1, \ldots, \bar{p}_n$ and the observed Q_c. Therefore,

$$w_{ic} = \alpha_i + \beta_i \log Q_c + (w_{ic} - \hat{w}_{ic}) + \epsilon_{ic} \tag{3.15}$$

where w_{ic} is the observed budget share of good i in country c (see the lower part of Table 2.3).

The Slutsky Matrix

The difference $w_{ic} - \hat{w}_{ic}$ in (3.15) results from the difference between the price vectors $[p_{ic}]$ and $[\bar{p}_i]$. It is shown in Section 3.3 that $w_{ic} - \hat{w}_{ic}$ can be written as the sum of two terms,

$$w_{ic} - \hat{w}_{ic} = w_{ic} \left(\log \frac{p_{ic}}{\bar{p}_i} - \sum_{j=1}^{n} w_{jc} \log \frac{p_{jc}}{\bar{p}_j} \right) + \sum_{j=1}^{n} \pi_{ij} \log \frac{p_{jc}}{\bar{p}_j} \tag{3.16}$$

where π_{ij} is an element of the $n \times n$ *Slutsky matrix* $[\pi_{ij}]$. The first term on the right in (3.16) represents the fact that the budget share of each good is affected by the change from $[\bar{p}_i]$ to $[p_{ic}]$ even when the consumer decides to buy the same quantities in spite of the price change. The second term recognizes that the consumer will *not* buy the same quantities because he will react to the price change by substitution. The coefficients of this substitution term are the elements of the Slutsky matrix $[\pi_{ij}]$, which is symmetric negative semidefinite and has rank $n - 1$. The symmetry amounts to

$$\pi_{ij} = \pi_{ji} \tag{3.17}$$

for all pairs (i, j); this property is commonly known as *Slutsky symmetry*. The rank $n - 1$ of $[\pi_{ij}]$ implies that the Slutsky matrix is singular. The cause of the singularity is

$$\sum_{j=1}^{n} \pi_{ij} = 0 \tag{3.18}$$

for $i = 1, ..., n$. This property is referred to as *demand homogeneity* and it amounts to unchanged quantities consumed when income and prices all change proportionately. We will have more to say about the homogeneity and symmetry properties in Section 3.3.

Substitution of (3.16) into (3.15) yields

$$y_{ic} = \alpha_i + \beta_i \log Q_c + \sum_{j=1}^{n} \pi_{ij} \log \frac{p_{jc}}{\overline{p}_j} + \epsilon_{ic} \tag{3.19}$$

where

$$y_{ic} = w_{ic} \left(1 - \log \frac{p_{ic}}{\overline{p}_i} + \sum_{j=1}^{n} w_{jc} \log \frac{p_{jc}}{\overline{p}_j}\right) \tag{3.20}$$

Note that the first right-hand term of (3.16) occurs on the left in (3.19). This switch is made because the term contains no unknown parameters. The formulation (3.19) has the convenient property of being linear in the parameters (α_i, β_i and the π_{ij}'s). The symmetry and homogeneity constraints (3.17) and (3.18) are also linear in the parameters, which should make the testing of these constraints in principle straightforward. How straightforward these tests actually are is a matter that will be considered in Sections 3.4 and 3.5 after we have derived the results (3.16) to (3.18).

3.3. Derivation of the Substitution Term

The result (3.16) can be derived from the so-called differential approach to consumption theory. This approach does not require a specification of the algebraic form of the utility function such as the Klein–Rubin form

(3.10). Rather, the approach deals with small displacements of the independent variables (income and prices) and it presents a system of demand equations in the form of the total differential of demand. The main steps are summarized below; further details can be found in Theil (1980a).

Barten's Fundamental Matrix Equation

Both the budget constraint (3.1) and the proportionality (3.9) of the marginal utilities and prices hold identically in income and prices. This enables us to differentiate (3.1) and (3.9) for $i = 1, ..., n$ with respect to $M, p_1, ..., p_n$. For example, when we differentiate both sides of (3.1) with respect to M and p_j, we obtain

$$\sum_{i=1}^{n} p_i \frac{\partial q_i}{\partial M} = 1, \qquad \sum_{i=1}^{n} p_i \frac{\partial q_i}{\partial p_j} + q_j = 0$$

We can write this result conveniently in the form of two matrix equations,

$$\boldsymbol{p}' \frac{\partial \boldsymbol{q}}{\partial M} = 1, \qquad \boldsymbol{p}' \frac{\partial \boldsymbol{q}}{\partial \boldsymbol{p}'} + \boldsymbol{q}' = \boldsymbol{0}$$

where $\boldsymbol{p}' = [p_1 \; ... \; p_n]$ and $\boldsymbol{q}' = [q_1 \; ... \; q_n]$ are the price and quantity vectors, the prime indicating transposition (transforming a column vector into a row vector), while $\partial \boldsymbol{q}/\partial M = [\partial q_i/\partial M]$ is the column vector of income derivatives of demand and $\partial \boldsymbol{q}/\partial \boldsymbol{p}' = [\partial q_i/\partial p_j]$ is the $n \times n$ matrix of price derivatives of demand.

To differentiate (3.9) with respect to M, we apply the chain rule on the left:

$$\sum_{k=1}^{n} \frac{\partial^2 u}{\partial q_i \partial q_k} \frac{\partial q_k}{\partial M} = p_i \frac{\partial \lambda}{\partial M}$$

This can be written in the form of a third matrix equation,

$$\boldsymbol{U} \frac{\partial \boldsymbol{q}}{\partial M} = \frac{\partial \lambda}{\partial M} \boldsymbol{p}$$

where $\boldsymbol{U} = [\partial^2 u/\partial q_i \partial q_j]$ is the Hessian matrix (the matrix of second derivatives) of the utility function. Finally, we differentiate (3.9) with respect to p_j. With δ_{ij} defined as the Kronecker delta ($\delta_{ij} = 1$ if $i = j$, 0 if $i \neq j$), we obtain

$$\sum_{k=1}^{n} \frac{\partial^2 u}{\partial q_i \partial q_k} \frac{\partial q_k}{\partial p_j} = p_i \frac{\partial \lambda}{\partial p_j} + \lambda \delta_{ij}$$

which yields another matrix equation,

$$\boldsymbol{U} \frac{\partial \boldsymbol{q}}{\partial \boldsymbol{p}'} = \boldsymbol{p} \frac{\partial \lambda}{\partial \boldsymbol{p}'} + \lambda \boldsymbol{I}$$

where $\partial\lambda/\partial\boldsymbol{p}' = [\partial\lambda/\partial p_1 \; ... \; \partial\lambda/\partial p_n]$ is the row vector of price derivatives of the marginal utility of income, while $\boldsymbol{I}$ is the unit matrix of order $n \times n$.

These four matrix equations can be conveniently combined in partitioned form,

$$\begin{bmatrix} \boldsymbol{U} & \boldsymbol{p} \\ \boldsymbol{p}' & 0 \end{bmatrix} \begin{bmatrix} \partial\boldsymbol{q}/\partial M & \partial\boldsymbol{q}/\partial\boldsymbol{p}' \\ -\partial\lambda/\partial M & -\partial\lambda/\partial\boldsymbol{p}' \end{bmatrix} = \begin{bmatrix} \boldsymbol{0} & \lambda\boldsymbol{I} \\ 1 & -\boldsymbol{q}' \end{bmatrix} \tag{3.21}$$

which is known as Barten's (1964) fundamental matrix equation in consumption theory. The matrix on the far left is the Hessian matrix $\boldsymbol{U}$ bordered by prices. The matrix immediately to the left of the equal sign contains the derivatives of all dependent variables ($\boldsymbol{q}$ and λ) with respect to all independent variables ($\boldsymbol{p}$ and M).

Solving the Matrix Equation

We assume that $\boldsymbol{U}$ is symmetric negative definite. This assumption is stronger than necessary; we can derive (3.16) from the weaker condition that the Hessian is definite under the budget constraint, but it will be convenient to make the stronger assumption in view of the developments on preference independence which follow later in this section. The inverse of the bordered Hessian on the far left in (3.21) can then be written as

$$\frac{1}{\boldsymbol{p}'\boldsymbol{U}^{-1}\boldsymbol{p}} \begin{bmatrix} (\boldsymbol{p}'\boldsymbol{U}^{-1}\boldsymbol{p})\boldsymbol{U}^{-1} - \boldsymbol{U}^{-1}\boldsymbol{p}(\boldsymbol{U}^{-1}\boldsymbol{p})' & \boldsymbol{U}^{-1}\boldsymbol{p} \\ (\boldsymbol{U}^{-1}\boldsymbol{p})' & -1 \end{bmatrix}$$

Thus, by premultiplying (3.21) by this matrix we obtain the derivatives of the dependent variables with respect to the independent variables. Three such derivatives will be needed:

$$\frac{\partial \lambda}{\partial M} = \frac{1}{\boldsymbol{p}'\boldsymbol{U}^{-1}\boldsymbol{p}} \tag{3.22}$$

$$\frac{\partial \boldsymbol{q}}{\partial M} = \frac{1}{\boldsymbol{p}'\boldsymbol{U}^{-1}\boldsymbol{p}}\, \boldsymbol{U}^{-1}\boldsymbol{p} \tag{3.23}$$

$$\frac{\partial \boldsymbol{q}}{\partial \boldsymbol{p}'} = \lambda \boldsymbol{U}^{-1} - \frac{\lambda}{\boldsymbol{p}'\boldsymbol{U}^{-1}\boldsymbol{p}}\, \boldsymbol{U}^{-1}\boldsymbol{p}(\boldsymbol{U}^{-1}\boldsymbol{p})' - \frac{1}{\boldsymbol{p}'\boldsymbol{U}^{-1}\boldsymbol{p}}\, \boldsymbol{U}^{-1}\boldsymbol{p}\boldsymbol{q}' \tag{3.24}$$

Substitution from (3.22) and (3.23) shows that the (i, j)th element of (3.24) can be written as

$$\frac{\partial q_i}{\partial p_j} = \lambda u^{ij} - \frac{\lambda}{\partial \lambda / \partial M} \frac{\partial q_i}{\partial M} \frac{\partial q_j}{\partial M} - \frac{\partial q_i}{\partial M} q_j \tag{3.25}$$

where $[u^{ij}] = \boldsymbol{U}^{-1}$. The last term in (3.25) represents the income effect of the change in p_j on the demand for good i, while the first two right-hand terms jointly represent the substitution effect of this change. The first term (λu^{ij}) represents the specific substitution effect and the second the general substitution effect. The latter effect is concerned with the competition of all goods for an extra dollar of the consumer's income, whereas the former deals with the utility interaction of goods i and j. The distinction between these two components of the substitution effect is from Houthakker (1960b).

The Total Differential of Demand

We can write the total differential of the demand for good i as

$$\mathrm{d}q_i = \frac{\partial q_i}{\partial M} \mathrm{d}M + \sum_{j=1}^{n} \frac{\partial q_i}{\partial p_j} \mathrm{d}p_j \tag{3.26}$$

and we can thus use (3.25) for the derivative $\partial q_i / \partial p_j$ in the price term of (3.26). However, a much more elegant result can be obtained when we select a formulation in budget shares, in agreement with eq. (3.16) which is to be proved. The differential of $w_i = p_i q_i / M$ can be written as

$$\mathrm{d}w_i = \frac{q_i}{M} \mathrm{d}p_i + \frac{p_i}{M} \mathrm{d}q_i - \frac{p_i q_i}{M^2} \mathrm{d}M$$

or, more elegantly, as

$$\mathrm{d}w_i = w_i \mathrm{d}(\log p_i) + w_i \mathrm{d}(\log q_i) - w_i \mathrm{d}(\log M) \tag{3.27}$$

which shows that $w_i \mathrm{d}(\log q_i) = (p_i/M)\,\mathrm{d}q_i$ may be viewed as the quantity component of $\mathrm{d}w_i$.

So, when we select this component as the variable on the left, (3.26) is changed into

$$w_i \mathrm{d}(\log q_i) = p_i \frac{\partial q_i}{\partial M} \mathrm{d}(\log M) + \sum_{j=1}^{n} \frac{p_i p_j}{M} \frac{\partial q_i}{\partial p_j} \mathrm{d}(\log p_j)$$

It follows from (3.6) and (3.25) that this can be written as

$$w_i \mathrm{d}(\log q_i) = \theta_i \mathrm{d}(\log M) + \sum_{j=1}^{n} \left(\frac{\lambda p_i p_j u^{ij}}{M} - \frac{\lambda/M}{\partial\lambda/\partial M} \theta_i \theta_j - \theta_i w_j \right) \mathrm{d}(\log p_j)$$

A third equivalent formulation is

$$w_i \mathrm{d}(\log q_i) = \theta_i \left[\mathrm{d}(\log M) - \sum_{j=1}^{n} w_j \mathrm{d}(\log p_j) \right] + \sum_{j=1}^{n} \left(\frac{\lambda p_i p_j u^{ij}}{M} - \frac{\lambda/M}{\partial\lambda/\partial M} \theta_i \theta_j \right) \mathrm{d}(\log p_j) \tag{3.28}$$

Note that in the expression in brackets on the first line, the income effect of the price changes serves as the deflator which transforms the change in money income into a real-income change. The expression on the second line is the substitution term. Also note that using the quantity component in (3.27) as the left-hand variable of a demand equation, rather than either of the two other components, can be justified by pointing out that the former component is the endogenous component of the budget share change from the consumer's viewpoint, whereas the latter two components are exogenous.

Simplifying the Substitution Term

To simplify the substitution term of (3.28) we define

$$\theta_{ij} = \frac{\lambda}{\phi M} p_i u^{ij} p_j \tag{3.29}$$

where

$$\frac{1}{\phi} = \frac{\partial \lambda}{\partial M} \frac{M}{\lambda} \tag{3.30}$$

Thus, ϕ is the reciprocal of the income elasticity of the marginal utility of income; for brevity, we shall refer to ϕ as the *income flexibility*. Substitution of (3.29) and (3.30) into (3.28) yields

$$w_i \mathrm{d}(\log q_i) = \theta_i \left[\mathrm{d}(\log M) - \sum_{j=1}^{n} w_j \mathrm{d}(\log p_j)\right] + \phi \sum_{j=1}^{n} (\theta_{ij} - \theta_i \theta_j) \mathrm{d}(\log p_j) \tag{3.31}$$

So, when we define

$$\pi_{ij} = \phi(\theta_{ij} - \theta_i \theta_j) \tag{3.32}$$

we can write (3.31) in the equivalent form

$$w_i \mathrm{d}(\log q_i) = \theta_i \left[\mathrm{d}(\log M) - \sum_{j=1}^{n} w_j \mathrm{d}(\log p_j)\right] + \sum_{j=1}^{n} \pi_{ij} \mathrm{d}(\log p_j) \tag{3.33}$$

To relate (3.33) to (3.16) we recall that the latter equation describes the change in the ith budget share caused by the price change from $[\overline{p}_i]$ to $[p_{ic}]$ when real income remains fixed at the level Q_c. Constancy of real income means in (3.33) that the expression in brackets vanishes so that

$$\mathrm{d}(\log M) = \sum_{j=1}^{n} w_j \mathrm{d}(\log p_j) \tag{3.34}$$

which means that (3.27) takes the form

$$\begin{aligned} \mathrm{d}w_i &= w_i \mathrm{d}(\log p_i) + w_i \mathrm{d}(\log q_i) - w_i \sum_{j=1}^{n} w_j \mathrm{d}(\log p_j) \\ &= w_i \left[\mathrm{d}(\log p_i) - \sum_{j=1}^{n} w_j \mathrm{d}(\log p_j)\right] + \sum_{j=1}^{n} \pi_{ij} \mathrm{d}(\log p_j) \end{aligned}$$

where the second step is based on (3.33) with the real-income change specified as zero in accordance with (3.34). Next we interpret $\mathrm{d}(\log p_i)$ as $\log p_{ic} - \log \overline{p}_i = \log (p_{ic}/\overline{p}_i)$ and apply the mean value theorem of differential calculus,

$$w_{ic} - \hat{w}_{ic} = w_i \left(\log \frac{p_{ic}}{\bar{p}_i} - \sum_{j=1}^{n} w_j \log \frac{p_{jc}}{\bar{p}_j} \right) + \sum_{j=1}^{n} \pi_{ij} \log \frac{p_{jc}}{\bar{p}_j}$$

where the w_i's and π_{ij}'s are the budget shares and Slutsky coefficients, respectively, evaluated at the per capita real income level of country c and at relative prices between those of $[\bar{p}_i]$ and $[p_{ic}]$. The specification $w_i = w_{ic}$ and π_{ij} = constant in (3.16) should be viewed as a first-order Taylor expansion.

Properties of the Slutsky Matrix

The symmetry property (3.17) follows directly from (3.32) and the symmetry of θ_{ij} defined in (3.29). The homogeneity property (3.18) follows from (3.32) and

$$\sum_{j=1}^{n} \theta_{ij} = \theta_i \tag{3.35}$$

for $i = 1, ..., n$. To verify (3.35) we use (3.29) and (3.30) in

$$\sum_{j=1}^{n} \theta_{ij} = \frac{\lambda p_i}{\phi M} \sum_{j=1}^{n} u^{ij} p_j = p_i \frac{\partial \lambda}{\partial M} \sum_{j=1}^{n} u^{ij} p_j$$

Since (3.22) and (3.23) imply $\partial \boldsymbol{q}/\partial M = (\partial \lambda/\partial M) \boldsymbol{U}^{-1} \boldsymbol{p}$, the sum of θ_{ij} over j is thus $p_i(\partial q_i/\partial M)$, after which (3.6) completes the proof of (3.35). Note that the homogeneity property (3.18) implies that a proportionate change in money income and all prices yields zero for both right-hand terms in (3.33) so that $\mathrm{d}(\log q_i)$ on the left then also vanishes.

It follows from (3.22) and the negative definiteness of $\boldsymbol{U}$ that $\partial \lambda/\partial M$ is negative. Therefore, given the positive sign of M and λ in (3.30),

$$\phi < 0 \tag{3.36}$$

while θ_{ij} in (3.29) is an element of the symmetric positive definite matrix $[\theta_{ij}]$ of order $n \times n$. The Slutsky matrix $[\pi_{ij}]$ obtained from (3.32) is symmetric negative semidefinite with rank $n - 1$, the negativity being due to the occurrence of ϕ on the right in (3.32). As stated in the discussion preceding (3.18), the semidefiniteness of $[\pi_{ij}]$ results from the homogeneity property $\Sigma_j \pi_{ij} = 0$. It is not difficult to verify that the rank of $[\pi_{ij}]$ cannot be smaller than $n - 1$.

Preference Independence

For the developments which follow in Section 3.5 it is convenient to consider here the special case in which the consumer's preferences can be represented by a utility function which is the sum of n functions, one for each good. The Klein–Rubin utility function (3.10) provides an example. The marginal utility of each good is then independent of the quantities consumed of all other goods, which is the reason why this preference structure is referred to as *preference independence*. ("Strong separability" is also frequently used.)

Under preference independence the Hessian matrix $\boldsymbol{U}$ is diagonal and so is $[\theta_{ij}]$ in view of (3.29), while (3.35) is simplified to $\theta_{ii} = \theta_i$. This means that we can now write the substitution term of (3.31) in the form

$$\phi\theta_i \mathrm{d}(\log p_i) - \phi\theta_i \sum_{j=1}^{n} \theta_j \mathrm{d}(\log p_j) = \phi\theta_i \left[\mathrm{d}(\log p_i) - \sum_{j=1}^{n} \theta_j \mathrm{d}(\log p_j)\right] \tag{3.37}$$

The expression in brackets is the logarithmic change in the relative price of good i, the deflator being

$$\sum_{j=1}^{n} \theta_j \mathrm{d}(\log p_j) \tag{3.38}$$

which differs from the deflator on the right in (3.34) that transforms money income into real income in (3.33). We shall refer to the deflator in (3.34) as the *Divisia price index* in differential form, and to (3.38) as the *Frisch price index*; see Divisia (1925) and Frisch (1932). Whereas the Divisia price index results from the income effect of the price changes, the Frisch price index represents the general substitution effect of these changes and the price change $\mathrm{d}(\log p_i)$, which is deflated in (3.37), represents the specific substitution effect. Since luxuries have marginal shares that exceed the budget shares, these goods have a greater weight in the Frisch price index (3.38) than in the Divisia price index shown in (3.34), while the opposite is true for necessities.

The Cost of Utility and the Indirect Utility Function

A different way of endowing Working's model with a substitution term is by means of the cost function $C(u, \boldsymbol{p})$, which specifies the smallest amount of expenditure needed to attain the utility level u when the price vector is $\boldsymbol{p}$. Shephard's lemma states that $\partial C/\partial \boldsymbol{p} = \boldsymbol{q}$, which means that the quantity vector can be obtained by differentiating the cost function with respect to the prices. The cost function should obviously be homogeneous (of degree 1) in the prices.

Deaton and Muellbauer (1980a, b) proposed a specific algebraic form, viz., $\log C = a(\boldsymbol{p}) + ub(\boldsymbol{p})$, where

$$a(\boldsymbol{p}) = \sum_{i=1}^{n} \alpha_i \log p_i + \frac{1}{2} \sum_{i=1}^{n} \sum_{j=1}^{n} \gamma_{ij} \log p_i \log p_j$$

$$b(\boldsymbol{p}) = \beta_0 \sum_{i=1}^{n} p_i^{\beta_i}$$

Homogeneity of this cost function requires $\Sigma_i\, \alpha_i = 1$ and $\Sigma_i\, \beta_i = 0$, as in (3.5), and $\Sigma_j\, \gamma_{ij} = \Sigma_i\, \gamma_{ij} = 0$, while Slutsky symmetry is satisfied when $\gamma_{ij} = \gamma_{ji}$. Using Shephard's lemma, Deaton and Muellbauer show that the implied budget shares take the form

$$w_i = \alpha_i + \beta_i \log \frac{M}{P} + \sum_{j=1}^{n} \gamma_{ij} \log p_j$$

where

$$\log P = \sum_{i=1}^{n} \alpha_i \log p_i + \frac{1}{2} \sum_{i=1}^{n} \sum_{j=1}^{n} \gamma_{ij} \log p_i \log p_j$$

Clearly, this budget share equation is equivalent to Working's specification (3.4) when we put the prices of all goods equal to 1 (which can be done by selecting appropriate units for the quantities of all goods). When prices change but money income M remains unchanged, the equation shows how this affects the budget shares given the underlying algebraic specification of the consumer's cost function.

The two previous paragraphs illustrate how the cost function can be used to generate a demand system. This should be contrasted with the approach which is based on an algebraic specification of the utility function, such as the Klein–Rubin function (3.10) which yields the linear expenditure system (3.11). A third approach is based on the indirect utility function $u_I(M, \boldsymbol{p})$, which specifies the highest utility level that can be attained given income M and the price vector $\boldsymbol{p}$. Roy's theorem states that the quantity of each good i can be obtained from the indirect utility function by taking minus the ratio of the price derivative $\partial u_I/\partial p_i$ to the income derivative $\partial u_I/\partial M$. Christensen et al. (1975) used this convenient property when they proposed an indirect utility function which is quadratic in the logarithms of the price–income ratios $p_1/M, ..., p_n/M$.

These three approaches have in common that the *first* step requires the algebraic specifications of some function: the utility function, the indirect utility function or the cost function. The differential approach discussed in the previous subsections differs from these in that it does not start with a specific algebraic form. For example, ϕ and θ_i in (3.37) need not be constant; they may be functions of the levels of income and prices. Of course, when the differential approach is applied to data, some parametrization is typically needed. However, this is done in the *last* step prior to the estimation or hypothesis testing, as will be illustrated in Sections 3.4 and 3.5.

Concluding Remarks

Remark 1. We mentioned in the discussion preceding (3.37) that (3.35) is simplified to $\theta_{ii} = \theta_i$ under preference independence. Since θ_{ii} is a diagonal element of a positive definite matrix, it is necessarily positive. Therefore, each θ_i is positive under preference independence, which excludes the possibility of inferior goods. This exclusion also applies to the linear expenditure system (3.11) which is based on the preference-independent Klein–Rubin utility function (3.10).

Remark 2. When we divide both sides of (3.33) by w_i, we obtain $d(\log q_i)$ on the left and the income elasticity θ_i/w_i multiplied by the logarithmic change in real income for the first term on the right. When we also replace the substitution term on the far right in (3.33) by (3.37), as is legitimate under preference independence, we obtain $\phi\theta_i/w_i$ multiplied by the Frisch-deflated logarithmic price change of good i. This shows that $\phi\theta_i/w_i$ can be viewed as the own-price elasticity of the demand for good i: the elasticity of the demand for this good with respect to its own Frisch-deflated price when real income remains constant.

Remark 3. Given that θ_i/w_i is the income elasticity of i, and given the interpretation of $\phi\theta_i/w_i$ as the own-price elasticity of i under preference independence, we can conclude that the latter elasticities are proportional to the former with the income flexibility ϕ as (negative) proportionality coefficient. Each cross-elasticity vanishes under preference independence; that is, the elasticity of the demand for a good with respect to the Frisch-deflated price of a different good, real income remaining constant. Thus, given the income elasticities of demand, the consumer's reaction to price changes is, under preference independence, determined by the income flexibility. This is a very convenient result, but it also shows that preference independence is a restrictive assumption.

Remark 4. A less restrictive assumption is that which imposes a separability on groups of goods (rather than individual goods); see e.g., Theil (1980a). This approach can be further extended by constructing conditional demand equations for goods within their group. It is then sometimes possible to structure the θ_{ij}'s within the group under certain conditions; for examples, see Meisner (1979b), Meisner and Clements (1979) and Theil (1979a).

Remark 5. We pointed out in the previous subsection that the cost function and the indirect utility function can also be used as a starting point for the generation of demand systems. Note that these functions are both obtained from the (direct) utility function in conjunction with the budget constraint. Hence they do not provide a "pure" description of the consumer's tastes; they provide a mixture of these tastes and of the opportunity set available to the consumer. This raises a problem when separability conditions are imposed on the cost function or the indirect utility function, since such a separability cannot claim to refer to the consumer's tastes only.

Remark 6. The differential approach can also be applied to the theory of the firm. If the firm operates under competitive conditions on the demand and supply side, this approach yields a system of input demand equations as well as a system of output supply equations. For details, see Laitinen (1980) and Theil (1980a).

3.4. *Problems in Testing Homogeneity and Symmetry*

We mentioned at the end of Section 3.2 that testing homogeneity and symmetry should be straightforward, but the fact of the matter is that many such tests have led to unexpected negative results; see, e.g., Barten (1969), Byron (1970), Christensen et al. (1975), Deaton (1974) and Lluch (1971). These tests are typically based on time series data. It is therefore appropriate to extend the relevant results of Section 3.3 to finite rather than infinitesimal displacements, but it will be more convenient to start with the formulation of a volume index similar to the Divisia price index shown in the right side of (3.34).

The Divisia Volume Index

We obtain $dM = \Sigma_j q_j dp_j + \Sigma_j p_j dq_j$ by taking the total differential of $M = \Sigma_j p_j q_j$. Division of both sides by M and use of (3.2) gives

$$\text{(3.39)} \qquad d(\log M) = \sum_{j=1}^{n} w_j d(\log p_j) + \sum_{j=1}^{n} w_j d(\log q_j)$$

The sum on the far right is the Divisia volume index. Thus, (3.39) states that the logarithmic change in total expenditure is the sum of the Divisia price and volume indexes, while (3.33) can now be written in the equivalent form

$$\text{(3.40)} \qquad w_i d(\log q_i) = \theta_i \sum_{j=1}^{n} w_j d(\log q_j) + \sum_{j=1}^{n} \pi_{ij} d(\log p_j)$$

in which the logarithmic change in real income is measured by the Divisia volume index.

Recall from (3.27) that the left side of (3.40) can be viewed as the quantity component of the change in the ith budget share. A comparison of the two terms immediately to the left and right of the equal sign in (3.40) shows that this left side has a second interpretation, viz., as the contribution of good i to the Divisia volume index. Thus, (3.40) describes this contribution as being equal to the ith marginal share of the Divisia volume index plus a substitution term.

By summing (3.40) over $i = 1, ..., n$ we obtain the Divisia volume index for the two terms facing the equal sign, and zero for the substitution term (because $\Sigma_i \pi_{ij} = 0$). This illustrates that (3.40) should be viewed as an allocation model: it describes how the change in total expenditure is allocated to the n goods, given the change in real income and the relative price changes.

The Rotterdam Model

For any positive variable x we write Dx_t for the finite log-change from period $t-1$ to period t: $Dx_t = \log x_t - \log x_{t-1} = \log(x_t/x_{t-1})$. The finite-change version of the substitution term in (3.40) is thus $\Sigma_j \pi_{ij} Dp_{jt}$, while $d(\log q_i)$ on the left similarly becomes Dq_{it}. For w_i we have two equally plausible choices: the budget share w_{it} in t and $w_{i,t-1}$ in $t-1$. We select their arithmetic average, $\bar{w}_{it} = (w_{it} + w_{i,t-1})/2$, and formulate the finite-change version of (3.40) as

$$\bar{w}_{it} Dq_{it} = \theta_i DQ_t + \sum_{j=1}^{n} \pi_{ij} Dp_{jt} + \epsilon_{it} \tag{3.41}$$

where ϵ_{it} is a random disturbance and $DQ_t = \Sigma_i \bar{w}_{it} Dq_{it}$. This DQ_t is the log-change in real income; it is a finite-change version of the Divisia volume index in (3.40). The model (3.41) with the θ_i's and π_{ij}'s interpreted as unknown parameters is known as the *Rotterdam model*. Details on this parametrization can be found in Barnett (1979) and Theil (1980a, Sec. 14.3 and 14.4).

Summation of (3.41) over i yields $DQ_t = DQ_t + 0 + 0$, which means that one of the equations (say the nth) can be deleted. Let t take the values $t = 1, ..., N$ so that N is the sample size. We assume that the vectors $(\epsilon_{1t}, ..., \epsilon_{n-1,t})$ are independently and normally distributed with zero means and a nonsingular covariance matrix Σ. Since (3.41) is linear in its parameters, and since it contains the same set of explanatory variables for each i, least squares is the best linear unbiased estimation method if the symmetry and homogeneity constraints (3.17) and (3.18) are ignored. It is assumed throughout the discussion which follows that the explanatory variables (the log-changes in real income and all prices) are "fixed variates", i.e., that they are constant in repeated samples.

Testing Homogeneity and Symmetry

The constraints (3.17) and (3.18) are linear in the parameters. Testing these constraints can be done straightforwardly by means of standard F tests if the disturbance covariance matrix Σ is known, but the problem is that Σ is typically unknown, in which case it is conventional to approximate Σ by the matrix S consisting of mean squares and products of least-squares residuals. This approximation affects the F ratio in two ways. First, its denominator becomes a constant so that the ratio is basically reduced to its numerator. Second, the distribution of this numerator is affected. When the true Σ is used, the numerator follows a χ^2 distribution if the null hypothesis is true, with a number of degrees of freedom equal to the number of constraints tested, but if S is substituted for Σ, the numerator thus modified follows this χ^2 distribution only asymptotically (for a sufficiently large sample). This raises the question of whether the asymptotic χ^2 distribution provides an adequate approximation to the actual distribution of the numerator.

Laitinen (1978) decided to attack this problem by means of a simulation experiment. He constructed a model of the form (3.41) which satisfies homogeneity with the ϵ_{it}'s obtained as pseudo-normal variates with a known matrix Σ. He used $N = 31$ observations and considered systems of $n = 5, 8, 11$ and 14 equations. Then he applied the conventional homogeneity test based on the estimate S, which amounts to the asymptotic χ^2 test described at the end of the previous paragraph. The numbers of rejections out of 100 trials at the 5 and 1 percent significance levels are shown in the upper left part of Table 3.1. Clearly, the test is heavily biased toward rejection of the null hypothesis, particularly for large systems. Since Laitinen knew his Σ, he could also apply an exact test based on Σ rather than an asymptotic test based on S. The result is shown in the upper middle part of Table 3.1 for the exact χ^2 tests of the numerator discussed in the previous paragraph, and in the upper right part for the exact F tests. The rejections shown in these parts of the table are in approximate agreement with the significance levels, thus suggesting that the use of S rather than Σ is the main cause of the numerous rejections of homogeneity in the literature.

Subsequently, Meisner (1979a) made a similar simulation experiment for the test of the symmetry constraint (3.17). His results are shown in the lower part of Table 3.1. For small n the bias of the test based on S toward rejection of symmetry is less than that of the homogeneity test, but the picture becomes worse when n increases. For $n = 14$ there are more than 90 rejections out of 100 at the 1 percent level, whereas the

Table 3.1
Rejections of homogeneity and symmetry

	Asymptotic χ^2 tests based on S		Exact χ^2 tests based on Σ		Exact F tests based on Σ	
	5%	1%	5%	1%	5%	1%
			Rejections of homogeneity			
5 goods	14	6	8	1	7	1
8 goods	30	16	5	2	8	2
11 goods	53	35	5	1	5	2
14 goods	87	81	6	1	4	2
			Rejections of symmetry			
5 goods	9	3	5	1	6	0
8 goods	26	8	5	1	5	2
11 goods	50	37	4	3	6	2
14 goods	96	91	6	0	4	2

rejections are in reasonable agreement with the significance levels when the symmetry test is based on the true Σ.

Alternative Procedures

Laitinen (1978) was able to derive the exact distribution of the homogeneity test statistic based on the estimate $\boldsymbol{S}$. This is Hotelling's T^2, which in this case is an F ratio whose denominator has a number of degrees of freedom equal to $N - 2n + 1$. This result indicates the problem of homogeneity testing when the number of equations n is not much below $\frac{1}{2}N$ (one-half the number of observations). The exact distribution of the symmetry test statistic is a much more complicated issue. The reason is that (3.17) is a cross-equation constraint, whereas (3.18) is confined to one equation, viz., the demand equation for good i.

The tests based on $\boldsymbol{S}$ fall under what is frequently referred to as Wald tests. Other tests are available such as likelihood ratio tests and the Lagrange multiplier or Rao tests; see, e.g., Judge et al. (1980, Sec. 17.5). The Wald test uses exclusively unconstrained coefficient estimates for testing the constraint. The likelihood ratio test uses both the constrained and the unconstrained estimates, while the Rao test uses exclusively constrained estimates. All three are asymptotic χ^2 tests, not F tests. In the Appendix to this monograph an attempt is made to restore the F test by means of an entirely different estimator of Σ, viz., an estimator derived from the maximum entropy distribution of the dependent and the independent variables of the demand system.

3.5. Maximum Likelihood Estimates under Preference Independence

Here we return to the demand system (3.19) for $i = 1, ..., n$. Each equation of this system contains n Slutsky coefficients in addition to the parameters α_i and β_i, thus yielding 10 coefficients per equation when we apply the system to the $n = 8$ goods of Table 2.2 and when we impose neither homogeneity nor symmetry. Given that there are observations for only $N = 15$ countries, we must conclude that the model (3.19) is overparametrized, particularly when we also consider the difficulties described in Section 3.4.

A Preference-Independent Demand System

The appropriate response to this situation is to introduce additional restrictions. Here we shall consider a replacement of (3.19) by a preference-independent model. The underlying idea is that the eight goods are actually broad aggregates. Therefore, it is worthwhile to explore the possibility that the per capita consumption data of the 15 countries conform to budget-constrained utility maxima with a utility function that is additive in these aggregates.

The preference independence specification affects the substitution term of (3.19). Recall that this specification changes the last term of (3.33) into (3.37), which we reproduce here:

$$\phi\theta_i \left[\mathrm{d}(\log p_i) - \sum_{j=1}^{n} \theta_j \mathrm{d}(\log p_j) \right]$$

This expression takes the following form when we use (3.7) to eliminate θ_n:

$$(3.42) \quad \phi\theta_i \left\{ \mathrm{d}(\log p_i) - \mathrm{d}(\log p_n) - \sum_{j=1}^{n-1} \theta_j \left[\mathrm{d}(\log p_j) - \mathrm{d}(\log p_n) \right] \right\}$$

Also recall from (3.8) that $\theta_i = w_i + \beta_i$ under Working's model; we use this property to write the marginal share of good i in country c as $w_{ic} + \beta_i$. Finally, when we proceed as in the paragraph following (3.33), we find that the substitution term (3.42) for country c can be written as

$$(3.43) \qquad \phi(w_{ic} + \beta_i) \, [\bar{x}_{ic} - \sum_{j=1}^{n-1} (w_{jc} + \beta_j) \bar{x}_{jc}]$$

where

$$(3.44) \qquad \bar{x}_{ic} = x_{ic} - x_{in}, \qquad x_{ic} = \log \frac{p_{ic}}{\bar{p}_i}$$

Therefore, when we replace the substitution term of (3.19) by (3.43), the model takes the form

$$(3.45) \qquad y_{ic} = \alpha_i + \beta_i \log Q_c + \phi(w_{ic} + \beta_i) \left[\bar{x}_{ic} - \sum_{j=1}^{n-1} (w_{jc} + \beta_j) \bar{x}_{jc} \right] + \epsilon_{ic}$$

As in the case of the Rotterdam model (3.41), we can delete the nth equation so that there are $2(n-1)$ parameters α_i and β_i to be estimated in addition to ϕ. Hence, with $n = 8$, the number of unconstrained parameters in the preference-independent demand system is 15. Each country supplies $n - 1$ degrees of freedom so that the total number of degrees of freedom prior to the estimation of the parameters is $N(n - 1) = 105$ and that which remains after the estimation is 90.

Frisch's Conjecture on the Income Flexibility

We shall actually want to raise the number of unconstrained parameters by one in order to allow for the possibility that the income flexibility ϕ varies with the level of real per capita income. In this connection, recall that the coefficients of the differential approach in Section 3.3 are not postulated to be constant but may vary with the levels of income and prices. One major reason for allowing the income flexibility to vary with income is the important role, already noted in Remark 3 at the end of Section 3.3, that this flexibility plays with respect to price effects under preference independence. Another reason is Frisch's (1959, p. 189) conjecture, quoted below, on the form of the relationship between the income elasticity of the marginal utility of income (the reciprocal of the income flexibility) and the level of real income. The words in brackets are adaptations to the terminology used here.

> "We may, perhaps, assume that in most cases the [income elasticity of the marginal utility of income] has values of the order of magnitude given below.
>
> −10 for an extremely poor and apathetic part of the population
> −4 for the slightly better off but still poor part of the population with a fairly pronounced desire to become better off
> −2 for the middle income bracket, 'the median part' of the population
> −.7 for the better off part of the population
> −.1 for the rich part of the population with ambitions towards 'conspicuous consumption.'
>
> It would be a very promising research project to determine [the income elasticity of the marginal utility of income] for different types of populations. A universal 'atlas' of the values of [this elasticity] should be constructed. It would serve an extremely useful purpose in demand analysis."

Thus, Frisch conjectures that the income elasticity of the marginal utility of income takes negative values which increase algebraically as income increases. Since ϕ is the reciprocal of this elasticity, the implication is that ϕ takes negative values which increase in absolute value as income increases. We shall allow such behavior by specifying the ϕ of country c as $\phi_0 + \phi_1 \log Q_c$; a negative value of ϕ_1 would thus be in qualitative agreement with Frisch's conjecture. The large dispersion of the income values in our sample, varying from the per capita value of India to that of the U.S., should enable us to verify Frisch's conjecture. Note that specifying ϕ as linear in the logarithm of income can be viewed as an extension of the corresponding properties (3.4) and (3.8) of the budget and marginal shares of Working's model.

We thus substitute $\phi_0 + \phi_1 \log Q_c$ for ϕ in (3.45) and estimate this model by maximum likelihood (ML) for $i = 1, ..., n-1$ and $c = 1, ..., N$ ($n = 8$ and $N = 15$) under the assumption that the disturbance vectors $(\epsilon_{1c}, ..., \epsilon_{n-1,c})$ are independently and normally distributed with zero means and nonsingular covariance matrix Σ. The ML estimates of ϕ_0 and ϕ_1 with asymptotic standard errors in parentheses are

$$\hat{\phi}_0 = -.705\ (.075), \qquad \hat{\phi}_1 = -.099\ (.059) \tag{3.46}$$

The derivation of these estimates is described in Section 3.6; here we confine ourselves to the discussion of numerical results. Note that the sign of the point estimate of ϕ_1 in (3.46) agrees with Frisch's conjecture. However, the asymptotic standard error of .059 suggests that the estimate is hardly significant.

There are several reasons for adopting a conservative view of significance in this case. First, the estimates are obtained under the convenient but restrictive assumption of preference independence. If a less restrictive assumption with a larger number of unknown parameters had been used, the asymptotic standard error of ϕ_1 could easily have been larger than that which is shown in (3.46). Second, the estimates are obtained from per capita data, whereas the theoretical developments in Section 3.3 are formulated for an individual consumer. This raises the problem of aggregation over consumers, which is ignored in the derivation of the ML estimates; we shall have more to say about this problem in Chapter 7. Third, the ML estimates are derived under the assumption that real income per capita and all prices are "fixed variates", which implies that these variables are not subject to random observational errors. We should admire the painstaking work done by Kravis and his colleagues, but it would be unwise to assume that there are no such errors.

Estimates for a Constant Income Flexibility

The arguments listed in the previous paragraph suggest that the ϕ_1 estimate of (3.46) presents no cogent evidence that the income flexibility varies monotonically with the level of income in spite of the fact that the sample of 15 countries displays such a large income variation. We shall consider this matter further in Section 4.3; here we apply Occam's razor by ignoring a possible dependence of ϕ on the level of real income. So we return to the specification (3.45) with ϕ treated as a constant. Its ML estimate is

$$\hat{\phi} = -.618\ (.051) \tag{3.47}$$

which is in good agreement with earlier estimates of the income flexibility; see, e.g., Clements and Nguyen (1980a), Fellner (1967), Stern (1977), Theil (1975–76, Sec. 5.4 and 6.3), Theil (1980a, Sec. 14.4) and Theil and Brooks (1970–71).

The ML estimates of the α_i's and β_i's of the model (3.45) for constant ϕ are shown in Table 3.2. The Q_c's are normalized so that Q_c of the U.S. equals 1, which means that the α_i estimates can be interpreted as estimated budget shares at the U.S. per capita income level and geometric mean prices. For comparison, the β_i estimates obtained when the differences in relative prices are ignored are shown in the last column; these are simply least-squares (LS) estimates in the regressions of w_{ic} on log Q_c. Note that the ML estimates of the β_i's are all closer to zero than the LS estimates with Furniture as a (numerically minor) exception. As we

Table 3.2
Parameter estimates of the preference-independent model

Good	ML estimates		LS estimate of β_i
	α_i	β_i	
Food	.2130 (.0130)	−.1526 (.0096)	−.1711
Clothing	.0893 (.0061)	.0042 (.0046)	.0060
Rent	.1514 (.0112)	.0261 (.0083)	.0270
Furniture	.0995 (.0079)	.0267 (.0060)	.0266
Medical care	.0881 (.0045)	.0258 (.0035)	.0260
Transport	.1050 (.0125)	.0210 (.0093)	.0228
Recreation	.1327 (.0076)	.0243 (.0064)	.0361
Other expenditure	.1209 (.0088)	.0246 (.0067)	.0266

Table 3.3
Estimates of β_i's from two sources

Group of goods	Izan and Clements	This study
Food	–.101	–.153
Clothing	.007	.004
Housing	.011	.053
Rest	.083	.096

shall see in Section 4.1, this effect has interesting implications for the income elasticities of the demand for the eight goods.

Izan and Clements (1979) applied Working's model to the estimated income elasticities which Houthakker (1957) computed from more than 50 family budget surveys conducted in a large number of countries. Four groups of goods are considered: Food, Clothing, Housing and the Rest. The estimated β_i's obtained by Izan and Clements are shown in the first column of Table 3.3, while the figures in the last column are obtained by adding the ML estimates of the β_i's of Table 3.2, Rent and Furniture being combined into Housing and the last four goods into the Rest. It will be noticed that the two sets of estimates are broadly similar. See also Russell (1967) for an earlier attempt to explain Houthakker's income elasticity estimates in terms of income levels and relative prices.

In Section 3.6 we shall derive the ML estimates and their asymptotic standard errors using the information matrix approach. The reader who is more interested in the discussion of numerical results is advised to proceed from here to Chapter 4.

3.6. Derivation of the Maximum Likelihood Estimates

Notation

We simplify the notation by introducing

$$q_c = \log Q_c \tag{3.48}$$

$$z_{ic} = (w_{ic} + \beta_i)\left[\bar{x}_{ic} - \sum_{j=1}^{n-1} (w_{jc} + \beta_j)\,\bar{x}_{jc}\right] \tag{3.49}$$

Thus, when we specify the ϕ of country c as $\phi_0 + \phi_1 \log Q_c$, we can write (3.45) in the form

(3.50) $$y_{ic} = \alpha_i + \beta_i q_c + (\phi_0 + \phi_1 q_c) z_{ic} + \epsilon_{ic}$$

To write (3.50) in matrix form, we define

(3.51) $$\alpha = \begin{bmatrix} \alpha_1 \\ \cdot \\ \cdot \\ \cdot \\ \alpha_{n-1} \end{bmatrix}, \quad \beta = \begin{bmatrix} \beta_1 \\ \cdot \\ \cdot \\ \cdot \\ \beta_{n-1} \end{bmatrix}, \quad \theta = \begin{bmatrix} \alpha \\ \beta \\ \\ \phi_0 \\ \phi_1 \end{bmatrix}$$

so that we can write (3.50) for $i = 1, ..., n - 1$ as

(3.52) $$\boldsymbol{y}_c = \boldsymbol{X}_c \theta + \boldsymbol{\epsilon}_c$$

where $\boldsymbol{y}_c$ and $\boldsymbol{\epsilon}_c$ are column vectors consisting of $n - 1$ elements, the ith being y_{ic} and ϵ_{ic}, respectively, while $\boldsymbol{X}_c$ can be written in partitioned form as

(3.53) $$\boldsymbol{X}_c = [\boldsymbol{I} \quad q_c \boldsymbol{I} \quad \boldsymbol{z}_c \quad q_c \boldsymbol{z}_c]$$

where $\boldsymbol{I}$ is the unit matrix of order $n - 1$ and $\boldsymbol{z}_c$ is a column vector with z_{ic} as ith element.

The Likelihood Equations and the Information Matrix

If $\boldsymbol{\epsilon}_1, ..., \boldsymbol{\epsilon}_N$ are independent normal vectors with zero mean and nonsingular covariance matrix $\boldsymbol{\Sigma}$, the log-likelihood function is

$$L = -\frac{(n-1)N}{2} \log 2\pi + \frac{N}{2} \log |\Sigma^{-1}| - \frac{1}{2} \sum_{c=1}^{N} (\boldsymbol{y}_c - \boldsymbol{X}_c \theta)' \Sigma^{-1} (\boldsymbol{y}_c - \boldsymbol{X}_c \theta)$$

which has the following derivatives with respect to Σ^{-1} and θ':

(3.54) $$\frac{\partial L}{\partial \Sigma^{-1}} = \frac{N}{2} \Sigma' - \frac{1}{2} \sum_{c=1}^{N} (\boldsymbol{y}_c - \boldsymbol{X}_c \theta)(\boldsymbol{y}_c - \boldsymbol{X}_c \theta)'$$

(3.55) $$\frac{\partial L}{\partial \theta'} = \sum_{c=1}^{N} (\boldsymbol{y}_c - \boldsymbol{X}_c \theta)' \Sigma^{-1} \frac{\partial (\boldsymbol{X}_c \theta)}{\partial \theta'}$$

It follows from (3.53) and the definition of θ in (3.51) that the derivative on the far right in (3.55) equals

$$(3.56) \qquad \frac{\partial(X_c\theta)}{\partial\theta'} = \left[I \quad q_c I + \phi \frac{\partial z_c}{\partial \beta'} \quad z_c \quad q_c z_c \right]$$

where $\partial z_c / \partial \beta'$ is a square matrix of order $n - 1$ with diagonal elements of the form

$$\frac{\partial z_{ic}}{\partial \beta_i} = (1 - w_{ic} - \beta_i)\bar{x}_{ic} - \sum_{j=1}^{n-1} (w_{jc} + \beta_j)\bar{x}_{jc}$$

and off-diagonal elements $\partial z_{ic}/\partial \beta_j = -(w_{ic} + \beta_i)\bar{x}_{jc}$.

It follows from (3.55) and the zero expectation of $y_c - X_c\theta = \epsilon_c$ that $\partial^2 L/\partial \theta_j \partial \Sigma^{-1}$ has zero expectation for each element θ_j of θ. Therefore, the information matrix is block-diagonal with respect to the elements of θ and those of Σ^{-1} so that the asymptotic covariance matrix of the ML estimator of θ is equal to minus the inverse of the expectation of the derivative $\partial^2 L/\partial\theta\,\partial\theta'$. This derivative is obtained by differentiating (3.55) with respect to θ, which yields

$$(3.57) \qquad M = -\sum_{c=1}^{N} \frac{\partial(X_c\theta)'}{\partial\theta} \Sigma^{-1} \frac{\partial(X_c\theta)}{\partial\theta'}$$

plus a matrix which is linear in $(y_c - X_c\theta)'$ for $c = 1, ..., N$. The latter matrix has zero expectation, whereas M is nonrandom. Hence, the asymptotic covariance matrix of the ML estimator of θ is $-M^{-1}$.

The ML estimates were obtained by means of Newton's method based on successive estimates of M. The asymptotic standard errors were calculated from the diagonal elements of $-M^{-1}$ with ML estimates substituted for the unknown parameters in M. When ϕ is postulated to be constant, the expressions are simplified because the last element of θ and the last column of $\partial(X_c\theta)/\partial\theta'$ can be deleted. The parameters α_n and β_n are not elements of θ in (3.51); their ML estimates and asymptotic standard errors are obtained from the constraint (3.5). The ML estimate of the disturbance covariance matrix Σ is shown in Table E.2 in Appendix E.

Chapter 4

INCOME AND PRICE ELASTICITIES AND INCOME FLEXIBILITIES

4.1. *The Income and Price Elasticities of Demand*

Elasticity Values Implied by the Maximum Likelihood Estimates

We know from (3.8) that the marginal share of good i equals $\theta_i = w_i + \beta_i$ under Working's model. So, when we also use this model in the form (3.4), $w_i = \alpha_i + \beta_i \log M$, we conclude that the income elasticity of the demand for good i under Working's model takes the form

$$\frac{\theta_i}{w_i} = 1 + \frac{\beta_i}{\alpha_i + \beta_i \log M} \tag{4.1}$$

Table 4.1 presents these income elasticities based on the ML estimates of the α_i's and β_i's given in Table 3.2. Each row of Table 4.1 provides the income elasticities of the eight goods which correspond to the per capita real income of one of the 15 countries and geometric mean prices. These per capita real incomes are substituted for M in (4.1). Their values, normalized so that the U.S. value equals 1, are shown in the first column of Table 4.1, followed by the income elasticities in the next eight columns.

A quick glance at these income elasticities shows that Food is a necessity in all countries and that all other goods are luxuries, although Clothing is barely so. The most luxurious goods are Medical care and Furniture, followed by Other expenditure, Transport and Recreation. The own-price elasticities are obtained by multiplying the corresponding income elasticity by the income flexibility (see Remark 3 at the end of Section 3.3). So, using the estimate (3.47), we find the own-price elasticity of each good at the relevant income level and geometric mean prices is obtained by multiplying the appropriate income elasticity in the relevant row of Table 4.1 by $-.618$. Each cross-price elasticity vanishes when interpreted similarly to the own-price elasticities, viz., as the elasticity of the demand for a good with respect to the Frisch-deflated price of a different good when real income remains constant. These simple rules for price elasticities are implied by the assumption of preference independence with a constant income flexibility.

The decline of the income elasticities when income rises should be noted. In particular, the income elasticity of the demand for Food in the

Table 4.1
Income elasticities of demand implied by the demand system

Country	Per capita real income[a]	Income elasticity of								Divisia variance of income elasticities
		Food	Cloth-ing	Rent	Furni-ture	Medical care	Trans-port	Recre-ation	Other	
U.S.	1.000	.28	1.05	1.17	1.27	1.29	1.20	1.18	1.20	.1424
Belgium	.700	.43	1.05	1.18	1.30	1.33	1.22	1.20	1.22	.1231
France	.666	.45	1.05	1.19	1.30	1.33	1.22	1.20	1.22	.1212
Germany	.651	.45	1.05	1.19	1.30	1.34	1.22	1.20	1.22	.1203
U.K.	.630	.46	1.05	1.19	1.31	1.34	1.22	1.20	1.22	.1192
Netherlands	.629	.46	1.05	1.19	1.31	1.34	1.22	1.20	1.22	.1191
Japan	.496	.52	1.05	1.20	1.33	1.37	1.23	1.21	1.24	.1123
Italy	.489	.53	1.05	1.20	1.33	1.37	1.23	1.21	1.24	.1119
Hungary	.416	.56	1.05	1.20	1.35	1.39	1.24	1.22	1.25	.1087
Iran	.200	.67	1.05	1.24	1.47	1.56	1.30	1.26	1.30	.1041
Colombia	.191	.67	1.05	1.24	1.48	1.57	1.30	1.26	1.31	.1043
Malaysia	.186	.68	1.05	1.24	1.49	1.58	1.30	1.26	1.31	.1045
Philippines	.137	.70	1.05	1.26	1.57	1.70	1.33	1.29	1.34	.1079
Korea	.128	.71	1.05	1.27	1.59	1.74	1.34	1.29	1.35	.1092
India	.072	.75	1.05	1.31	1.90	2.28	1.42	1.35	1.44	.1317

[a] Obtained by dividing the entries of line 9 of Table 2.3 by the U.S. value.

Table 4.2
Income elasticities obtained when cross-country price differences are ignored

Country	Per capita real income[a]	Income elasticity of: Food	Clothing	Rent	Furniture	Medical care	Transport	Recreation	Other	Divisia variance of income elasticities
U.S.	1.000	.10	1.07	1.18	1.27	1.29	1.21	1.25	1.22	.1934
Belgium	.700	.32	1.07	1.19	1.30	1.32	1.23	1.27	1.23	.1595
France	.666	.34	1.07	1.19	1.30	1.33	1.23	1.27	1.24	.1563
Germany	.651	.35	1.07	1.19	1.30	1.33	1.23	1.27	1.24	.1549
U.K.	.630	.36	1.07	1.19	1.30	1.34	1.23	1.28	1.24	.1530
Netherlands	.629	.36	1.07	1.19	1.30	1.34	1.23	1.28	1.24	.1529
Japan	.496	.45	1.07	1.20	1.33	1.36	1.25	1.30	1.26	.1417
Italy	.489	.45	1.07	1.20	1.33	1.37	1.25	1.30	1.26	.1412
Hungary	.416	.50	1.07	1.21	1.35	1.39	1.26	1.31	1.27	.1359
Iran	.200	.63	1.07	1.25	1.47	1.55	1.32	1.41	1.33	.1275
Colombia	.191	.64	1.07	1.25	1.48	1.56	1.33	1.41	1.34	.1277
Malaysia	.186	.64	1.07	1.25	1.48	1.57	1.33	1.42	1.34	.1278
Philippines	.137	.68	1.08	1.28	1.57	1.69	1.36	1.48	1.38	.1317
Korea	.128	.68	1.08	1.28	1.59	1.72	1.37	1.49	1.39	.1332
India	.072	.73	1.08	1.33	1.89	2.22	1.48	1.69	1.50	.1600

[a] See footnote a below Table 4.1.

U.S. is just over one-third of the Indian value. This should be compared with the qualitatively opposite result that we would have obtained if we had used the linear expenditure system rather than Working's model (see the last paragraph of Section 3.1). In fact, the decline of an income elasticity as income rises is a general property of Working's model, which may be verified by differentiating (4.1) with respect to $\log M$:

$$\frac{\partial(\theta_i/w_i)}{\partial(\log M)} = -\frac{\beta_i^2}{(\alpha_i + \beta_i \log M)^2} = -\left(\frac{\beta_i}{w_i}\right)^2 \tag{4.2}$$

If $\beta_i > 0$ so that good i is a luxury, an income increase reduces its income elasticity in the direction of 1. If $\beta_i < 0$ so that good i is a necessity, its income elasticity is also reduced when income rises, and ultimately the good becomes inferior when the income increase is large enough. Only when $\beta_i = 0$ does the income increase not affect the elasticity; for such a good the income elasticity remains constant at the unitary level.

Elasticity Values Implied by the Least-Squares Estimates

Table 4.2 is similar to Table 4.1 except that it uses estimates of α_i and β_i which ignore the differences between the relative prices of the different countries. These estimates are obtained from LS regressions of budget shares on the logarithm of per capita real income (see the last column of Table 3.2 for such estimates of the β_i's). A comparison of the income elasticities of Table 4.2 with the corresponding figures in Table 4.1 indicates that, for most goods, ignoring the cross-country relative price differences yields income elasticities that are farther from 1. In particular, the income elasticity of the demand for Food in the U.S. becomes only .10. This is an unrealistically small value and it illustrates the importance of taking the differences in relative prices into account. On the other hand, it should be admitted that the elasticity values in Table 4.1 for Recreation (which includes education) are a bit on the small side.

We shall have more to say about the effect of ignoring cross-country price differences in Section 4.2. Here we note that a convenient measure for the degree to which the income elasticities differ from 1 is their variance which is shown in the last column of Tables 4.1 and 4.2. To explain this variance we mention the well-known fact that the weighted mean of the n income elasticities with budget shares as weights is always 1:

$$(4.3) \qquad \sum_{i=1}^{n} w_i \frac{\theta_i}{w_i} = \sum_{i=1}^{n} \theta_i = 1$$

The extension of this weighted mean to the rth moment is

$$(4.4) \qquad \mu_r = \sum_{i=1}^{n} w_i \left(\frac{\theta_i}{w_i} - 1 \right)^r$$

which will be referred to as the rth order *Divisia moment* about the mean of the n income elasticities, the weights $w_1, \ldots, w_n$ being the same as those of the Divisia price and volume indexes which occur on the right in (3.39). In particular, when Working's model holds, we can use (4.1) to write (4.4) for $r = 2$ as

$$(4.5) \qquad \mu_2 = \sum_{i=1}^{n} \frac{\beta_i^2}{\alpha_i + \beta_i \log M}$$

which is the Divisia variance of the income elasticities under Working's model. These variances are shown in the last column of Tables 4.1 and 4.2 with the entries in the first column substituted for M and the two alternative sets of estimates substituted for the parameters. The Divisia variances in Table 4.2 are systematically larger than the corresponding values in Table 4.1, thus confirming that ignoring the relative price differences across countries tends to increase the dispersion of the estimated income elasticities.

Also notice that there is a systematic effect on the Divisia variance of a change in real income. In both Tables 4.1 and 4.2, when we start at the Indian level and move up to Iran, the Divisia variance declines and then increases when we consider higher income levels. Since it will appear in Chapter 5 that the Divisia variance of the income elasticities plays an important role in the analysis of the demand for the quality of consumption, it is worthwhile to pursue this matter a little further. We differentiate the right side of (4.5) with respect to $\log M$,

$$-\sum_{i=1}^{n} \frac{\beta_i^3}{(\alpha_i + \beta_i \log M)^2} = -\sum_{i=1}^{n} w_i \left(\frac{\beta_i}{w_i} \right)^3 = -\sum_{i=1}^{n} w_i \left(\frac{\theta_i}{w_i} - 1 \right)^3$$

and hence, in view of (4.4), we have

$$(4.6) \qquad \frac{\partial \mu_2}{\partial (\log M)} = -\mu_3$$

which shows that under Working's model the derivative with respect to log M of the Divisia variance of the income elasticities is equal to minus their third-order Divisia moment about the mean. Thus, the Divisia-weighted distributions of the income elasticities have different types of skewness at income levels above and below Iran's.

Concluding Remarks

Remark 1. We mentioned in the discussion preceding (4.2) that under Working's model the income elasticities decline as income rises. But (4.3) shows that the Divisia mean of these elasticities remains constant at the unit level. How can this be reconciled with a decline of all individual income elasticities? The answer is that the Divisia mean is a weighted mean with budget shares as weights, and that these budget shares change as income increases, those of luxuries going up and those of necessities going down.

Remark 2. Recall from Remark 1 at the end of Section 2.3 that the income elasticities in Table 2.5 have a zero weighted mean when the weights used are $\bar{w}_1, \ldots, \bar{w}_n$. These weights are similar to those of the Divisia moments, and we shall meet several other Divisia moments in the analysis which follows. We shall also meet Frisch moments with weights equal to the marginal rather than the budget shares, in agreement with the marginal shares that occur in the Frisch price index (3.38). Sometimes the two sets of moments are related. An example is

$$\sum_{i=1}^{n} \theta_i \frac{\theta_i}{w_i} = \sum_{i=1}^{n} w_i \left(\frac{\theta_i}{w_i}\right)^2$$

which equates the Frisch mean of the income elasticities to their second-order Divisia moment. Since the latter moment equals the Divisia variance plus the square of the Divisia mean, and since the Divisia mean equals 1 in view of (4.3), the implication is that the Frisch mean of the income elasticities is larger than 1 except when all goods have unitary elasticities.

4.2. The Effect of Ignoring Cross-Country Price Differences

The closer proximity to 1 of the income elasticities of Table 4.1 relative to those of Table 4.2 is due, of course, to the fact that the ML estimates of the β_i's in Table 3.2 tend to be closer to zero [cf. (4.1)] than the LS estimates which ignore the relative price differences between the various countries. The real question is, therefore, why does ignoring these price differences yield β_i estimates that are so systematically different?

Specification Analysis of Two Omitted Variables

The answer to this question is provided by our finding in Section 2.3 that, in the sample of 15 countries, luxuries tend to become more expensive relative to necessities when we move from poor to richer countries. This means that the independent variables of the demand system (relative prices and real income per capita) are correlated, so that ignoring the effect of relative prices on demand constitutes a specification error in the estimation of the effect of income.

To analyze this specification error we note that when the effect of relative prices is ignored, Working's model is estimated by applying least squares to

$$w_{ic} = \alpha_i + \beta_i \log Q_c + \epsilon_{ic} \tag{4.7}$$

A comparison with (3.19) and (3.20) shows that two terms are missing on the right in (4.7), viz.,

$$w_{ic}\left(\log\frac{p_{ic}}{\overline{p}_i} - \sum_{j=1}^{n} w_{jc}\log\frac{p_{jc}}{\overline{p}_j}\right) \tag{4.8}$$

and the substitution term $\Sigma_j\, \pi_{ij} \log (p_{jc}/\overline{p}_j)$. Since we operate under preference independence, we can express the latter term in the income flexibility and the marginal shares as shown in (3.37) for differentials. Using Working's model by equating the marginal shares of good i in country c to $w_{ic} + \beta_i$, we can then write the substitution term in the form

$$\phi(w_{ic} + \beta_i)\left[\log\frac{p_{ic}}{\overline{p}_i} - \sum_{j=1}^{n} (w_{jc} + \beta_j)\log\frac{p_{jc}}{\overline{p}_j}\right] \tag{4.9}$$

Thus, when we use the specification (4.7), we omit two variables, the values of which are shown in (4.8) and (4.9) for good i in country c. Consider in particular Food ($i = 1$). It is clear from Table 2.5 in Section 2.3 that the expression in parentheses in (4.8) for $i = 1$ is negatively correlated with $\log Q_c$. Since w_{1c} is positive, the variable (4.8) for $i = 1$ is thus an omitted variable which is negatively correlated with the independent variable log Q_c in (4.7).

For $i = 1$, the expression in brackets in (4.9) is also negatively correlated with log Q_c, but note that this expression is multiplied by the negative coefficient $\phi(w_{1c} + \beta_1)$ so that (4.9) represents an omitted variable which is positively correlated with log Q_c. However, the negative coefficient $\phi(w_{1c} + \beta_1)$ is smaller (probably substantially smaller) in absolute value than w_{1c} if we assume that Engel's law prevails, the income elasticity $(w_{1c} + \beta_1)/w_{1c}$ of Food being smaller than 1, and that ϕ is between -1 and 0. This suggests that (4.8) dominates (4.9) for $i = 1$ in the sense that their sum is negatively correlated with log Q_c. When this sum is omitted, as is the case in (4.7), we should expect that the coefficient of log Q_c is downwardly biased, which agrees with the two β_1 estimates shown in the first line of Table 3.2. Since the β_i's have zero sum in view of (3.5), we should expect that the least-squares estimates of most of the other β_i's are upwardly biased, which is also confirmed by Table 3.2.

Comparison of Divisia and Frisch Price Indexes

The magnitude of the difference in relative prices across countries should not be underestimated. It is frequently presumed that a modest change in weights will have only a slight effect on a price index, but this is not the case here when we compare Divisia and Frisch price indexes. We subtract the Divisia price index shown in (3.34) from the Frisch price index (3.38):

$$\sum_{i=1}^{n} \theta_i \mathrm{d}(\log p_i) - \sum_{i=1}^{n} w_i \mathrm{d}(\log p_i) = \sum_{i=1}^{n} w_i \left(\frac{\theta_i}{w_i} - 1\right) \mathrm{d}(\log p_i) \tag{4.10}$$

The expression on the right may be viewed as the Divisia covariance (the budget-share-weighted covariance) of the income elasticities $\theta_1/w_1, \ldots, \theta_n/w_n$ and the logarithmic price changes $\mathrm{d}(\log p_1), \ldots, \mathrm{d}(\log p_n)$ of the n goods. Therefore, when the prices of luxuries increase relative to those of necessities, the Divisia covariance in (4.10) is positive and thus implies a positive excess of the Frisch price index over the Divisia price index on the left.

To implement this development for our data we consider a move from any country c to any country d. We define the Divisia price index (in logarithmic form) associated with this move as

$$P_{cd} = \sum_{i=1}^{n} w_{icd} \log \frac{p_{id}}{p_{ic}} \tag{4.11}$$

where $w_{icd} = (w_{ic} + w_{id})/2$. [The use of this arithmetic average budget share is similar to that of $\bar{w}_{it}$ in the Rotterdam model (3.41).] Since Working's model implies that the marginal share of good i equals $w_i + \beta_i$, we define the Frisch price index of the move from country c to country d as

$$P'_{cd} = \sum_{i=1}^{n} \theta_{icd} \log \frac{p_{id}}{p_{ic}} \tag{4.12}$$

where $\theta_{icd} = w_{icd} + \beta_i$, while the prime attached to P indicates "marginal weighting." Thus, the excess of the Frisch over the Divisia price index of the move from c to d is

$$P'_{cd} - P_{cd} = \sum_{i=1}^{n} \beta_i \log \frac{p_{id}}{p_{ic}} \tag{4.13}$$

which will be interpreted as the finite-move version of the left side of (4.10) under Working's model. Note that the Divisia and Frisch indexes (4.11) and (4.12) involve the currencies of countries c and d, but that their difference (4.13) is independent of these currencies. To show this we assume that the currency unit of c changes so that p_{ic} becomes $k_c p_{ic}$ for each i, and that the currency unit of d changes so that p_{id} becomes $k_d p_{id}$ for each i. It is readily verified that this has the effect of adding $\log (k_d/k_c)$ to the right sides of (4.11) and (4.12), and that it leaves the difference (4.13) unchanged.

Table 4.3 contains the excess (4.13) of the Frisch over the Divisia price index for pairs of countries, based on the ML estimates of the β_i's shown in Table 3.2. The picture of Table 4.3 is that of a "matrix comparison" of country pairs, which we shall find useful on several other occasions as well. In the present case, the full 15 x 15 matrix $[P'_{cd} - P_{cd}]$ is skew-symmetric and only the triangular array below the main diagonal is shown. The diagonal elements of the full matrix are obviously zero and those above the diagonal are equal to the corresponding elements in transposed position apart from sign. The figures shown in Table 4.3 are multiplied by 100 so that they approximately represent percentage differences between the Frisch and Divisia price indexes (given our use of natural logarithms).

Table 4.3
Frisch price indexes minus Divisia price indexes for all eight goods[a]

	U.S.	Belgium	France	Germany	U.K.	Netherlands
Belgium	3.71					
France	1.58	−2.13				
Germany	4.03	.32	2.45			
U.K.	3.90	.19	2.32	− .12		
Netherlands	3.13	− .58	1.55	− .90	− .77	
Japan	7.80	4.09	6.22	3.77	3.90	4.67
Italy	5.64	1.93	4.06	1.61	1.74	2.51
Hungary	7.79	4.08	6.21	3.77	3.89	4.66
Iran	9.69	5.98	8.10	5.66	5.78	6.55
Colombia	4.14	.43	2.56	.11	.24	1.01
Malaysia	5.21	1.50	3.63	1.19	1.31	2.08
Philippines	8.59	4.88	7.01	4.56	4.68	5.46
Korea	9.69	5.98	8.11	5.66	5.79	6.56
India	12.31	8.60	10.73	8.28	8.41	9.18

[a] All entries should be divided by 100.

Recall that the 15 countries are listed in the order of declining per capita income. Therefore, all figures shown in Table 4.3 correspond to a move from a less affluent to a more affluent country. A substantial majority (89 out of 105 cases, or about 85 percent) of the figures is positive. Hence, going back to the Divisia covariance in (4.10), we may conclude that there is indeed a clear tendency of the prices of luxuries to increase relative to those of necessities when we move from a country c to a more affluent country d. The figures are particularly large (of the order of 10 percent) in the lower left corner of the table where the difference in affluence between c and d is substantial.

The Effect of Food on the Differences Between the Indexes

It is appropriate to ask whether the systematic effect displayed by Table 4.3 is mainly the result of Food. In many countries Food plays a dominant role in the consumer's budget (see the budget shares of Table 2.3) and it is also the case that the relative price of Food has the largest negative income elasticity (see Table 2.5). Table 4.4 answers this question by comparing the Frisch and Divisia price indexes when Food is deleted. With $n = 8$ and Food indicated by $i = 1$, the Divisia price index then changes from (4.11) to

Japan	Italy	Hun-gary	Iran	Colom-bia	Malay-sia	Philip-pines	Korea
−2.16							
− .01	2.15						
1.88	4.05	1.89					
−3.66	−1.50	−3.65	−5.54				
−2.59	− .43	−2.58	−4.47	1.07			
.79	2.95	.79	−1.10	4.45	3.37		
1.89	4.05	1.90	.01	5.55	4.48	1.10	
4.51	6.67	4.52	2.62	8.17	7.10	3.72	2.62

$$\sum_{i=2}^{8} \frac{w_{icd}}{1 - w_{1cd}} \log \frac{p_{id}}{p_{ic}} \tag{4.14}$$

while the Frisch price index (4.12) becomes

$$\sum_{i=2}^{8} \frac{\theta_{icd}}{1 - \theta_{1cd}} \log \frac{p_{id}}{p_{ic}} \tag{4.15}$$

Table 4.4 contains the excess of (4.15) over (4.14) multiplied by 100. A comparison with Table 4.3 shows that the positive majority is reduced from 85 to just over 60 percent and that most of the figures are much smaller. Thus, the tendency of luxuries to increase in price relative to necessities in the more affluent countries is mainly the result of the fact that Food tends to be relatively cheaper in the rich countries of our sample.

4.3. A Matrix Comparison of Income Flexibilities

Since the income flexibility plays a crucial role in the assessment of price effects on demand, it is appropriate that we pay some further at-

Table 4.4
Frisch price indexes minus Divisia price indexes for seven goods with Food deleted[a]

	U.S.	Belgium	France	Germany	U.K.	Netherlands
Belgium	.87					
France	.78	.21				
Germany	.84	– .03	– .14			
U.K.	.71	– .17	– .36	– .22		
Netherlands	.86	.19	– .18	.04	.34	
Japan	.76	.38	– .25	.11	.65	.08
Italy	.98	.20	– .09	.06	.35	.08
Hungary	1.13	1.07	.24	.85	.73	.54
Iran	.15	– .87	– .62	– .60	– .82	– .44
Colombia	1.09	.09	– .13	.05	.49	– .27
Malaysia	1.37	– .02	– .29	– .14	.38	– .47
Philippines	– .41	– .97	–1.22	– .95	–1.48	–1.58
Korea	2.06	1.25	.53	.98	1.73	.54
India	2.19	1.38	.94	1.51	1.71	.63

[a] All entries should be divided by 100.

tention to this parameter. It will appear that this can be done in an instructive way by means of a matrix comparison similar to that of Table 4.3.

The Price–Quantity Covariance

A convenient starting point is the Divisia covariance of the logarithmic price and quantity changes of the n goods. This covariance, to be called the price–quantity covariance for short, is defined as

$$\Gamma = \sum_{i=1}^{n} w_i \left[d(\log p_i) - \sum_{j=1}^{n} w_j d(\log p_j) \right] \times \left[d(\log q_i) - \sum_{j=1}^{n} w_j d(\log q_j) \right]$$

Since the value of a covariance is not affected when we measure only one of the variables as a deviation from its mean, we can simplify Γ to

$$\Gamma = \sum_{i=1}^{n} w_i \left[d(\log p_i) - \sum_{j=1}^{n} w_j d(\log p_j) \right] d(\log q_i) \tag{4.16}$$

Japan	Italy	Hungary	Iran	Colombia	Malaysia	Philippines	Korea
.03							
.92	.26						
−1.12	−.81	−1.58					
.67	−.16	−1.30	2.12				
−.74	−.22	−1.21	1.02	.39			
−1.50	−1.78	−2.22	.02	−1.58	−1.77		
1.15	.95	−.11	3.56	1.11	1.61	3.97	
.93	1.45	.10	4.18	1.86	1.74	3.76	.24

A comparison of (4.16) with (3.40) shows that we can express Γ in terms of income and price changes by multiplying (3.40) by the Divisia-deflated logarithmic price change of good i and then summing over i. In particular, when we assume preference independence so that the substitution term of (3.40) takes the form (3.37), we find after minor rearrangements that Γ is equal to a real-income component of the form

$$(4.17) \qquad \left[\sum_{i=1}^{n} \theta_i \mathrm{d}(\log p_i) - \sum_{i=1}^{n} w_i \mathrm{d}(\log p_i) \right] \sum_{i=1}^{n} w_i \mathrm{d}(\log q_i)$$

plus the following relative-price component:

$$(4.18) \qquad \phi \sum_{i=1}^{n} \theta_i \left[\mathrm{d}(\log p_i) - \sum_{j=1}^{n} \theta_j \mathrm{d}(\log p_j) \right]^2$$

Note that the real-income component (4.17) is nothing but the excess of the Frisch over the Divisia price index shown in (4.10), multiplied by the Divisia volume index, while the relative-price component (4.18) is a multiple ϕ of the Frisch variance of the logarithmic price changes of the n goods (see Remark 2 at the end of Section 4.1).

To implement these developments for our data, we write the preference-independent version of (3.40) under Working's model for the move from country c to country d as

$$(4.19)\quad w_{icd}\log\frac{q_{id}}{q_{ic}} = \theta_{icd}Q_{cd} + \phi\theta_{icd}\left(\log\frac{p_{id}}{p_{ic}} - P'_{cd}\right) + \epsilon_{icd}$$

where ϵ_{icd} is a disturbance and Q_{cd} is the finite-move version of the Divisia volume index:

$$(4.20)\qquad Q_{cd} = \sum_{i=1}^{n} w_{icd}\log\frac{q_{id}}{q_{ic}}$$

The price–quantity covariance of the move from c to d is defined as

$$(4.21)\qquad \Gamma_{cd} = \sum_{i=1}^{n} w_{icd}\left(\log\frac{p_{id}}{p_{ic}} - P_{cd}\right)\left(\log\frac{q_{id}}{q_{ic}} - Q_{cd}\right)$$

As in (4.16), we can delete the volume index on the far right in (4.21). Next we multiply (4.19) by $\log(p_{id}/p_{ic})$ deflated by P_{cd}, and sum over i:

$$(4.22)\qquad \Gamma_{cd} = (P'_{cd} - P_{cd})\,Q_{cd} + \phi\Pi'_{cd} + \sum_{i=1}^{n}\epsilon_{icd}\log\frac{p_{id}}{p_{ic}}$$

The successive terms on the right are the real-income, relative-price and disturbance components of Γ_{cd}, with Π'_{cd} defined as

$$(4.23)\qquad \Pi'_{cd} = \sum_{i=1}^{n}\theta_{icd}\left(\log\frac{p_{id}}{p_{ic}} - P'_{cd}\right)^2$$

which is the Frisch variance of the logarithmic price differences between country c and country d. As in (4.12), the prime attached to Π indicates marginal weighting.

A Matrix Comparison of Income Flexibility Estimates

By subtracting the real-income component from Γ_{cd}, we obtain the relative price component $\phi\Pi'_{cd}$ plus the disturbance component. If the price ratios can be viewed as independent variables and if the ϵ_{icd}'s have zero expectation, so has the disturbance component of (4.22). This suggests that we can estimate the income flexibility for any pair of countries by correcting the price–quantity covariance for its real-income component and then dividing by the Frisch price variance:

$$\hat{\phi}_{cd} = \frac{\Gamma_{cd} - (P'_{cd} - P_{cd})\, Q_{cd}}{\Pi'_{cd}} \tag{4.24}$$

The estimates $\hat{\phi}_{cd}$ are given in Table 4.5. The figures shown are the elements below the diagonal of a symmetric 15 x 15 matrix whose diagonal is undefined (the diagonal elements are of the form 0/0). Note that P'_{cd} and Π'_{cd} in (4.24) involve the marginal shares and hence the β_i's of Working's model; the values used for the β_i's are the ML estimates of Table 3.2 so the income flexibility values of Table 4.5 are conditional on these estimates. Also, the values in Table 4.5 in the same row or the same column are obviously not independent, and we should expect that the sampling variability of $\hat{\phi}_{cd}$ will vary inversely with the variance Π'_{cd} that occurs in the denominator of (4.24).

In spite of these limitations it is the case that the income flexibility estimates of Table 4.5 present an interesting picture. There are only seven positive values out of 105 and most of these positive values are close to zero. There are 12 negative values larger than 1 in absolute value so that there is a majority in excess of 80 percent in the interval (–1, 0). There is a slight tendency of the figures in the lower right corner to be closer to zero than those in the upper left corner, which could explain the negative point estimate of ϕ_1 in (3.46), but the picture of Table 4.5 does not support Frisch's conjecture (see Section 3.5) which would imply values of the order of –.1 and –2 in the lower right and upper left corners, respectively, of the table. On the whole, the estimates of Table 4.5 are sufficiently dispersed to warrant the assumption of a constant income flexibility as a first approximation, at least until additional evidence becomes available.

Concluding Remarks

Remark 1. We concluded in the discussion following (4.18) that the substitution component of the price–quantity covariance equals ϕ multiplied by the Frisch price variance. Note that this result involves the assumption of preference independence. When there is no preference independence, the substitution component of the price–quantity covariance is equal to a negative semidefinite quadratic form in the logarithmic price changes. It is possible to apply a preference independence

Table 4.5
Income flexibility estimates for pairs of countries

	U.S.	Belgium	France	Germany	U.K.	Netherlands
Belgium	− .83					
France	− .91	− .98				
Germany	− .88	−1.61	−2.76			
U.K.	− .48	−1.58	− .56	−.79		
Netherlands	− .67	− .49	− .32	−.04	− .33	
Japan	−1.01	− .96	− .79	−.80	−1.60	−.68
Italy	− .52	−1.07	− .47	−.21	− .26	.05
Hungary	− .62	− .58	− .70	−.74	− .42	−.63
Iran	− .88	− .93	− .90	−.58	−1.00	−.29
Colombia	− .95	−1.01	−1.03	−.92	−1.01	−.61
Malaysia	− .55	− .64	− .47	.11	− .16	.03
Philippines	− .56	− .47	− .69	−.55	− .50	−.46
Korea	− .55	− .81	− .66	−.49	− .85	−.45
India	− .48	− .59	− .53	−.43	− .59	−.38

Table 4.6
Divisia price variances for all eight goods[a]

	U.S.	Belgium	France	Germany	U.K.	Netherlands
Belgium	760					
France	673	241				
Germany	573	115	89			
U.K.	624	179	287	115		
Netherlands	711	339	97	125	329	
Japan	1905	651	1221	800	512	915
Italy	981	352	237	119	191	181
Hungary	2427	854	1055	954	857	1324
Iran	1033	616	984	540	686	795
Colombia	862	595	963	667	513	1192
Malaysia	1315	343	582	381	270	509
Philippines	1481	756	1324	843	746	1500
Korea	2006	674	1296	791	547	1335
India	3052	1217	2003	1408	1290	2283

[a] All entries should be divided by 10,000.

Japan	Italy	Hungary	Iran	Colombia	Malaysia	Philippines	Korea
–.93							
–.39	–.79						
–.97	–.85	–.49					
–.85	–.79	–.65	–1.31				
–.12	.06	–.02	– .09	–.39			
–.80	–.71	–.19	–1.36	–.83	.13		
–.69	–.88	–.25	–1.09	–.37	.17	–.44	
–.55	–.70	.07	– .94	–.52	–.13	–.38	–.52

Japan	Italy	Hungary	Iran	Colombia	Malaysia	Philippines	Korea
815							
1391	640						
1090	601	979					
996	950	1342	1137				
542	323	908	861	1136			
1206	825	612	250	802	792		
471	664	546	783	555	671	449	
1184	1190	525	763	1145	1153	381	268

transformation which changes this quadratic form into ϕ times the Frisch price variance; see Theil (1980a, Chap. 10–11) and Theil and Laitinen (1981) for details on this transformation.

Remark 2. The estimator (4.24) can be obtained directly from (4.19) for $i = 1, ..., n$ by means of a Frisch-weighted regression, and such regressions have optimal properties under the conditions of the theory of rational random behavior. For details on these regressions see Theil (1975–76, Chap. 15); for details on rational random behavior see Theil (1980a, Chap. 7–8).

Remark 3. It is assumed in this monograph that prices can be viewed as exogenous variables. However, it is possible to extend the differential approach to consumption theory so that the prices become endogenous rather than exogenous; see Theil (1975–76, Chap. 9–10).

4.4. *Divisia and Frisch Price Variances*

In (4.23) we met the Frisch price variance of countries c and d, but there exists also a Divisia price variance,

$$\Pi_{cd} = \sum_{i=1}^{n} w_{icd} \left(\log \frac{p_{id}}{p_{ic}} - P_{cd} \right)^2 \tag{4.25}$$

in which the prime is deleted from Π and P for obvious reasons. Such variances are convenient summary measures because they describe the extent to which the relative prices in the two countries differ. Table 4.6 contains the Divisia variances (4.25) for country pairs and Table 4.7 contains the Frisch variances (4.23). The figures are multiplied by 10^4 so that their square roots approximately represent standard deviations in percentage form.

It should come as no surprise that many of these price variances are large, particularly those which correspond to countries with widely different levels of per capita real income. Nor should it come as a surprise that the variances involving Hungary with its communist regime are large relative to Hungary's position on the real-income scale. It is intriguing that the Frisch price variances tend to be larger than the Divisia price variances. There are only 10 exceptions (out of 105) to the rule that the Frisch price variance in Table 4.7 exceeds the corresponding Divisia variance in Table 4.6. Returning to the last paragraph of Section 4.2, we may wonder whether this results mainly from Food, although the reason would be different in this case. A price variance cannot be very large when it assigns an overwhelming weight to the price of one of the n goods. Food has a large budget share in poor countries, but its marginal share is smaller because this is obtained from the budget share by adding a negative β_i (see the ML estimate of Food's β_i in Table 3.2). Thus, we would expect that $\Pi'_{cd} > \Pi_{cd}$ holds more often when c and d are both poor countries than when either c or d is a more affluent country. This is corroborated by the fact that none of the above-mentioned 10 exceptions to the rule $\Pi'_{cd} > \Pi_{cd}$ is located in the lower right corners of Tables 4.6 and 4.7 consisting of the last eight columns.

A second check is provided by a comparison of Divisia and Frisch price variances when Food is deleted. With $n = 8$ and Food indicated by $i = 1$, the variances (4.25) and (4.23) then become

$$\sum_{i=2}^{8} \frac{w_{icd}}{1 - w_{1cd}} \left(\log \frac{p_{id}}{p_{ic}} - P_{\mathrm{F}cd} \right)^2 \tag{4.26}$$

$$\sum_{i=2}^{8} \frac{\theta_{icd}}{1 - \theta_{1cd}} \left(\log \frac{p_{id}}{p_{ic}} - P'_{\mathrm{F}cd} \right)^2 \tag{4.27}$$

where $P_{\mathrm{F}cd}$ and $P'_{\mathrm{F}cd}$ are the Divisia and Frisch price indexes (4.14) and (4.15), respectively, with the subscript F indicating the deleted Food category. The variances (4.26) and (4.27) are shown in Tables 4.8 and 4.9. These tables still show a majority of Frisch price variances which exceed the corresponding Divisia variances. But since this majority is only about 55 percent, it seems reasonable to conclude that the corresponding excesses of Frisch over Divisia price variances for $n = 8$ in Tables 4.6 and 4.7 mainly result from the dominating position of Food in the Divisia variance.

4.5. The Price–Quantity Covariance Further Considered

In Section 4.3 we used the price–quantity covariance Γ_{cd} to obtain an estimate of the income flexibility for each pair of countries, but it is also of interest to consider these covariances directly. They are shown in Table 4.10, where they are multiplied by 10^4 in order to make them comparable to the corresponding Divisia price variances of Table 4.6. Note that 41 of the 105 covariances are positive and that many of these positive values

(*text continues on p. 74*)

Table 4.7
Frisch price variances for all eight goods[a]

	U.S.	Belgium	France	Germany	U.K.	Netherlands
Belgium	874					
France	809	258				
Germany	634	138	66			
U.K.	731	218	296	137		
Netherlands	852	401	93	142	380	
Japan	2075	724	1232	894	573	995
Italy	1107	424	198	139	220	189
Hungary	2743	1019	1113	1127	977	1484
Iran	769	540	844	478	665	759
Colombia	982	727	1152	818	628	1456
Malaysia	1555	400	600	433	313	569
Philippines	1427	801	1357	923	798	1640
Korea	2264	771	1360	896	612	1479
India	3361	1326	2135	1575	1418	2506

[a] All entries should be divided by 10,000.

Table 4.8
Divisia price variances for seven goods with Food deleted[a]

	U.S.	Belgium	France	Germany	U.K.	Netherlands
Belgium	891					
France	855	267				
Germany	627	150	48			
U.K.	708	245	315	155		
Netherlands	856	450	98	156	440	
Japan	1996	740	1206	943	592	1025
Italy	1083	473	114	138	257	184
Hungary	2777	1100	1049	1231	1119	1677
Iran	263	277	392	265	435	506
Colombia	1081	883	1338	968	784	1749
Malaysia	1654	481	663	535	402	677
Philippines	1091	731	1149	922	698	1771
Korea	2142	692	1151	893	577	1591
India	3198	1104	1719	1545	1397	2726

[a] All entries should be divided by 10,000.

Japan	Italy	Hungary	Iran	Colombia	Malaysia	Philippines	Korea
962							
1647	772						
1350	696	1260					
1162	1190	1743	1162				
653	369	1052	991	1366			
1555	1009	815	336	891	967		
561	799	710	1077	688	767	708	
1407	1419	623	1112	1378	1314	590	340

Japan	Italy	Hungary	Iran	Colombia	Malaysia	Philippines	Korea
1180							
2097	949						
1674	650	1498					
1284	1515	2037	1073				
792	531	1426	1024	1892			
2103	1207	1026	489	917	1111		
821	1014	929	1493	589	1061	989	
2020	1743	638	1760	1322	1657	915	529

Table 4.9
Frisch price variances for seven goods with Food deleted[a]

	U.S.	Belgium	France	Germany	U.K.	Netherlands
Belgium	908					
France	865	265				
Germany	643	151	47			
U.K.	756	248	303	153		
Netherlands	893	445	91	153	428	
Japan	2080	754	1187	947	599	1028
Italy	1134	485	117	147	251	183
Hungary	2856	1132	1074	1248	1096	1633
Iran	263	300	412	288	474	541
Colombia	1067	880	1348	971	778	1751
Malaysia	1698	471	620	507	382	650
Philippines	1095	751	1168	944	740	1758
Korea	2235	735	1159	913	572	1560
India	3190	1101	1703	1531	1314	2590

[a] All entries should be divided by 10,000.

Table 4.10
Price–quantity covariances[a]

	U.S.	Belgium	France	Germany	U.K.	Netherlands
Belgium	− 585					
France	− 674	− 263				
Germany	− 388	− 221	− 180			
U.K.	− 167	− 343	− 155	− 108		
Netherlands	− 428	− 204	− 23	− 9	−126	
Japan	−1518	− 534	− 777	− 599	−799	−550
Italy	− 167	− 384	34	18	− 11	76
Hungary	−1019	− 371	− 477	− 653	−241	−740
Iran	890	246	236	393	7	554
Colombia	− 227	− 675	− 860	− 735	−605	−762
Malaysia	30	− 60	178	194	110	270
Philippines	916	418	185	210	319	76
Korea	731	388	433	473	405	375
India	1578	1144	1232	1105	962	994

[a] All entries should be divided by 10,000.

Japan	Italy	Hungary	Iran	Colombia	Malaysia	Philippines	Korea
1157							
2023	945						
1714	717	1611					
1317	1532	2167	1066				
789	484	1333	1075	1815			
2161	1272	1124	508	936	1189		
769	996	971	1636	674	958	1192	
1899	1681	663	1885	1353	1483	996	504

Japan	Italy	Hungary	Iran	Colombia	Malaysia	Philippines	Korea
−890							
−639	−575						
−1146	−220	−476					
−1338	−1088	−1403	−1569				
−309	−19	−220	−102	−526			
−1147	−336	−72	−497	−592	245		
−142	−163	37	−1169	−45	308	−308	
47	266	804	−789	70	498	7	−30

Table 4.11
Price–quantity covariances excluding their real-income components[a]

	U.S.	Belgium	France	Germany	U.K.	Netherlands
Belgium	− 722					
France	− 740	−252				
Germany	− 559	−223	− 181			
U.K.	− 349	−344	− 166	−108		
Netherlands	− 575	−198	− 30	− 5	−125	
Japan	−2090	−692	− 977	−716	−915	−680
Italy	− 574	−454	− 93	− 29	− 56	10
Hungary	−1708	−595	− 774	−831	−410	−941
Iran	− 673	−501	− 759	−279	−662	−218
Colombia	− 932	−732	−1187	−749	−635	−885
Malaysia	− 858	−258	− 285	46	− 51	18
Philippines	− 794	−378	− 942	−503	−398	−756
Korea	−1251	−622	− 900	−438	−519	−660
India	−1608	−780	−1141	−682	−840	−963

[a] All entries should be divided by 10,000.

Table 4.12
Divisia volume indexes minus logarithmic total expenditure ratios in international dollars[a,b]

	U.S.	Belgium	France	Germany	U.K.	Netherlands
Belgium	1.19					
France	.94	.45				
Germany	− .36	−1.16	−1.52			
U.K.	.50	− .60	− .73	.15		
Netherlands	.46	− .07	−1.33	.39	.45	
Japan	3.17	4.17	2.67	3.84	5.82	3.83
Italy	.76	.45	.50	.53	1.02	1.14
Hungary	.67	2.82	.81	2.56	2.07	1.66
Iran	.28	− .26	2.42	.60	.91	2.93
Colombia	4.36	2.33	2.90	2.86	3.94	2.36
Malaysia	2.23	− .88	− .07	− .48	.54	−1.20
Philippines	.59	.42	2.97	.66	.62	.20
Korea	− .70	− .68	− .12	−1.45	.71	−1.12
India	−3.86	−3.24	− .77	−3.99	−2.09	−3.22

[a] $Q_{cd} - \log (Q_d/Q_c)$, where Q_{cd} is defined in (4.20) and Q_c is the cth entry of line 9 of Table 2.3.

[b] All entries should be divided by 100.

Japan	Italy	Hungary	Iran	Colombia	Malaysia	Philippines	Korea
−896							
−639	−612						
−1309	−590	−612					
−989	−945	−1126	−1526				
−77	21	−24	−86	−528			
−1243	−712	−157	−457	−740	129		
−386	−700	−177	−1169	−257	134	−315	
−777	−993	42	−1046	−711	−176	−221	−177

Japan	Italy	Hungary	Iran	Colombia	Malaysia	Philippines	Korea
−4.17							
−.84	.74						
−4.71	1.75	−1.82					
−.16	1.27	−2.38	3.04				
−8.41	−1.39	−4.65	−3.47	−1.14			
−6.09	.51	−2.92	−1.25	.58	3.96		
−5.98	−1.36	−4.77	−.91	−1.39	1.80	−.17	
−9.70	−2.49	−6.28	−3.56	−1.40	.36	−2.78	−1.38

are substantial, particularly those in the lower left corner of Table 4.10. One would expect that a price–quantity covariance is "normally" negative because of the consumer's tendency to substitute in favor of those goods that are relatively cheaper. The answer to this argument is, of course, that it takes only the substitution effect into account, not the real-income effect which is large in the lower left corner to the table where the countries compared have widely different per capita incomes.

To correct for this effect, recall from (4.22) that Γ_{cd} has a real-income component equal to the difference between the Frisch and the Divisia price indexes multiplied by the Divisia volume index Q_{cd} which is defined in (4.20). When c is less affluent than d, as is the case in the lower left corner of Table 4.10, we should expect Q_{cd} to be positive. Also recall from Table 4.3 that the excess of the Frisch over the Divisia price indexes tends to take large positive values in the same lower left corner. Consequently, the product of Q_{cd} and this excess (the real-income component of Γ_{cd}) will also tend to be positive in this corner. Table 4.11 pursues this matter by presenting

$$\Gamma_{cd} - (P'_{cd} - P_{cd})\, Q_{cd} \tag{4.28}$$

which is the price–quantity covariance corrected for the difference in affluence between the two countries. Most of the figures in the lower left corner of Table 4.11 are negative and many of these negative values exceed the corresponding positive values of Table 4.10 in absolute value. The real-income correction reduces the number of positive covariances from 41 to 7; of course, these seven cases are the same as those which have a positive income flexibility estimate in Table 4.5.

The corrected price–quantity covariance (4.28) should not be identified with the substitution component of Γ_{cd} because (4.28) is actually equal to the sum of the substitution and the disturbance components in (4.22); we shall go further into this matter in Chapter 6. Here we should mention that the Divisia volume index Q_{cd} is not identical to the corresponding index implied by the methodology used by Kravis and his colleagues. The latter index takes the form $\log (Q_d/Q_c)$, where the single-subscript Q's are the entries in line 9 of Table 2.3. However, the difference is not large for most country pairs. This is pursued in Table 4.12, which contains the discrepancy

$$Q_{cd} - \log (Q_d/Q_c) \tag{4.29}$$

multiplied by 100 (so that the figures shown approximately represent percentage discrepancies). Most of the figures indicate discrepancies of a few percentage points or less, although some of the values which compare Japan and Hungary with the poorest countries are larger. However, even those values are small relative to the per capita real-income differences implied by line 9 of Table 2.3.

The price–quantity covariance may be compared with an analogous covariance which appears in Bortkiewicz's (1923) theorem. The latter covariance is related to the Laspeyres and Paasche price and volume indexes, whereas Γ_{cd} is related to the Divisia indexes; see Theil (1975–76, Chap. 11). The Divisia methodology and the associated Frisch methodology have the advantage relative to Laspeyres and Paasche of treating the two countries that are compared symmetrically and of doing so in simple logarithmic terms. This implies that we can easily implement the results of the differential approach to consumption theory.

Chapter 5

THE QUALITY OF CONSUMPTION

5.1. *The Measurement of Quality*

Can the Quality of Consumption Be Measured?

The measurement of the quality of consumption is a controversial matter. There have been several similar controversial issues in the past. One example is the measurement of utility, which was taken for granted by many economists in the 19th century and in the early 20th century until the work of Hicks and Allen (1934) led to a more critical attitude. The later work of Von Neumann and Morgenstern (1947) convinced most economists that utility measurement is acceptable under conditions of uncertainty, but utility measurement under certainty remains controversial. An even more instructive example is that of the measurement of heat. Many 19th century physicists considered "warmth" too subjective to be measured, but later on a general agreement emerged that there are two different useful ways of measuring this phenomenon, viz., in the form of heat measured in calories and in the form of temperature measured along the Celsius or Kelvin scale.

Three Ways of Measuring Quality

Here we adopt the view that there are at least three ways in which the quality of consumption can be measured. The most direct approach is based on an enumeration of the attractive features of a good, such as the horsepower and the size of an automobile (unattractive features may also be included and should be counted negatively). In fact, this is the approach used in the theory of hedonic price indexes to explain price differentials of automobiles and other goods; see, e.g., Griliches (1971). But this approach is less practical when the analyst is interested in several goods simultaneously as is the case here (because we shall want to make quality assessments based on the composition of the per capita consumption of different countries). It is then more attractive to summarize quality by means of one single number. The procedures described in the next two paragraphs are different ways to achieve this objective.

One approach, suggested independently by Houthakker (1953) and

Theil (1953), is based on the average price paid for a composite (i.e., nonhomogeneous) good. Let coffee be such a good, consisting of various grades. Since high-quality coffee commands a higher price than low-quality coffee, the average price which a family pays for a pound of coffee (the total expenditure on coffee divided by the total quantity in pounds) is a measure of the quality of the coffee bought. Such an indicator is useful for a cross-section study when the prices of the individual coffee grades are approximately constant during the short period covered by such a study. However, this method is applicable only to narrowly defined composite goods, since dimensional considerations prevent us from averaging the prices of coffee and dental services. It is more attractive to measure quality by means of dimensionless concepts.

The distinction between luxuries and necessities based on income elasticities provides a solution. Consider the Divisia volume index which occurs in (3.39) as well as the Frisch volume index $\Sigma_i \theta_i \mathrm{d}(\log q_i)$ which we have not yet met. The excess of the latter index over the former can be written as

$$(5.1)\quad \sum_{i=1}^{n} \theta_i \mathrm{d}(\log q_i) - \sum_{i=1}^{n} w_i \mathrm{d}(\log q_i) = \sum_{i=1}^{n} w_i \left(\frac{\theta_i}{w_i} - 1\right) \mathrm{d}(\log q_i)$$

The right side of this equation is the Divisia covariance of the income elasticities and the logarithmic quantity changes in the same way that the right side of (4.10) is the Divisia covariance of the income elasticities and the logarithmic price changes. Thus, when the quantities consumed of luxuries increase relative to those of necessities, both sides of (5.1) are positive. The consumer reveals by his behavior that he considers luxuries more desirable than necessities, because he spends a larger fraction of his income on the former goods and a smaller fraction on the latter when he becomes more affluent and prices remain unchanged. Hence, a positive (negative) value of either side of (5.1) indicates that the consumer's basket has increased (decreased) in desirability. Accordingly, we shall refer to (5.1) as the *quality index* of the consumer's basket in differential form.

The approaches of the two previous paragraphs, based respectively on the average price paid for a composite good and on the income elasticities of all n goods, are both behavioral in the sense that they do not involve an outside value judgment on what is "good" for the consumer. This is in contrast to the approach implicit in the hedonic price index theory, which may be viewed as claiming that "a powerful big car is good for you." Also, the former two approaches may be presumed to yield results that are positively correlated with each other. This may be illustrated with income elasticities [quoted from Cramer (1973)] obtained from a European household survey in 1963–64. In Germany, where beer is cheap relative to wine, the income elasticity of beer is only .5 and that of wine is 1.3, but in Italy (where beer is expensive relative to wine) the income elasticity of beer is 1.1 and that of wine is only .7.

The Components of the Quality Index

For the move from country c to country d we interpret the left side of (5.1) as $Q'_{cd} - Q_{cd}$, where Q_{cd} is the Divisia volume index defined in (4.20) and

$$Q'_{cd} = \sum_{i=1}^{n} \theta_{icd} \log \frac{q_{id}}{q_{ic}} \tag{5.2}$$

is the corresponding Frisch volume index. To express $Q'_{cd} - Q_{cd}$ in terms of the incomes and prices of the two countries, we use the demand model (4.19) which is reproduced here:

$$w_{icd} \log \frac{q_{id}}{q_{ic}} = \theta_{icd} Q_{cd} + \phi\theta_{icd} \left(\log \frac{p_{id}}{p_{ic}} - P'_{cd} \right) + \epsilon_{icd} \tag{5.3}$$

The further developments are described in Sections 5.2 and 5.3, but the final result can be conveniently discussed here.

The first column of Table 5.1 contains the quality index of consumption of the eight goods in the 15 countries. This index is obtained by taking the antilog of $Q'_{cd} - Q_{cd}$ and then normalizing so that the U.S. value equals 1 (see Section 5.3 for further details). All countries other than the U.S. have a lower quality index (although Germany comes close) and the range is from 1 to less than .8. Note that this range is much smaller than that of the real-income index which is shown in the first column of Table 4.1. Real income is a measure of the total quantity of consumption, whereas Table 5.1 is concerned with the quality of consumption measured in terms of the luxury-necessity composition of the consumer's basket.

Since the quality index of Table 5.1 is obtained by taking antilogs, it is equal to the product (rather than the sum) of three component indexes: one for the effect of real income, a second for the substitution effect of relative prices, and a third which results from the ϵ_{icd}'s in (5.3). As could be expected, the behavior of the third (residual) component is largely irregular. The substitution component is not irregular at all because it tends to decline as we move from less affluent to more affluent countries

Table 5.1
The quality of consumption index and its components

Country	Quality	Component indexes		
		Real income	Substitution	Residual
U.S.	1.000	1.000	1.000	1.000
Belgium	.961	.951	1.014	.996
France	.937	.945	1.007	.985
Germany	.990	.944	1.016	1.033
U.K.	.929	.942	1.014	.973
Netherlands	.954	.940	1.013	1.003
Japan	.947	.910	1.033	1.008
Italy	.895	.914	1.023	.958
Hungary	.921	.895	1.034	.995
Iran	.868	.831	1.040	1.006
Colombia	.870	.823	1.015	1.042
Malaysia	.869	.824	1.021	1.033
Philippines	.815	.801	1.034	.984
Korea	.813	.794	1.050	.976
India	.785	.750	1.067	.982

This results from the tendency of luxuries to increase in price relative to necessities when we move in this direction (see Section 2.3), and it has the effect of reducing the quality index in the more affluent countries below the level that would have been attained if there were no such tendency. However, the substitution component is overcompensated by the real-income component which dominates the quality index. Ideally the real-income component should decline in the order of the countries shown, but there are two exceptions to this rule (Japan–Italy and Colombia–Malaysia) which will be explained in Section 5.3. The figures in Table 5.1 are based on the ML estimates discussed in Section 3.5.

5.2. *Quality Indexes for Pairs of Countries*

We obtain Q'_{cd} of (5.2) by multiplying (5.3) by the income elasticity θ_{icd}/w_{icd} and then summing over i,

$$(5.4)\qquad Q'_{cd} = Q_{cd} \sum_{i=1}^{n} \frac{\theta_{icd}^2}{w_{icd}} + \phi \sum_{i=1}^{n} \frac{\theta_{icd}^2}{w_{icd}} \left(\log \frac{p_{id}}{p_{ic}} - P'_{cd} \right) + \sum_{i=1}^{n} \frac{\theta_{icd}\,\epsilon_{icd}}{w_{icd}}$$

after which the logarithmic quality index $Q'_{cd} - Q_{cd}$ is obtained by subtracting Q_{cd} from both sides. This changes the real-income term in (5.4) to

$$Q_{cd} \sum_{i=1}^{n} w_{icd} \left(\frac{\theta_{icd}}{w_{icd}} \right)^2 - Q_{cd} = Q_{cd} \sum_{i=1}^{n} w_{icd} \left(\frac{\theta_{icd}}{w_{icd}} - 1 \right)^2$$

It follows from (4.4) that the right side of this equation may be written as $\mu_{2cd} Q_{cd}$, where

$$\mu_{2cd} = \sum_{i=1}^{n} w_{icd} \left(\frac{\theta_{icd}}{w_{icd}} - 1 \right)^2 \tag{5.5}$$

is the Divisia variance of the income elasticities in the move from country c to country d. Therefore,

$$Q'_{cd} - Q_{cd} = \mu_{2cd} Q_{cd} + \phi \sum_{i=1}^{n} \theta_{icd} \left(\log \frac{p_{id}}{p_{ic}} - P'_{cd} \right) \frac{\theta_{icd}}{w_{icd}} + \sum_{i=1}^{n} \frac{\theta_{icd}}{w_{icd}} \epsilon_{icd} \tag{5.6}$$

The three successive terms on the right in (5.6) are the real-income, the substitution and the residual components of $Q'_{cd} - Q_{cd}$. Since $Q'_{cd} - Q_{cd}$ measures the quality difference between c and d and since Q_{cd} measures the real-income difference, both in logarithmic terms, the Divisia variance μ_{2cd} of the income elasticities which is the coefficient of Q_{cd} thus has the interpretation of the *income elasticity of the demand for quality*. Therefore, when all n goods have income elasticities close to 1 so that there is not much of a distinction between luxuries and necessities, the demand for quality has a small income elasticity. On the other hand, if the income elasticities of the n goods are greatly dispersed, a given change in real income has a much more substantial impact on the quality of the consumer's basket in terms of its luxury-necessity composition.

The substitution component in (5.6) can be viewed as a multiple ϕ of the Frisch covariance of the income elasticities and the logarithmic price ratios in the two countries. Therefore, given the negative sign of ϕ, a move from c to d yields a lower quality of consumption index when the prices of luxuries relative to those of necessities are higher in d than in c. Such an effect agrees with what we should expect the substitution effect to perform with respect to the luxury-necessity composition of the consumer's basket. Recall that we met a covariance of income elasticities and logarithmic price displacements earlier, viz., in (4.10) where we considered the difference between the Frisch and the Divisia price indexes. However, note that the covariance in (4.10) is a Divisia covariance, whereas the covariance in the substitution term of (5.6) is a Frisch covariance. Finally, the residual component of (5.6) may be viewed as a weighted sum of the ϵ_{icd}'s of (5.3) with the income elasticities as weights.

For the implementation of (5.6) we use Working's model in the form $\theta_{icd} = w_{icd} + \beta_i$, which implies that (5.5) can be simplified to

$$\mu_{2cd} = \sum_{i=1}^{n} \frac{\beta_i^2}{w_{icd}} \tag{5.7}$$

and that the quality index takes the form

$$Q'_{cd} - Q_{cd} = \sum_{i=1}^{n} \beta_i \log \frac{q_{id}}{q_{ic}} \tag{5.8}$$

Table 5.2 contains $Q'_{cd} - Q_{cd}$ for pairs of countries, and the next three tables give its real-income, substitution and residual components. The entries in these four tables are all multiplied by 100 and they are based on the ML estimates of Section 3.5. The entry upper left in Table 5.2 is 3.98,

Table 5.2
Quality of consumption indexes for pairs of countries[a]

	U.S.	Belgium	France	Germany	U.K.	Netherlands
Belgium	3.98					
France	6.52	2.54				
Germany	.96	− 3.02	− 5.56			
U.K.	7.35	3.37	.83	6.38		
Netherlands	4.67	.69	− 1.85	3.70	− 2.68	
Japan	5.40	1.42	− 1.12	4.44	− 1.95	.73
Italy	11.05	7.07	4.53	10.08	3.70	6.38
Hungary	8.24	4.26	1.72	7.28	.89	3.57
Iran	14.12	10.14	7.60	13.16	6.77	9.45
Colombia	13.89	9.91	7.37	12.92	6.54	9.22
Malaysia	14.02	10.04	7.50	13.06	6.67	9.35
Philippines	20.47	16.49	13.95	19.51	13.12	15.80
Korea	20.69	16.71	14.17	19.72	13.34	16.02
India	24.18	20.20	17.66	23.21	16.83	19.51

[a] All entries should be divided by 100.

which means that the U.S. quality of consumption index exceeds the Belgian level by about 4 percent. The corresponding elements in the next three tables indicate that this results from a real-income component slightly in excess of 5 percent, compensated by a substitution component of a little over 1 percent, while the residual component takes a value close to zero in this case. Table 5.6 contains the Divisia variance (5.7) of the income elasticities of the $n = 8$ goods. The values of this variance range from .10 to .15; this order of magnitude is similar to that of the Divisia variances in the last column of Table 4.1.

The entries in Table 5.2 are positive with only nine exceptions out of 105. This is so because the countries are listed in the order of declining affluence and because of the dominant role of the real-income components. The latter components are shown in Table 5.3 and are all positive (see Section 5.3 for the Japan–Italy exception). The substitution components in Table 5.4 are in majority (over 80 percent) negative, which results from the tendency of luxuries to increase in price relative to necessities when we move to a more affluent country. Note that the triangular arrays of Tables 5.2 to 5.5 all consist of the elements below the diagonal of a skew-symmetric matrix of order 15 x 15, whereas the elements of Table 5.6 are those of a symmetric matrix.

Japan	Italy	Hungary	Iran	Colombia	Malaysia	Philippines	Korea
5.65							
2.84	–2.81						
8.72	3.07	5.88					
8.49	2.84	5.65	–.23				
8.62	2.97	5.78	–.10	.13			
15.07	9.42	12.23	6.35	6.59	6.45		
15.29	9.64	12.45	6.57	6.80	6.67	.21	
18.78	13.13	15.94	10.06	10.29	10.16	3.71	3.49

Table 5.3
Real-income components of the quality indexes for pairs of countries[a]

	U.S.	Belgium	France	Germany	U.K.	Netherlands
Belgium	5.23					
France	5.84	.67				
Germany	6.35	.79	.09			
U.K.	6.34	1.21	.58	.43		
Netherlands	6.63	1.33	.53	.50	.07	
Japan	9.47	4.56	3.76	3.77	3.44	3.28
Italy	8.91	4.11	3.53	3.38	2.98	2.99
Hungary	11.04	6.36	5.48	5.60	4.95	5.00
Iran	18.46	13.56	13.22	12.98	12.65	12.69
Colombia	20.37	14.76	14.14	14.29	13.64	13.57
Malaysia	20.38	14.72	14.03	14.14	13.76	13.45
Philippines	21.10	16.96	16.39	16.13	16.01	15.79
Korea	22.49	17.94	17.28	17.01	17.47	16.71
India	27.00	22.97	22.44	21.98	22.92	21.81

[a] All entries should be divided by 100.

Table 5.4
Substitution components of the quality indexes for pairs of countries[a]

	U.S.	Belgium	France	Germany	U.K.	Netherlands
Belgium	−1.27					
France	− .73	.57				
Germany	−1.17	− .08	− .64			
U.K.	−1.37	− .04	− .67	.11		
Netherlands	−1.14	.06	− .43	.21	.12	
Japan	−2.61	−1.71	−2.22	−1.37	−1.78	−1.75
Italy	−2.28	− .88	−1.60	− .63	− .86	−1.01
Hungary	−2.89	−1.97	−2.43	−1.65	−1.76	−1.92
Iran	−3.89	−2.37	−3.47	−2.22	−2.40	−2.74
Colombia	−1.87	− .17	−1.00	− .03	− .20	− .24
Malaysia	−2.50	− .75	−1.51	− .51	− .79	− .78
Philippines	−3.73	−2.09	−3.12	−1.88	−1.86	−2.18
Korea	−5.06	−3.44	−4.20	−3.03	−3.51	−3.41
India	−6.75	−5.02	−5.99	−4.70	−5.07	−5.04

[a] All entries should be divided by 100.

Japan	Italy	Hungary	Iran	Colombia	Malaysia	Philippines	Korea
– .31							
1.87	1.83						
9.30	9.72	7.63					
10.22	10.14	8.13	.81				
9.55	10.27	8.16	.39	.14			
12.93	13.11	11.38	3.94	3.41	3.59		
13.64	14.34	12.14	1.87	4.05	4.32	.74	
18.88	20.20	17.85	11.20	10.11	10.55	7.14	7.09

Japan	Italy	Hungary	Iran	Colombia	Malaysia	Philippines	Korea
.97							
– .13	– .95						
– .53	–1.77	– .55					
1.51	.81	2.11	2.28				
1.39	.20	1.43	1.83	– .81			
.11	–1.04	.16	.68	–2.07	–1.12		
–1.20	–2.47	–1.14	– .97	–3.50	–2.89	–1.92	
–2.57	–4.17	–2.65	–2.55	–5.32	–4.54	–3.41	–1.61

Table 5.5
Residual components of the quality indexes for pairs of countries[a]

	U.S.	Belgium	France	Germany	U.K.	Netherlands
Belgium	.03					
France	1.42	1.29				
Germany	−4.22	−3.72	−5.01			
U.K.	2.38	2.19	.92	5.84		
Netherlands	− .82	− .70	−1.96	3.00	−2.87	
Japan	−1.47	−1.44	−2.66	2.03	−3.60	− .80
Italy	4.42	3.83	2.60	7.34	1.58	4.40
Hungary	.09	− .13	−1.33	3.33	−2.29	.49
Iran	− .45	−1.05	−2.15	2.39	−3.48	− .50
Colombia	−4.61	−4.68	−5.77	−1.33	−6.91	−4.11
Malaysia	−3.85	−3.93	−5.03	− .58	−6.30	−3.32
Philippines	3.10	1.62	.69	5.25	−1.03	2.20
Korea	3.26	2.20	1.09	5.74	− .62	2.72
India	3.93	2.24	1.21	5.94	−1.02	2.74

[a] All entries should be divided by 100.

Table 5.6
Divisia variances of income elasticities for pairs of countries

	U.S.	Belgium	France	Germany	U.K.	Netherlands
Belgium	.1416					
France	.1402	.1244				
Germany	.1493	.1310	.1292			
U.K.	.1358	.1224	.1209	.1261		
Netherlands	.1418	.1265	.1247	.1314	.1223	
Japan	.1292	.1181	.1169	.1213	.1153	.1185
Italy	.1233	.1134	.1127	.1159	.1131	.1134
Hungary	.1250	.1160	.1145	.1183	.1135	.1162
Iran	.1144	.1084	.1076	.1094	.1093	.1078
Colombia	.1197	.1115	.1105	.1136	.1105	.1114
Malaysia	.1195	.1118	.1101	.1133	.1123	.1114
Philippines	.1060	.1039	.1019	.1032	.1047	.1036
Korea	.1100	.1063	.1051	.1058	.1094	.1059
India	.1043	.1026	.1014	.1018	.1069	.1023

Japan	Italy	Hungary	Iran	Colombia	Malaysia	Philippines	Korea
4.98							
1.10	−3.69						
− .05	−4.87	−1.20					
−3.24	−8.11	−4.59	−3.32				
−2.32	−7.49	−3.81	−2.33	.80			
2.03	−2.65	.68	1.73	5.24	3.98		
2.85	−2.22	1.45	2.67	6.24	5.23	1.39	
2.47	−2.90	.74	1.40	5.50	4.15	− .03	−1.99

Japan	Italy	Hungary	Iran	Colombia	Malaysia	Philippines	Korea
.1089							
.1119	.1083						
.1079	.1064	.1067					
.1071	.1061	.1074	.1050				
.1066	.1077	.1075	.1064	.1060			
.1058	.1028	.1055	.1089	.1022	.1047		
.1057	.1083	.1077	.1127	.1065	.1114	.1141	
.1032	.1070	.1058	.1142	.1058	.1112	.1162	.1262

5.3. Single-Subscript Quality Indexes

We can write (5.8) in the form

$$Q'_{cd} - Q_{cd} = y_d - y_c \tag{5.9}$$

where

$$y_c = \sum_{i=1}^{n} \beta_i \left(\log q_{ic} - \frac{1}{15} \sum_{d=1}^{15} \log q_{id} \right) \tag{5.10}$$

which satisfies

$$\sum_{c=1}^{15} y_c = 0 \tag{5.11}$$

Writing the logarithmic quality difference between countries c and d in the form $y_d - y_c$ amounts to defining a quality index y_c for each individual country. These y_c's are shown in the first column of Table 5.7.

Table 5.7
A logarithmic single-subscript quality index and its components

		Component indexes		
Country	Quality	Real income	Substitution	Residual
U.S.	.1037	.1264	–.0249	.0021
Belgium	.0639	.0765	–.0111	–.0015
France	.0385	.0700	–.0181	–.0134
Germany	.0941	.0687	–.0092	.0346
U.K.	.0302	.0662	–.0108	–.0252
Netherlands	.0570	.0642	–.0119	.0048
Japan	.0497	.0319	.0073	.0105
Italy	–.0068	.0360	–.0021	–.0407
Hungary	.0213	.0154	.0087	–.0029
Iran	–.0375	–.0593	.0141	.0077
Colombia	–.0352	–.0682	–.0099	.0430
Malaysia	–.0365	–.0670	–.0038	.0343
Philippines	–.1010	–.0952	.0085	–.0143
Korea	–.1032	–.1039	.0234	–.0227
India	–.1381	–.1614	.0396	–.0163

Approximate Single-Subscript Component Indexes

The additive decomposition in terms of the country subscripts c and d shown in (5.9) does not hold exactly but rather closely for the three components of the quality index (see Remark 1 below for the degree of accuracy). Let us write x_{rcd} for the three terms on the right in (5.6), where $r = 1$ refers to the real-income component of $Q'_{cd} - Q_{cd}$, $r = 2$ to the substitution component and $r = 3$ to the residual component, and consider

$$x_{rcd} = x_{rd} - x_{rc} + v_{rcd} \tag{5.12}$$

where v_{rcd} is a residual from the additive decomposition of the rth component of $Q'_{cd} - Q_{cd}$. The least-squares solution of x_{rd} constrained by $\Sigma_d\, x_{rd} = 0$ is

$$x_{rd} = \frac{1}{15} \sum_{c=1}^{15} x_{rcd} \tag{5.13}$$

To verify this solution we construct the Lagrangean function

$$\frac{1}{4} \sum_{c=1}^{15} \sum_{d=1}^{15} (x_{rcd} - x_{rd} + x_{rc})^2 - \mu \sum_{d=1}^{15} x_{rd}$$

We differentiate this function with respect to x_{rf}, where $f = 1, ..., 15$, and equate the result to zero:

$$-\frac{1}{2} \sum_{c=1}^{15} (x_{rcf} - x_{rf} + x_{rc}) + \frac{1}{2} \sum_{d=1}^{15} (x_{rfd} - x_{rd} + x_{rf}) - \mu = 0$$

Since the two sums on the left are equal apart from sign (because $x_{rcf} = -x_{rfc}$), we can simplify this equation to

$$-\sum_{c=1}^{15} (x_{rcf} - x_{rf} + x_{rc}) = \mu$$

and hence, since $\Sigma_c\, x_{rc} = 0$, to

$$-\sum_{c=1}^{15} (x_{rcf} - x_{rf}) = \mu \tag{5.14}$$

The sum of the left side over $f = 1, ..., 15$ is zero because the sum of all elements of a skew-symmetry matrix such as $[x_{rcf}]$ for $r = 1$, 2, and 3 vanishes. Therefore, $\mu = 0$, after which (5.13) follows directly from (5.14).

The zero value of the Lagrangean multiplier μ reflects the fact that raising x_{rf} by any k for each $f = 1, \ldots, 15$ does not affect $x_{rd} - x_{rc}$ in (5.12) for any pair (c, d).

Also note that the solution (5.13) satisfies

$$y_d = \sum_{r=1}^{3} x_{rd} \tag{5.15}$$

which amounts to an additive decomposition of the single-subscript quality index in terms of real-income, substitution and residual components in which the v_{rcd}'s of (5.12) play no role. The proof of (5.15) is a matter of successively applying (5.13), $Q'_{cd} - Q_{cd} = \Sigma_r x_{rcd}$, (5.9), and (5.11):

$$\sum_{r=1}^{3} x_{rd} = \frac{1}{15} \sum_{c=1}^{15} \sum_{r=1}^{3} x_{rcd} = \frac{1}{15} \sum_{c=1}^{15} (Q'_{cd} - Q_{cd})$$

$$= \frac{1}{15} \sum_{c=1}^{15} (y_d - y_c) = y_d$$

The last three columns of Table 5.7 contain the x_{rd}'s and Table 5.1 is obtained from Table 5.7 by taking antilogs and renormalizing so that the U.S. values equal 1. Recall that Japan–Italy and Colombia–Malaysia are exceptions to the rule that the real-income components decline in the successive rows of Table 5.1; also recall that the negative element in the Italian row and Japanese column of Table 5.3 represents a similar exception. Such exceptions result from the use of the Divisia volume index Q_{cd} in the real-income term of (5.6), which does not quite agree with the order of declining affluence measured by expenditures in international dollars (see Table 4.12), and also from the residuals v_{rcd} for $r = 1$. As is usual with index numbers, the third decimal places in Table 5.1 should be mistrusted.

Concluding Remarks

Remark 1. Since the solution (5.13) is obtained by least squares, a natural measure of fit is the sum of squares of the v_{rcd}'s in (5.12) divided by the sum of squares of the x_{rcd}'s. The ratio equals .0014 for $r = 1$ (real income), .0073 for $r = 2$ (substitution) and .0197 for $r = 3$ (residual), thus confirming that the single-subscript component indexes account for a major proportion of the observed variation of their double-subscript counterparts.

Remark 2. The additive decomposition (5.9) of the quality index in the subscripts c and d results from Working's model which implies that each marginal share exceeds the corresponding budget share by the constant β_i. This implies that all entries in Table 5.2 can be obtained from the first column of Table 5.7. The reason why Table 5.2 is nevertheless presented is that it allows a direct comparison with the component indexes in Table 5.3 and 5.5. A similar result holds for the excess of Frisch over Divisia price indexes in Table 4.3 and 4.4. The additive decomposition holds exactly for Table 4.3 but not for Table 4.4.

Remark 3. The quality index can also be applied to groups of goods under appropriate separability conditions, which leads to the problem of how to measure quality variations between and within groups. See Theil (1975–76, Chap. 14) for details on this matter, including an application to data in a time series context.

Chapter 6

FURTHER INTERNATIONAL CONSUMPTION COMPARISONS

6.1. *Equivalent Income Changes and Their Frisch Moments*

Equivalent Income Changes

We reproduce the demand equation (5.3),

$$(6.1)\quad w_{icd} \log \frac{q_{id}}{q_{ic}} = \theta_{icd} Q_{cd} + \phi\theta_{icd} \left(\log \frac{p_{id}}{p_{ic}} - P'_{cd} \right) + \epsilon_{icd}$$

and divide both sides by θ_{icd}:

$$(6.2)\quad \frac{\log (q_{id}/q_{ic})}{\theta_{icd}/w_{icd}} = Q_{cd} + \phi \left(\log \frac{p_{id}}{p_{ic}} - P'_{cd} \right) + \frac{\epsilon_{icd}}{\theta_{icd}}$$

Note that the right side of (6.2) is much simpler than that of (6.1) in that the coefficients of Q_{cd} and of the relative price term in parentheses are 1 and ϕ, respectively, and are hence the same for all n goods. The ratio on the left in (6.2) is the logarithmic difference between the quantities bought of good i in the two countries (c and d) divided by the income elasticity of this good. To interpret this ratio, imagine that the last two terms in (6.2) both vanish. Then, by solving for Q_{cd}, we find that the left side of (6.2) is equal to the value of Q_{cd} that would yield the observed q_{id}/q_{ic} if the difference in real income were the only difference between c and d, i.e., if the relative prices of all goods were the same in the two countries and if ϵ_{icd} were zero. Accordingly, the ratio on the left of (6.2) was referred to by Theil (1967, Chap. 7) as the *equivalent income change* of good i in the move from country c to country d.

Three Moments Involving Equivalent Income Changes

By weighing the equivalent income changes with the marginal shares we obtain

$$(6.3)\quad \sum_{i=1}^{n} \theta_{icd} \frac{\log (q_{id}/q_{ic})}{\theta_{icd}/w_{icd}} = \sum_{i=1}^{n} w_{icd} \log \frac{q_{id}}{q_{ic}} = Q_{cd}$$

so that the Frisch-weighted mean of the equivalent income changes is simply equal to the Divisia volume index. Next we consider the Frisch covariance of the equivalent income changes and the logarithmic price differences:

$$C'_{cd} = \sum_{i=1}^{n} \theta_{icd} \left[\frac{\log(q_{id}/q_{ic})}{\theta_{icd}/w_{icd}} - Q_{cd} \right] \log \frac{p_{id}}{p_{ic}} \tag{6.4}$$

It follows from (6.2) that this covariance can be written as

$$C'_{cd} = \phi \Pi'_{cd} + \sum_{i=1}^{n} \epsilon_{icd} \log \frac{p_{id}}{p_{ic}} \tag{6.5}$$

where Π'_{cd} is the Frisch price variance defined in (4.23). A comparison of (6.5) and (4.22) shows that the Frisch covariance of the equivalent income changes and the logarithmic price differences is nothing but the corrected Divisia covariance of the logarithmic price and quantity differences (corrected for real-income differences) which was shown in Table 4.11.

Similarly, the Frisch covariance of the equivalent income changes and the income elasticities is

$$\sum_{i=1}^{n} \theta_{icd} \left[\frac{\log(q_{id}/q_{ic})}{\theta_{icd}/w_{icd}} - Q_{cd} \right] \frac{\theta_{icd}}{w_{icd}} \tag{6.6}$$

Again we use (6.2) to conclude that this expression may be written as

$$\phi \sum_{i=1}^{n} \theta_{icd} \left(\log \frac{p_{id}}{p_{ic}} - P'_{cd} \right) \frac{\theta_{icd}}{w_{icd}} + \sum_{i=1}^{n} \frac{\theta_{icd}}{w_{icd}} \epsilon_{icd} \tag{6.7}$$

On comparing this with (5.6) we conclude that the Frisch covariance of the equivalent income changes and the income elasticities is nothing but the quality index $Q'_{cd} - Q_{cd}$ excluding the real-income component $\mu_{2cd} Q_{cd}$ of this index.

The Frisch Variance of the Equivalent Income Changes

The two previous paragraphs provide interesting connections between Frisch moments of equivalent income changes and earlier measures, but the Frisch variance of the equivalent income changes,

$$V'_{cd} = \sum_{i=1}^{n} \theta_{icd} \left[\frac{\log (q_{id}/q_{ic})}{\theta_{icd}/w_{icd}} - Q_{cd} \right]^2 \tag{6.8}$$

is a new measure because it describes the extent to which the real-income difference between two countries fails to account for the observed consumption differences of the n goods. This may be clarified by substitution from (6.2), which shows that V'_{cd} can be written as the sum of three components:

$$V'_{cd} = \phi^2 \Pi'_{cd} + \sum_{i=1}^{n} \frac{\epsilon_{icd}^2}{\theta_{icd}} + 2\phi \sum_{i=1}^{n} \epsilon_{icd} \log \frac{p_{id}}{p_{ic}} \tag{6.9}$$

None of these three components has anything to do with the difference in real income between the two countries. Instead, the first component results from the substitution effect of the relative price differences, the second from the ϵ_{icd}'s, and the third from the interaction of the substitution effect and the ϵ_{icd}'s. The first two components are both positive, whereas the third is not restricted in sign.

Tables 6.1 to 6.4 contain the Frisch variance and its three components, based on the ML estimates of Section 3.5 and multiplied by 10^4, for each pair of countries. Note that there is no clear tendency for the figures in Table 6.1 to increase when we move to the lower left corner. This results from the absence of a real-income component. We obtain a better perspective of these tables by discussing them in conjunction with the Divisia quantity variance.

6.2. *Divisia Variances of Quantities and Budget Shares*

The Divisia Quantity Variance

The Divisia quantity variance of the move from country c to country d is defined as

$$K_{cd} = \sum_{i=1}^{n} w_{icd} \left(\log \frac{q_{id}}{q_{ic}} - Q_{cd} \right)^2 \tag{6.10}$$

This variance, which is simply the quantity counterpart of the Divisia price variance (4.25), measures the degree to which the n logarithmic quantity differences differ from the Divisia volume index Q_{cd} or, equiva-

Table 6.1
Frisch variances of equivalent income changes[a]

	U.S.	Belgium	France	Germany	U.K.	Netherlands
Belgium	1004					
France	968	464				
Germany	1255	691	892			
U.K.	328	792	480	907		
Netherlands	1014	327	430	233	588	
Japan	3027	1086	1336	1218	2069	914
Italy	691	919	238	927	149	542
Hungary	2199	776	1058	1382	1353	998
Iran	1481	1163	1366	976	1494	1171
Colombia	1540	1252	1722	881	1743	1163
Malaysia	797	937	1065	308	622	654
Philippines	1675	453	1130	1256	1013	752
Korea	1222	910	873	852	770	605
India	1249	816	769	816	778	647

[a] All entries should be divided by 10,000.

Table 6.2
Substitution components of Frisch variances of equivalent income changes[a]

	U.S.	Belgium	France	Germany	U.K.	Netherlands
Belgium	334					
France	309	99				
Germany	242	53	25			
U.K.	279	83	113	52		
Netherlands	326	153	36	54	145	
Japan	793	277	471	341	219	380
Italy	423	162	76	53	84	72
Hungary	1048	389	425	430	373	567
Iran	294	206	322	182	254	290
Colombia	375	278	440	312	240	556
Malaysia	594	153	229	165	120	217
Philippines	545	306	518	352	305	626
Korea	865	295	519	342	234	565
India	1284	507	815	602	542	957

[a] All entries should be divided by 10,000.

Japan	Italy	Hungary	Iran	Colombia	Malaysia	Philippines	Korea
1813							
484	1424						
1751	1465	1574					
1772	1740	1441	2740				
1734	791	1333	1393	627			
1239	1284	429	1176	1771	1366		
897	750	466	2043	697	508	719	
1242	851	711	1721	966	447	506	356

Japan	Italy	Hungary	Iran	Colombia	Malaysia	Philippines	Korea
368							
629	295						
516	266	481					
444	455	666	444				
249	141	402	379	522			
594	385	311	128	340	369		
214	305	271	411	263	293	271	
537	542	238	425	526	502	225	130

Table 6.3
Residual components of Frisch variances of equivalent income changes[a]

	U.S.	Belgium	France	Germany	U.K.	Netherlands
Belgium	445					
France	362	252				
Germany	806	469	692			
U.K.	175	449	388	826		
Netherlands	629	235	429	281	578	
Japan	1237	508	599	674	1157	454
Italy	405	519	199	944	164	627
Hungary	1136	430	526	785	1219	402
Iran	943	750	750	813	929	1192
Colombia	764	624	694	267	1198	625
Malaysia	329	771	942	530	679	894
Philippines	1239	293	484	987	826	444
Korea	541	436	280	652	362	355
India	546	358	173	575	281	414

[a] All entries should be divided by 10,000.

Table 6.4
Substitution-residual interaction components of Frisch variances of equivalent income changes[a]

	U.S.	Belgium	France	Germany	U.K.	Netherlands
Belgium	225					
France	297	114				
Germany	206	170	174			
U.K.	−127	259	− 22	28		
Netherlands	59	− 62	− 35	−102	−136	
Japan	998	302	266	203	694	80
Italy	−136	237	− 37	− 70	− 98	−157
Hungary	15	− 44	107	167	−240	29
Iran	245	207	294	− 20	311	−311
Colombia	402	350	588	302	305	− 18
Malaysia	−127	13	−107	−387	−177	−458
Philippines	−109	−145	128	− 83	−118	−318
Korea	−184	179	74	−142	174	−315
India	−580	− 49	−220	−360	− 45	−724

[a] All entries should be divided by 10,000.

Japan	Italy	Hungary	Iran	Colombia	Malaysia	Philippines	Korea
1073							
324	962						
649	1002	1299					
994	1026	715	1297				
1888	958	1705	1666	497			
297	790	546	739	1196	1895		
633	190	519	1009	643	966	600	
818	165	1001	852	613	731	458	267

Japan	Italy	Hungary	Iran	Colombia	Malaysia	Philippines	Korea
373							
–469	166						
586	197	–207					
334	259	60	999				
–403	–308	–774	–651	–391			
348	109	–428	309	234	–898		
49	254	–324	622	–208	–751	–152	
–114	144	–528	444	–174	–786	–177	–41

lently, it measures the inequality among these differences. We should contrast this with the variance V'_{cd} of (6.8), which measures the extent to which Q_{cd} fails to account for these differences (taking into consideration that different goods have different income elasticities).

When we substitute the demand model (6.1) into (6.10), we find that K_{cd} consists of six components. Three of these are positive components, which should be compared with the first two terms on the right in (6.9), and the three others are interaction components, to be compared with the last term in (6.9). The three positive components are

$$\text{(6.11)} \qquad \text{Real income:} \quad Q_{cd}^2 \sum_{i=1}^{n} w_{icd} \left(\frac{\theta_{icd}}{w_{icd}} - 1 \right)^2$$

$$\text{(6.12)} \qquad \text{Substitution:} \quad \phi^2 \sum_{i=1}^{n} \theta_{icd} \left(\log \frac{p_{id}}{p_{ic}} - P'_{cd} \right)^2 \frac{\theta_{icd}}{w_{icd}}$$

$$\text{(6.13)} \qquad \text{Residuals:} \quad \sum_{i=1}^{n} \frac{\epsilon_{icd}^2}{w_{icd}}$$

A comparison with (5.5) and (5.6) shows that the real-income component (6.11) of K_{cd} is a multiple Q_{cd} of the real-income component of the quality index. The substitution component (6.12) is a multiple ϕ^2 of a Frisch-weighted third-order moment of income elasticities and logarithmic price differences.

The three interaction components of K_{cd} are

$$\text{(6.14)} \qquad \text{Income-substitution:} \quad 2\phi Q_{cd} \sum_{i=1}^{n} \theta_{icd} \left(\log \frac{p_{id}}{p_{ic}} - P'_{cd} \right) \frac{\theta_{icd}}{w_{icd}}$$

$$\text{(6.15)} \qquad \text{Income-residual:} \quad 2 Q_{cd} \sum_{i=1}^{n} \frac{\theta_{icd}}{w_{icd}} \epsilon_{icd}$$

$$\text{(6.16)} \qquad \text{Substitution-residual:} \quad 2\phi \sum_{i=1}^{n} \frac{\theta_{icd}}{w_{icd}} \left(\log \frac{p_{id}}{p_{ic}} - P'_{cd} \right) \epsilon_{icd}$$

Note that the interaction components (6.14) and (6.15) are equal to a multiple $2Q_{cd}$ of the substitution and residual components, respectively, of the quality index in (5.6).

The Divisia Budget-Share Variance

Before presenting this six-way decomposition of K_{cd} numerically, we should discuss how K_{cd} and its price counterpart appear naturally in the Divisia variance of the budget shares. Consider $w_{jd} = p_{jd} q_{jd}/M_d$, where M_d is total per capita consumption expenditure of country d expressed in national currency. When taking logs of this equation and subtracting the corresponding equation for country c, we obtain

$$\log \frac{w_{jd}}{w_{jc}} = \log \frac{p_{jd}}{p_{jc}} + \log \frac{q_{jd}}{q_{jc}} - \log \frac{M_d}{M_c} \tag{6.17}$$

Multiplication of this equation by w_{jcd} and summation over j gives

$$\sum_{j=1}^{n} w_{jcd} \log \frac{w_{jd}}{w_{jc}} = P_{cd} + Q_{cd} - \log \frac{M_d}{M_c}$$

We subtract this from (6.17), where we replace j by i:

$$\log \frac{w_{id}}{w_{ic}} - \sum_{j=1}^{n} w_{jcd} \log \frac{w_{jd}}{w_{jc}} = \left(\log \frac{p_{id}}{p_{ic}} - P_{cd}\right) + \left(\log \frac{q_{id}}{q_{ic}} - Q_{cd}\right)$$

Next we square both sides of this equation, multiply by w_{icd} and sum over i. The result can be written as

$$W_{cd} = \Pi_{cd} + K_{cd} + 2\Gamma_{cd} \tag{6.18}$$

where Π_{cd}, K_{cd} and Γ_{cd} are the Divisia price and quantity variances and covariance, while

$$W_{cd} = \sum_{i=1}^{n} w_{icd} \left(\log \frac{w_{id}}{w_{ic}} - \sum_{j=1}^{n} w_{jcd} \log \frac{w_{jd}}{w_{jc}}\right)^2 \tag{6.19}$$

is the Divisia variance of the budget shares of countries c and d. This variance is a simple measure of the degree to which the allocation of total expenditure to the n goods is different in the two countries.

In summary, the Divisia budget-share variance can be decomposed in terms of price and quantity variances and the price–quantity covariance as shown in (6.18), while the Divisia quantity variance consists of the six components (6.11) to (6.16) and the price–quantity covariance consists of the three components given in (4.22). Thus, a complete display

Table 6.5
Decomposition of the Divisia budget-share variance for the U.S. and each of 14 other countries[a]

	W_{cd}	Π_{cd}	K_{cd}	Positive components of K_{cd}		
				I	S	R
Belgium	899	760	1310	193	400	548
France	752	673	1428	243	374	374
Germany	707	573	909	270	290	646
U.K.	1059	624	769	296	348	149
Netherlands	1200	711	1346	310	402	754
Japan	2554	1905	3685	695	940	1497
Italy	2381	981	1734	644	510	276
Hungary	3510	2427	3121	976	1256	1361
Iran	6000	1033	3188	2979	238	1135
Colombia	3308	862	2900	3465	439	785
Malaysia	3457	1315	2081	3474	727	301
Philippines	9366	1481	6053	4202	564	1498
Korea	8857	2006	5389	4600	1034	581
India	13347	3052	7138	6991	1477	570

[a] All entries should be divided by 10,000.

Table 6.6
Decomposition of the Divisia budget-share variance for India and each of 14 other countries[a]

	W_{cd}	Π_{cd}	K_{cd}	Positive components of K_{cd}		
				I	S	R
U.S.	13347	3052	7138	6991	1477	570
Belgium	8532	1217	5026	5140	577	455
France	8214	2003	3746	4966	902	224
Germany	9903	1408	6285	4744	697	537
U.K.	6547	1290	3332	4915	611	394
Netherlands	8737	2283	4466	4650	1078	475
Japan	6274	1184	4996	3452	647	1060
Italy	3915	1190	2193	3812	657	245
Hungary	5420	525	3286	3011	292	1260
Iran	2293	763	3107	1099	625	1050
Colombia	3562	1145	2277	967	656	681
Malaysia	3653	1153	1505	1001	580	815
Philippines	1234	381	838	439	361	691
Korea	651	268	442	398	167	365

[a] All entries should be divided by 10,000.

Interaction components of K_{cd}			$2\Gamma_{cd}$	Components of $2\Gamma_{cd}$		
IS	IR	SR		I	S	R
− 94	2	261	−1171	274	−1080	− 365
− 61	118	380	−1349	132	−1000	− 480
− 100	− 359	162	− 775	343	− 784	− 334
− 128	222	− 119	− 334	365	− 903	205
− 107	− 77	63	− 857	293	−1054	− 96
− 383	− 215	1151	−3036	1144	−2565	−1615
− 330	639	− 5	− 333	815	−1369	220
− 511	16	24	−2038	1377	−3390	− 25
−1256	− 146	237	1779	3125	− 950	− 396
− 635	−1569	415	− 454	1409	−1213	− 650
− 853	−1314	254	60	1777	−1922	205
−1486	1236	39	1832	3420	−1764	177
−2070	1332	− 87	1462	3964	−2799	297
−3495	2033	− 437	3157	6373	−4155	939

Interaction components of K_{cd}			$2\Gamma_{cd}$	Components of $2\Gamma_{cd}$		
IS	IR	SR		I	S	R
−3495	2033	− 437	3157	6373	−4155	939
−2245	1004	96	2288	3848	−1639	79
−2651	534	− 228	2465	4748	−2638	356
−2031	2563	− 226	2210	3575	−1947	582
−2175	− 436	24	1925	3605	−1752	72
−2149	1167	− 757	1988	3914	−3097	1171
− 939	904	− 127	94	1649	−1739	185
−1574	−1094	147	532	2518	−1754	− 232
− 895	251	− 634	1609	1524	− 769	854
− 500	275	558	−1578	515	−1374	− 719
−1017	1050	− 60	139	1561	−1704	282
− 862	787	− 816	995	1346	−1624	1272
− 419	− 3	− 230	15	457	− 729	286
− 181	− 223	− 84	− 59	294	− 420	67

of the Divisia budget-share variances and its components and subcomponents involves 13 matrices, all of order 15 x 15, which is a bit bulky. Tables 6.5 and 6.6 provide a condensed picture involving only the first and last rows (or columns) of these 13 matrices. This amounts to comparisons of the U.S. (the most affluent of the 15 countries) with each of the 14 other countries and of India (the least affluent country) with all others. In both tables, the first three columns show the Divisia variances of the budget shares, prices and quantities, followed by the components (6.11) to (6.16) of the quantity variance in the next six columns, while the last four columns contain twice the price–quantity covariance and its three components. The positive components (6.11) to (6.13) of the quantity variance are indicated by I (income), S (substitution) and R (residual), while the interaction components (6.14) to (6.16) are indicated by pairs of these letters. All entries in Table 6.5 and 6.6 have been obtained by multiplying by 10^4 and are based on the ML estimates of Section 3.5.

Numerical Discussion

The first column of Tables 6.5 and 6.6 shows how the Divisia variance of the budget shares increases, from about 10^{-1} to about 1, when the two countries are farther apart on the real-income scale. A comparison of the next two columns indicates that the Divisia quantity variance exceeds the corresponding price variance in all cases. This excess confirms similar results obtained before; see Theil (1967, Chap. 4) for other international cross-section data and Meisner (1979c) for a time series version of (6.18) applied to industry data.

The quantity variances in the third column of Tables 6.5 and 6.6 exceed, with only one exception (U.S.–Germany), the corresponding Frisch variances of equivalent income changes in the first column and the last row, respectively, of Table 6.1. The main cause of this excess is the fact that the former variances have a real-income component which the latter do not have. The fourth column of Tables 6.5 and 6.6 contains the real-income component (6.11) which increases quickly when the two countries compared are more different in terms of affluence. The substitution component (6.12) in the next column shows a similar increase although it is not nearly as large, and the residual component (6.13) displays no such trend at all. Also, note that the substitution components (6.12) in Tables 6.5 and 6.6 exceed the substitution components of the Frisch variances of the equivalent income changes in the first column and the last row, respectively, of Table 6.2 in all cases except one (U.S.–Iran).

The income-substitution interaction components (6.14) of the K_{cd}'s in Tables 6.5 and 6.6 are all negative. This is so because each such component is equal to one of the entries in the first column or the last row of Table 5.4, all of which are negative, multiplied by $2Q_{cd} > 0$. The negative values in the first column and last row of Table 5.4 result from the tendency of luxuries to increase in price relative to necessities when we move from less to more affluent countries (see Section 5.2), while the positive values of the Q_{cd}'s in Table 6.5 are implied by the move from a less affluent country c to the U.S. and in Table 6.6 by the move from India to a more affluent country d. The income-residual components of the K_{cd}'s in these two tables are obviously heteroscedastic because of the factor Q_{cd} which occurs before the summation sign in (6.15).

In the first several rows of Table 6.5, the sum of the Divisia price and quantity variances exceeds the budget-share variance. As (6.18) indicates, this results from a negative price–quantity covariance, which is confirmed by the fourth column from the right in Table 6.5. When we move downward in Table 6.5 and upward in Table 6.6, we find that the price–quantity covariances tend to increase algebraically due to increasing positive real-income components which result from the tendency of luxuries to increase in price relative to necessities when we move to a more affluent country. The result, both in the last few rows of Table 6.5 and in the first several rows of Table 6.6, is that the price–quantity covariance is positive for countries that are far apart on the real-income scale so that the Divisia budget-share variance is then larger than the sum of the Divisia price and quantity variances.

6.3. *An Extension to All Pairs of Countries*

A more complete display of Divisia budget-share variances and their components is provided by Tables 6.7 to 6.18. All entries in these tables are multiplied by 10^4; when relevant, these entries are based on the ML estimates of Section 3.5.

Table 6.7 shows that the Divisia variances of the budget shares increase when we move toward the lower left corner, i.e., when we consider two countries whose per capita real incomes are more different. Also note that the entries in the lower right corner are on the average larger than those in the upper left corner. This means that the allocation patterns of

(*text continues on p. 118*)

Table 6.7
Divisia budget-share variances[a]

	U.S.	Belgium	France	Germany	U.K.	Netherlands
Belgium	899					
France	752	267				
Germany	707	278	342			
U.K.	1059	514	565	770		
Netherlands	1200	323	449	291	771	
Japan	2554	783	776	1284	1123	842
Italy	2381	1050	769	1442	465	1192
Hungary	3510	1193	1101	1763	1817	1138
Iran	6000	3162	2977	4100	2377	3936
Colombia	3308	1271	1050	1713	1172	1543
Malaysia	3457	1918	1967	2624	996	2317
Philippines	9366	4778	4930	6406	4229	5005
Korea	8857	5248	4937	6413	3786	5284
India	13347	8532	8214	9903	6547	8737

[a] All entries should be divided by 10,000.

Table 6.8
Divisia quantity variances[a]

	U.S.	Belgium	France	Germany	U.K.	Netherlands
Belgium	1310					
France	1428	552				
Germany	909	605	613			
U.K.	769	1021	588	871		
Netherlands	1346	391	398	183	694	
Japan	3685	1200	1110	1682	2209	1027
Italy	1734	1466	463	1288	295	858
Hungary	3121	1081	1000	2114	1442	1295
Iran	3188	2053	1522	2775	1677	2034
Colombia	2900	2026	1806	2515	1870	1875
Malaysia	2081	1695	1029	1856	506	1268
Philippines	6053	3185	3237	5143	2845	3352
Korea	5389	3798	2774	4677	2429	3199
India	7138	5026	3746	6285	3332	4466

[a] All entries should be divided by 10,000.

Japan	Italy	Hungary	Iran	Colombia	Malaysia	Philippines	Korea
1014							
748	951						
1667	1348	2256					
1242	269	590	1354				
2742	577	2325	2362	873			
2612	2500	2463	1024	2259	3302		
3552	1856	2656	1315	1735	2249	846	
6274	3915	5420	2293	3562	3653	1234	651

Japan	Italy	Hungary	Iran	Colombia	Malaysia	Philippines	Korea
1980							
635	1461						
2870	1187	2228					
2922	1495	2053	3356				
2819	292	1857	1705	790			
3699	2347	1995	1768	2641	2019		
3365	1518	2035	2870	1272	962	1012	
4996	2193	3286	3107	2277	1505	838	442

Table 6.9
Real-income components of Divisia quantity variances[a]

	U.S.	Belgium	France	Germany	U.K.	Netherlands
Belgium	193					
France	243	4				
Germany	270	5	0			
U.K.	296	12	3	1		
Netherlands	310	14	2	2	0	
Japan	695	176	121	117	102	91
Italy	644	149	111	98	78	79
Hungary	976	348	262	265	216	215
Iran	2979	1696	1623	1542	1464	1493
Colombia	3465	1954	1810	1796	1685	1653
Malaysia	3474	1937	1789	1765	1686	1623
Philippines	4202	2767	2635	2521	2449	2407
Korea	4600	3028	2840	2736	2791	2636
India	6991	5140	4966	4744	4915	4650

[a] All entries should be divided by 10,000.

Table 6.10
Substitution components of Divisia quantity variances[a]

	U.S.	Belgium	France	Germany	U.K.	Netherlands
Belgium	400					
France	374	112				
Germany	290	64	23			
U.K.	348	102	124	63		
Netherlands	402	182	37	64	170	
Japan	940	327	514	400	257	438
Italy	510	200	71	65	99	80
Hungary	1256	479	484	522	440	656
Iran	238	199	300	180	271	304
Colombia	439	340	535	383	296	682
Malaysia	727	185	248	192	141	250
Philippines	564	344	562	406	348	714
Korea	1034	359	574	406	274	650
India	1477	577	902	697	611	1078

[a] All entries should be divided by 10,000.

Japan	Italy	Hungary	Iran	Colombia	Malaysia	Philippines	Korea
1							
31	31						
801	887	546					
975	968	615	6				
856	979	619	1	0			
1581	1672	1228	143	114	123		
1760	1897	1368	211	154	167	5	
3452	3812	3011	1099	967	1001	439	398

Japan	Italy	Hungary	Iran	Colombia	Malaysia	Philippines	Korea
440							
750	362						
652	328	640					
540	573	874	476				
304	161	472	462	636			
775	489	432	174	395	476		
257	374	359	583	347	340	440	
647	657	292	625	656	580	361	167

Table 6.11
Residual components of Divisia quantity variances[a]

	U.S.	Belgium	France	Germany	U.K.	Netherlands
Belgium	548					
France	374	298				
Germany	646	384	487			
U.K.	149	537	484	719		
Netherlands	754	273	456	234	660	
Japan	1497	614	638	829	1377	566
Italy	276	559	218	743	172	639
Hungary	1361	510	585	901	1450	491
Iran	1135	893	817	996	1087	1443
Colombia	785	611	573	315	1270	653
Malaysia	301	795	909	616	629	966
Philippines	1498	375	644	1084	1100	527
Korea	581	539	336	718	436	450
India	570	455	224	537	394	475

[a] All entries should be divided by 10,000.

Table 6.12
Income-substitution interaction components of Divisia quantity variances[a]

	U.S.	Belgium	France	Germany	U.K.	Netherlands
Belgium	− 94					
France	− 61	6				
Germany	− 100	− 1	− 1			
U.K.	− 128	− 1	− 6	1		
Netherlands	− 107	1	− 4	2	0	
Japan	− 383	− 132	− 142	− 85	− 106	− 97
Italy	− 330	− 63	− 100	− 37	− 45	− 53
Hungary	− 511	− 216	− 232	− 156	− 154	− 166
Iran	−1256	− 593	− 852	− 527	− 555	− 644
Colombia	− 635	− 46	− 256	− 7	− 49	− 58
Malaysia	− 853	− 197	− 384	− 126	− 193	− 188
Philippines	−1486	− 682	−1004	− 586	− 568	− 666
Korea	−2070	−1160	−1382	− 974	−1123	−1076
India	−3495	−2245	−2651	−2031	−2175	−2149

[a] All entries should be divided by 10,000.

Japan	Italy	Hungary	Iran	Colombia	Malaysia	Philippines	Korea
1188							
408	1084						
818	1092	1585					
1237	966	815	1610				
2260	873	1973	2021	609			
326	1043	642	899	1443	2262		
844	208	669	1241	764	1062	810	
1060	245	1260	1050	681	815	691	365

Japan	Italy	Hungary	Iran	Colombia	Malaysia	Philippines	Korea
– 6							
– 4	– 32						
– 91	– 324	– 79					
288	155	319	35				
249	38	217	14	– 2			
27	– 265	35	49	– 138	– 77		
–310	– 655	–257	– 84	– 266	–224	– 25	
–939	–1574	–895	–500	–1017	–862	–419	–181

Table 6.13
Income-residual interaction components of Divisia quantity variances[a]

	U.S.	Belgium	France	Germany	U.K.	Netherlands
Belgium	2					
France	118	14				
Germany	– 359	– 45	– 7			
U.K.	222	43	9	40		
Netherlands	– 77	– 15	– 17	23	– 3	
Japan	– 215	– 111	– 171	126	– 215	– 44
Italy	639	278	163	428	83	232
Hungary	16	– 14	– 127	315	– 200	42
Iran	– 146	– 263	– 528	567	– 806	– 118
Colombia	–1569	–1240	–1478	– 335	–1706	–1001
Malaysia	–1314	–1034	–1282	– 145	–1544	– 800
Philippines	1236	530	220	1642	– 314	670
Korea	1332	743	358	1846	– 199	859
India	2033	1004	534	2563	– 436	1167

[a] All entries should be divided by 10,000.

Table 6.14
Substitution-residual interaction components of Divisia quantity variances[a]

	U.S.	Belgium	France	Germany	U.K.	Netherlands
Belgium	261					
France	380	118				
Germany	162	198	110			
U.K.	– 119	327	– 26	47		
Netherlands	63	– 64	– 77	–140	–134	
Japan	1151	326	150	295	793	74
Italy	– 5	344	1	– 9	– 93	–119
Hungary	24	– 27	29	267	–309	55
Iran	237	121	162	16	215	–444
Colombia	415	407	622	364	374	– 54
Malaysia	– 254	10	–251	–446	–213	–582
Philippines	39	–149	179	76	–169	–300
Korea	– 87	289	47	– 56	248	–321
India	– 437	96	–228	–226	24	–757

[a] All entries should be divided by 10,000.

Japan	Italy	Hungary	Iran	Colombia	Malaysia	Philippines	Korea
– 28							
37	– 125						
– 8	– 889	–171					
–619	–1549	–695	– 52				
–417	–1429	–578	– 17	2			
496	– 676	148	125	350	273		
736	– 588	327	231	475	406	18	
904	–1094	251	275	1050	787	– 3	–223

Japan	Italy	Hungary	Iran	Colombia	Malaysia	Philippines	Korea
384							
–587	141						
698	94	–291					
499	382	124	1279				
–434	–329	–847	– 776	–454			
493	83	–490	378	478	–1038		
80	282	–431	688	–202	– 789	–236	
–127	147	–634	558	– 60	– 816	–230	–84

Table 6.15
Twice the price–quantity covariances[a]

	U.S.	Belgium	France	Germany	U.K.	Netherlands
Belgium	−1171					
France	−1349	− 526				
Germany	− 775	− 442	− 359			
U.K.	− 334	− 685	− 309	− 216		
Netherlands	− 857	− 407	− 46	− 17	− 252	
Japan	−3036	−1068	−1554	−1198	−1598	−1100
Italy	− 333	− 768	69	36	− 21	153
Hungary	−2038	− 742	− 955	−1306	− 481	−1481
Iran	1779	493	472	786	14	1107
Colombia	− 454	−1351	−1720	−1470	−1210	−1524
Malaysia	60	− 120	356	387	219	539
Philippines	1832	836	369	419	638	152
Korea	1462	776	866	946	811	751
India	3157	2288	2465	2210	1925	1988

[a] All entries should be divided by 10,000.

Table 6.16
Real-income components of twice the price–quantity covariances[a]

	U.S.	Belgium	France	Germany	U.K.	Netherlands
Belgium	274					
France	132	− 23				
Germany	343	4	3			
U.K.	365	4	22	− 1		
Netherlands	293	− 12	13	− 7	− 1	
Japan	1144	316	400	235	232	259
Italy	815	140	254	94	91	132
Hungary	1377	448	594	357	339	402
Iran	3125	1495	1990	1344	1339	1543
Colombia	1409	114	655	29	59	246
Malaysia	1777	396	926	296	321	503
Philippines	3420	1592	2253	1425	1433	1663
Korea	3964	2019	2667	1822	1849	2070
India	6373	3848	4748	3575	3605	3914

[a] All entries should be divided by 10,000.

Japan	Italy	Hungary	Iran	Colombia	Malaysia	Philippines	Korea
−1780							
−1277	−1151						
−2293	− 441	− 952					
−2676	−2177	−2805	−3139				
− 619	− 38	− 439	− 205	−1053			
2293	− 672	− 143	− 994	−1184	490		
− 285	− 327	75	−2338	− 91	615	−616	
94	532	1609	−1578	139	995	15	−59

Japan	Italy	Hungary	Iran	Colombia	Malaysia	Philippines	Korea
12							
− 0	73						
325	739	271					
− 699	− 286	− 553	− 86				
− 464	− 81	− 392	− 33	3			
192	752	171	− 80	296	231		
488	1073	428	1	422	347	14	
1649	2518	1524	515	1561	1346	457	294

Table 6.17
Substitution components of twice the price–quantity covariances[a]

	U.S.	Belgium	France	Germany	U.K.	Netherlands
Belgium	−1080					
France	−1000	− 319				
Germany	− 784	− 171	− 81			
U.K.	− 903	− 269	− 366	− 169		
Netherlands	−1054	− 495	− 115	− 176	− 470	
Japan	−2565	− 895	−1523	−1105	− 708	−1230
Italy	−1369	− 524	− 245	− 171	− 272	− 233
Hungary	−3390	−1260	−1376	−1393	−1208	−1835
Iran	− 950	− 668	−1043	− 590	− 822	− 939
Colombia	−1213	− 899	−1424	−1011	− 776	−1799
Malaysia	−1922	− 495	− 742	− 535	− 387	− 704
Philippines	−1764	− 991	−1677	−1140	− 986	−2026
Korea	−2799	− 953	−1681	−1107	− 756	−1829
India	−4155	−1639	−2638	−1947	−1752	−3097

[a] All entries should be divided by 10,000.

Table 6.18
Residual components of twice the price–quantity covariances[a]

	U.S.	Belgium	France	Germany	U.K.	Netherlands
Belgium	− 365					
France	− 480	−184				
Germany	− 334	−275	−282			
U.K.	205	−420	35	− 46		
Netherlands	− 96	100	56	165	220	
Japan	−1615	−489	−431	−328	−1122	− 129
Italy	220	−384	60	113	159	254
Hungary	− 25	70	−173	−270	388	− 48
Iran	− 396	−334	−475	32	− 503	503
Colombia	− 650	−566	−951	−488	− 493	29
Malaysia	205	− 20	172	627	286	740
Philippines	177	235	−207	134	191	515
Korea	297	−290	−119	231	− 282	509
India	939	79	356	582	72	1171

[a] All entries should be divided by 10,000.

Japan	Italy	Hungary	Iran	Colombia	Malaysia	Philippines	Korea
−1190							
−2036	− 955						
−1669	− 861	−1558					
−1437	−1471	−2155	−1436				
− 807	− 456	−1300	−1225	−1689			
−1922	−1247	−1007	− 415	−1102	−1195		
− 693	− 988	− 878	−1331	− 850	− 948	−876	
−1739	−1754	− 769	−1374	−1704	−1624	−729	−420

Japan	Italy	Hungary	Iran	Colombia	Malaysia	Philippines	Korea
−603							
759	−269						
−949	−319	334					
−540	−419	− 98	−1617				
652	498	1252	1054	633			
−564	−177	692	− 499	−378	1454		
− 79	−411	524	−1007	337	1216	245	
185	−232	854	− 719	282	1272	286	67

total consumption of two poor countries tend to be more different than those of two affluent countries.

A comparison of the Divisia quantity variances in Table 6.8 with the corresponding price variances in Table 4.6 confirms the rule that the former exceed the latter, the number of exceptions being only six out of 105. Also, the Divisia quantity variances exceed the corresponding Frisch variances of the equivalent income changes in Table 6.1 in 92 cases out of 105. The income-substitution interaction components in Table 6.12 are negative in about 85 percent of all cases, several of the exceptions being actually close to zero, particularly in the upper left part of the table.

Chapter 7

EPILOGUE

It has become customary in recent years to extend consumption and utility theory so that it includes intertemporal demand analysis and labor supply, while taxation and social choice are other topics related to utility theory. It would be of interest to explore these topics using international data, but much of such a research program will require extensions of the data that are presently available. Even when we confine ourselves to the more limited framework used in this monograph, there are several aspects worthy of further consideration. For example, prices may be endogenous rather than exogenous (see Remark 3 at the end of Section 4.3). Even when prices are exogenous if measured correctly, they may actually be measured with error; see Theil (1979b) and Clements and Meisner (1979) for first attempts to explore the implications of measurement errors in demand systems. Such features represent complications for statistical procedures which (as we know from Section 3.4) are not simple even when there are no such complications.

Aggregation over Consumers

Muellbauer (1975) considered the problem of how Working's model can be aggregated over consumers. He did this under the simplifying assumption that all N_c consumers of country c have identical tastes and face the same prices $p_{1c}, ..., p_{nc}$ at any given point in time. For consumer h in country c, let M_{ch} be his income (expressed in the currency of country c) and let $w_{ich} = p_{ic} q_{ich}/M_{ch}$ be his budget share of good i, where q_{ich} is the quantity of good i bought by this consumer. We write Working's model for this consumer as

$$w_{ich} = \alpha_i + \beta_i \log M_{ch} \tag{7.1}$$

Total personal income of country c is $\Sigma_h M_{ch} = N_c M_c$, where M_c is per capita income, and the total amount spent on good i is $p_{ic} \Sigma_h q_{ich} = \Sigma_h M_{ch} w_{ich}$ so that the per capita budget share of good i in country c, written w_{ic}, equals $\Sigma_h M_{ch} w_{ich}$ divided by $N_c M_c$. Substitution from (7.1) and minor rearrangements then yields

$$w_{ic} = \alpha_i + \beta_i (\log M_c + I_c) \tag{7.2}$$

where $I_c = \Sigma_h (M_{ch}/N_c M_c) \log (M_{ch}/M_c)$ is one of two informational measures of income inequality proposed by Theil (1967, Chap. 4).

In Chapter 3 we estimated the demand system using per capita data and thus ignored I_c in (7.2). This amounts to a specification error. If I_c is known for each country c, the correction is easily made, but I_c is frequently not known. If I_c is a constant independent of c, the specification error affects the constant term α_i in (7.2) but it does not affect the more crucial slope coefficient β_i. However, Kuznetz's work suggests that income inequality is more likely to be less at a very low and at a high per capita income level than at intermediate levels, and it would be of interest to explore the implications of this relationship for the estimation of Working's model.

The Measurement of Disutility

The previous paragraphs deal with extensions and qualifications of the approach of this monograph. Alternatively, we can proceed from the other end and assume optimistically that the demand system fitted in Section 3.5 provides an essentially correct picture of consumer behavior in all countries. The simplest approach is then based on the indirect utility function $u_I(M, \boldsymbol{p})$, which measures the highest utility level that can be obtained when income is M and prices are $\boldsymbol{p}$. Let us fix the prices at the geometric means (2.6) so that our problem becomes how to express the indirect utility function in terms of M.

Recall from Section 3.3 that the marginal utility of income has an income elasticity equal to $1/\phi$. So, if ϕ is a constant, this marginal utility takes the form $BM^{1/\phi}$, where B is a positive constant. Since the marginal utility of income is the derivative of the indirect utility function with respect to income, we find by integration that this function takes the form

$$B_1 - B_2 M^{-\alpha} \tag{7.3}$$

where $\alpha = -1 - 1/\phi$ and $B_2 = B/\alpha$. Using the estimate $\hat{\phi} = -.618$ of (3.47), we obtain $\hat{\alpha} = .62$. For such a positive value of α, the indirect utility function (7.3) increases and converges to the bliss level B_1 when M increases indefinitely. The excess of this bliss level over the actual level, $B_1 - (B_1$

$- B_2M^{-\alpha}) = B_2M^{-\alpha}$, measures the consumer's disutility when his income is M. We can write this disutility function in the simpler form

$$\Delta(M) = M^{-\alpha} \tag{7.4}$$

because specifying $B_2 = 1$ is a matter of appropriate selection of the utility unit.

As a generalization of (7.3), we may want to consider an indirect utility function of the form

$$B_1 - B_2(M - M_0)^{-\alpha} \tag{7.5}$$

where M_0 is interpreted as the smallest amount of income below which sustained life is impossible (say, 40 percent of India's per capita income in 1970). By differentiating the function (7.5) with respect to M we obtain the implied marginal utility of income:

$$\lambda = \alpha B_2(M - M_0)^{-\alpha - 1}$$

It is then readily verified that the income elasticity of this marginal utility is

$$\frac{\partial\lambda}{\partial M}\frac{M}{\lambda} = -\frac{(\alpha + 1)M}{M - M_0} \tag{7.6}$$

which is approximately constant (equal to $-\alpha - 1$) when M_0/M is close to zero. When M is not much larger than M_0, the elasticity (7.6) takes a large negative value, which agrees with Frisch's conjecture quoted on page 42. For the developments which follow, we note that (7.5) can be reduced to (7.3) by the simple device of measuring income from M_0 rather than zero.

Per Capita Disutilities and Disutility Inequalities

We proceed to apply (7.4) in order to derive per capita disutilities of countries and of the world under appropriately simplifying conditions. Assume that the income distribution within each country is lognormal. Let the mean and the variance of the logarithm of income in country c be μ_c and σ_c^2, respectively, so that this country's per capita income is

(7.7) $$M_c = \exp \{\mu_c + \tfrac{1}{2}\, \sigma_c^2\}$$

Under (7.4) the disutility distribution is then also lognormal and the mean and variance of log Δ are $-\alpha\mu_c$ and $\alpha^2\sigma_c^2$ so that the per capita disutility of country c is

(7.8) $$\Delta_c = \exp \{-\alpha\mu_c + \tfrac{1}{2}\, \alpha^2\sigma_c^2\}$$

On combining this with (7.4) and (7.7) we obtain

(7.9) $$\Delta_c = \Delta(M_c) \exp \{\tfrac{1}{2}\, \alpha(\alpha + 1)\sigma_c^2\}$$

We can estimate $\Delta(M_c)$ by raising per capita income in Kravis's international dollars to the power $-\alpha$. The exponent in (7.9) is approximately equal to that of $\frac{1}{2}\,\sigma_c^2$ for α close to .6 [see the discussion following (7.3)]. Thus, a fairly rough estimate of σ_c suffices to obtain an estimate of Δ_c.

Let π_c be the share of country c in the world population so that $\Delta = \Sigma_c\, \pi_c \Delta_c$ is world per capita disutility. This could be extended by the computation of regional per capita disutilities. Another extension would be the measurement of disutility inequality. One such measure is

(7.10) $$\sum_c \pi_c \log \frac{\Delta}{\Delta_c}$$

which is the logarithm of the ratio of arithmetic mean disutility to geometric mean disutility. This expression measures the inequality among the per capita disutilities of the countries of the world and it allows a simple decomposition between and within regions; see Theil (1967, Chap. 4).

Computing per capita disutilities and disutility inequalities for countries and regions would be an attractive research project. Using Frisch's language quoted on page 42, we suggest that a universal 'atlas' of these measures be constructed. It would serve a useful purpose for the analysis of the distribution of disutility and its development over time.

APPENDIX

by

JAMES F. MEISNER

Appendix A

THE F TESTS AND THE CONSTRAINED ESTIMATORS

Notation

Our objective is to test and impose the properties of homogeneity and Slutsky symmetry for the demand system described in Section 3.2. To make the exposition self-contained, we start with a brief summary of the notation used.

The 15 countries are indicated by the subscript $c = 1, ..., 15$ and the consumer goods by $i = 1, ..., n$. We write w_{ic} and p_{ic} for the budget share and the price, respectively, of good i in country c, and $\overline{p}_i$ for the geometric mean of the prices $p_{i1}, ..., p_{i,15}$ of good i in the 15 countries. The dependent variable of the demand equation for good i in country c is then

$$y_{ic} = w_{ic} \left(1 - x_{ic} + \sum_{j=1}^{n} w_{jc} x_{jc}\right) \tag{A.1}$$

where

$$x_{ic} = \log \frac{p_{ic}}{\overline{p}_i} \tag{A.2}$$

with log interpreted as natural log.

The demand equation for good i in country c takes the form

$$y_{ic} = \alpha_i + \beta_i q_c + \sum_{j=1}^{n} \pi_{ij} x_{jc} + \epsilon_{ic} \tag{A.3}$$

where q_c is the log of per capita real income in country c and ϵ_{ic} is a random disturbance, while $\alpha_i, \beta_i, \pi_{i1}, ..., \pi_{in}$ are unknown parameters. Note that (A.3) is linear in these parameters. The property of homogeneity amounts to

$$\sum_{j=1}^{n} \pi_{ij} = 0 \tag{A.4}$$

for $i = 1, ..., n$, while Slutsky symmetry amounts to

$$\pi_{ij} = \pi_{ji} \tag{A.5}$$

for all pairs (i, j), $i \neq j$.

The Maintained Hypothesis

We assume that the per capita real incomes and all prices, and hence the q_c's and all x_{ic}'s, are constant in repeated samples. Also, we assume that there is no extreme multicollinearity among the q_c's and x_{ic}'s, nor among the q_c's and the $\bar{x}_{ic}$'s in eq. (A.16) below. The 15 vectors $[\epsilon_{1c} \ldots \epsilon_{nc}]$ are assumed to be independent random drawings from a multivariate normal population with zero means. The covariance matrix of this distribution is singular because

$$\sum_{i=1}^{n} \epsilon_{ic} = 0 \tag{A.6}$$

holds with probability 1. To verify this result it is sufficient to note that the unit sum of the budget shares $w_{1c}, \ldots, w_{nc}$ implies that the values $y_{1c}, \ldots, y_{nc}$ of the dependent variables of each country also have unit sum [see (A.1)]. In fact, summation of (A.3) over $i = 1, \ldots, n$ yields $1 = 1 + 0 + 0 + 0$ because of (A.6) and

$$\sum_{i=1}^{n} \alpha_i = 1, \qquad \sum_{i=1}^{n} \beta_i = 0, \qquad \sum_{i=1}^{n} \pi_{ij} = 0 \tag{A.7}$$

The problem raised by this linear dependence is solved by simply deleting one of the n equations, say, the last (the nth). This reduces each of the disturbance vectors to one consisting of $n - 1$ elements, $\epsilon_{1c}, \ldots, \epsilon_{n-1,c}$. It is assumed that these vectors have an unknown nonsingular covariance matrix, to be written Σ. If Σ were singular, the implication would be that there is a second linear dependence among the n demand equations, but such a second dependence will be excluded.

The F Test for Homogeneity

Let $\boldsymbol{Y}$ be the $15 \times (n - 1)$ matrix whose cth row consists of the elements $y_{1c}, \ldots, y_{n-1,c}$; let $\boldsymbol{X}$ be the $15 \times (n + 2)$ matrix with $1, q_c, x_{1c}, \ldots, x_{nc}$ as successive elements in the cth row. Then, under the assumptions made and if neither homogeneity nor symmetry is imposed, the best linear unbiased estimators of the coefficients of (A.3) for $i = 1, \ldots, n - 1$ are the elements of the least-squares matrix $(\boldsymbol{X}'\boldsymbol{X})^{-1}\boldsymbol{X}'\boldsymbol{Y}$. We define

$$\boldsymbol{b} = \text{vec}\,(\boldsymbol{X}'\boldsymbol{X})^{-1}\boldsymbol{X}'\boldsymbol{Y} \tag{A.8}$$

which is a column vector consisting of $n - 1$ subvectors, the ith subvector being the ith column of $(X'X)^{-1}X'Y$. We also define the Kronecker product

(A.9) $$R = I_{n-1} \otimes v'$$

where v' is a row vector with two zero and n unit elements:

(A.10) $$v' = [0 \quad 0 \quad 1 \quad \ldots \quad 1]$$

Given these definitions, $Rb = 0$ holds if and only if b satisfies the homogeneity property (A.4); but, in fact, Rb is a random vector with covariance matrix

(A.11) $$R\mathscr{V}(b)R' = R[\Sigma \otimes (X'X)^{-1}]R'$$

where $\mathscr{V}(\cdot)$ stands for the covariance matrix of any random vector with finite variances. If (A.4) is true, Rb has zero expectation. The test for homogeneity involves a quadratic form in Rb whose matrix equals the inverse of the covariance matrix (A.11). It follows from (A.9) that this quadratic form can be written as

(A.12) $$\frac{b'R'\Sigma^{-1}Rb}{v'(X'X)^{-1}v}$$

The distribution of this expression is $\chi^2(n-1)$ if (A.4) is true.

Finally, we define

(A.13) $$S = \frac{1}{15-(n+2)} Y'[I - X(X'X)^{-1}X']Y$$

which is an unbiased estimator of Σ, while

(A.14) $$(13-n) \operatorname{tr} \Sigma^{-1} S$$

is distributed as χ^2 with $(n-1)(13-n)$ degrees of freedom. The ratio of (A.12) to (A.14), each divided by its degrees of freedom, is

(A.15) $$\frac{b'R'\Sigma^{-1}Rb/v'(X'X)^{-1}v}{\operatorname{tr} \Sigma^{-1} S}$$

which is distributed as $F(n-1, 13-n)$ if (A.4) is true. The ratio (A.15) is known as the F statistic for testing homogeneity.

The F Test for Symmetry Given Homogeneity

If we assume that the homogeneity property (A.4) is true, we can equate π_{in} to $-\pi_{i1} - \ldots - \pi_{i,n-1}$, after which substitution into (A.3) yields

$$y_{ic} = \alpha_i + \beta_i q_c + \sum_{j=1}^{n-1} \pi_{ij} \bar{x}_{jc} + \epsilon_{ic} \tag{A.16}$$

where

$$\bar{x}_{jc} = x_{jc} - x_{nc} \tag{A.17}$$

Our objective is now to test the symmetry property (A.5), which can be conveniently done by means of appropriate modifications of the results described in the previous subsection. First, we replace $\boldsymbol{X}$ by $\bar{\boldsymbol{X}}$, which is a $15 \times (n+1)$ matrix whose cth row consists of $1, q_c, \bar{x}_{1c}, \ldots, \bar{x}_{n-1,c}$ as successive elements, and we change (A.13) into

$$\boldsymbol{S} = \frac{1}{15-(n+1)} \boldsymbol{Y}'[\boldsymbol{I} - \bar{\boldsymbol{X}}(\bar{\boldsymbol{X}}'\bar{\boldsymbol{X}})^{-1}\bar{\boldsymbol{X}}']\boldsymbol{Y} \tag{A.18}$$

with the result that

$$(14-n) \operatorname{tr} \boldsymbol{\Sigma}^{-1}\boldsymbol{S} \tag{A.19}$$

is distributed as χ^2 with $(n-1)(14-n)$ degrees of freedom.

Second, we change (A.8) into

$$\hat{\beta} = \operatorname{vec}(\bar{\boldsymbol{X}}'\bar{\boldsymbol{X}})^{-1}\bar{\boldsymbol{X}}'\boldsymbol{Y} \tag{A.20}$$

and we note that the specification (A.9) is no longer appropriate when the constraint to be tested is Slutsky symmetry. With the nth equation deleted, (A.5) for all pairs $i \neq j$ amounts to $\frac{1}{2}(n-1)(n-2)$ constraints. Thus, the $\boldsymbol{R}$ to be used for testing Slutsky symmetry has $\frac{1}{2}(n-1)(n-2)$ rows and $(n-1)(n+1)$ columns, each row consisting of zero elements except for a 1 corresponding to some π_{ij} with $i \neq j$ and a -1 corresponding to π_{ji}. For example, $\boldsymbol{R}$ takes the following 3×15 form for $n = 4$:

$$
\begin{array}{ccccccccccccccc}
\alpha_1 & \beta_1 & \pi_{11} & \pi_{12} & \pi_{13} & \alpha_2 & \beta_2 & \pi_{21} & \pi_{22} & \pi_{23} & \alpha_3 & \beta_3 & \pi_{31} & \pi_{32} & \pi_{33}
\end{array}
$$

$$
\begin{bmatrix}
0 & 0 & 0 & 1 & 0 & 0 & 0 & -1 & 0 & 0 & 0 & 0 & 0 & 0 & 0 \\
0 & 0 & 0 & 0 & 1 & 0 & 0 & 0 & 0 & 0 & 0 & 0 & -1 & 0 & 0 \\
0 & 0 & 0 & 0 & 0 & 0 & 0 & 0 & 0 & 1 & 0 & 0 & 0 & -1 & 0
\end{bmatrix}
$$

If (A.5) is true for all pairs (i, j), $\boldsymbol{R}\hat{\boldsymbol{\beta}}$ has zero expectation and covariance matrix $\boldsymbol{R}\boldsymbol{C}(\boldsymbol{\Sigma})\boldsymbol{R}'$, where

$$\boldsymbol{C}(\boldsymbol{\Sigma}) = \boldsymbol{\Sigma} \otimes (\overline{\boldsymbol{X}}'\overline{\boldsymbol{X}})^{-1} \tag{A.21}$$

and the quadratic form

$$\hat{\boldsymbol{\beta}}'\boldsymbol{R}'[\boldsymbol{R}\boldsymbol{C}(\boldsymbol{\Sigma})\boldsymbol{R}']^{-1}\boldsymbol{R}\hat{\boldsymbol{\beta}} \tag{A.22}$$

is then distributed as χ^2 with $\frac{1}{2}$ $(n-1)(n-2)$ degrees of freedom. The ratio of (A.22) to (A.19), each divided by its degrees of freedom, is

$$\frac{\hat{\boldsymbol{\beta}}'\boldsymbol{R}'[\boldsymbol{R}\boldsymbol{C}(\boldsymbol{\Sigma})\boldsymbol{R}']^{-1}\boldsymbol{R}\hat{\boldsymbol{\beta}}}{\frac{1}{2}(n-2)\operatorname{tr}\boldsymbol{\Sigma}^{-1}\boldsymbol{S}} \tag{A.23}$$

which is distributed as F with $\frac{1}{2}$ $(n-1)(n-2)$ and $(n-1)(14-n)$ degrees of freedom if (A.5) is true for each (i, j). The ratio (A.23) is known as the F statistic for testing Slutsky symmetry.

Homogeneity- and Symmetry-Constrained Coefficient Estimators

Homogeneity-constrained coefficient estimates are directly obtained from (A.16). It is true that (A.16) does not yield estimates of the eliminated parameters π_{in}, but such estimates can be easily obtained from the constraints used for the elimination.

The situation of symmetry-constrained coefficient estimates is more complicated because (A.5) provides a link between coefficients which occur in two different equations. The best linear unbiased coefficient estimator which is constrained to satisfy Slutsky symmetry involves the disturbance covariance matrix $\boldsymbol{\Sigma}$; see, e.g., Theil (1971, Sec. 6.8). The result is that the symmetry-constrained coefficient estimator takes the form

$$\hat{\boldsymbol{\beta}}^* = \hat{\boldsymbol{\beta}} - \boldsymbol{C}(\boldsymbol{\Sigma})\boldsymbol{R}'[\boldsymbol{R}\boldsymbol{C}(\boldsymbol{\Sigma})\boldsymbol{R}']^{-1}\boldsymbol{R}\hat{\boldsymbol{\beta}} \tag{A.24}$$

and that its covariance matrix is

$$\text{(A.25)} \qquad \mathscr{V}(\hat{\beta}^*) = C(\Sigma) - C(\Sigma)R'[RC(\Sigma)R']^{-1}RC(\Sigma)$$

where $\hat{\beta}$ and $C(\Sigma)$ are defined in (A.20) and (A.21), respectively, while R takes the form described in the discussion following (A.20).

Applications

The problem with the F statistics (A.15) and (A.23) is that their values cannot be computed if, as is assumed here and is generally the case, Σ is an unknown matrix. Of course, we have the same problem with respect to the symmetry-constrained estimator (A.24) and its covariance matrix (A.25).

The standard solution of this problem is to approximate Σ by the estimator S, which is given in (A.13) for the test of homogeneity and in (A.18) for the test of symmetry given homogeneity. It may be shown [see, e.g., Theil (1971, Sec. 8.6)] that this approximation is acceptable when the number of observations is sufficiently large, but in our applications this number is only 15, each country supplying one observation. Also, asymptotic distribution theory typically does not give an explicit answer to the question: How large a sample is large enough for an asymptotic result to provide an adequate approximation?

Sometimes the approximation of Σ by S does not even work at all, which we shall illustrate for the test of homogeneity. Substitution of $\Sigma = S$ into (A.14) yields a constant, so that the F statistic (A.15) is reduced to its numerator shown in (A.12). By substituting $\Sigma = S$ into (A.12) we obtain

$$\text{(A.26)} \qquad \frac{b'R'S^{-1}Rb}{v'(X'X)^{-1}v}$$

which is asymptotically distributed as $\chi^2(n-1)$ if the homogeneity hypothesis is true. Take the case $n = 8$ so that $\chi^2(n-1)$ becomes $\chi^2(7)$, while X and Y become of order 15×9 and 15×7, respectively. Then S of (A.13) has order 7×7, but the matrix in brackets in (A.13) has rank $15 - 9 = 6$ so that S is singular, which means that the ratio (A.26) does not exist. The proposition that this ratio is asymptotically distributed as $\chi^2(7)$ has, of course, little meaning when it fails to exist. Laitinen (1978) proved that the exact distribution of (A.26) is that of Hotelling's T^2, but this result is empty if (as is the case here for $n = 8$) the T^2 statistic involves a zero or negative number of degrees of freedom.

Next consider the test against Slutsky symmetry so that $\boldsymbol{S}$ takes the form (A.18). Substitution of $\boldsymbol{\Sigma} = \boldsymbol{S}$ into (A.19) yields a constant, so that the F statistic (A.23) is reduced to its numerator shown in (A.22). By substituting $\boldsymbol{\Sigma} = \boldsymbol{S}$ into (A.22) we obtain

$$\hat{\beta}'\boldsymbol{R}'[\boldsymbol{R}C(\boldsymbol{S})\boldsymbol{R}']^{-1}\boldsymbol{R}\hat{\beta} \tag{A.27}$$

which is asymptotically distributed as χ^2 with $\frac{1}{2}(n-1)(n-2)$ degrees of freedom if the symmetry hypothesis is true. For $n = 8$, this is $\chi^2(21)$ with a one-half percent significance point equal to 41.4. When we apply (A.27) to the $n = 8$ goods considered in the text of this monograph, we obtain 200.25, which suggests "overwhelming evidence" against the symmetry hypothesis. It is obvious, however, that the use of $\boldsymbol{S}$ rather than $\boldsymbol{\Sigma}$ in the test statistic (A.27) requires much more caution than the words in quotation marks indicate.

A Link with Canonical Correlation Theory

The basic problem is the fact that the disturbance covariance matrix $\boldsymbol{\Sigma}$ is unknown. Further progress can be made by linking $\boldsymbol{\Sigma}$ to the covariance matrix of the dependent and the independent variables of the demand model. We write the latter matrix in partitioned form:

$$\begin{bmatrix} \boldsymbol{\Sigma}_{11} & \boldsymbol{\Sigma}_{12} \\ \boldsymbol{\Sigma}_{12}' & \boldsymbol{\Sigma}_{22} \end{bmatrix} \quad \begin{matrix} n-1 \text{ dependent variables} \\ n+1 \text{ or } n \text{ independent variables} \end{matrix} \tag{A.28}$$

In both (A.3) and (A.16) the dependent variables take the values $y_{1c}, ..., y_{n-1,c}$ for country c. In (A.3), there are $n + 1$ independent variables; their values are $q_c, x_{1c}, ..., x_{nc}$ for country c. (The 'unit variable' corresponding to the constant term α_i will be handled by using variances and covariances rather than second moments around zero.) In (A.16), there are n independent variables, with values $q_c, \bar{x}_{1c}, ..., \bar{x}_{n-1,c}$ for country c. Note that the matrix (A.28) is interpreted as consisting of population moments, not sample moments; estimation problems will not be considered until the next subsection. A little reflection shows that under this population interpretation, the disturbance covariance matrix Σ is related to the matrix (A.28) by

$$\Sigma = \Sigma_{11} - \Sigma_{12}\Sigma_{22}^{-1}\Sigma_{12}' \tag{A.29}$$

Let $\rho_1, ..., \rho_{n-1}$ be the canonical correlation coefficients of the dependent and the independent variables. It is well known [see, e.g., Anderson (1958, Chap. 12)] that these ρ_i's can be obtained from the determinantal equation

$$|\Sigma_{12}\Sigma_{22}^{-1}\Sigma_{12}' - \rho_i^2\Sigma_{11}| = 0 \tag{A.30}$$

A comparison with (A.29) shows that

$$|\Sigma - (1 - \rho_i^2)\Sigma_{11}| = 0 \tag{A.31}$$

which provides a link between the disturbance covariance matrix Σ and the canonical correlation coefficients of the dependent and the independent variables of the demand system: for $i = 1, ..., n - 1$, one minus each squared canonical correlation coefficient is a latent root of the diagonalization of Σ relative to the covariance matrix Σ_{11} of the dependent variables.

Correcting Sample Canonical Correlations

The clue for the developments which follow is the fact that canonical correlation coefficients are generalizations of the multiple correlation coefficient. Hence, the root $1 - \rho_i^2$ in (A.31) can be viewed as (the population value of) a generalization of $1 - R^2$, where R is the multiple correlation coefficient associated with the regression of one dependent variable on a number of independent variables. It is well known that R tends to overestimate the fit of the regression, particularly when the number of independent variables is not small relative to the number of observations. Several proposals have been made to correct for this bias, e.g.,

$$1 - \bar{R}^2 = \frac{N-1}{N-K-1}(1 - R^2) \tag{A.32}$$

where $\bar{R}$ is the corrected multiple correlation coefficient, N is the number of observations, K is the number of independent variables, and $K + 1$

is the number of coefficients adjusted (including a constant term).

It is of interest to consider whether it is similarly possible to correct sample canonical correlation coefficients for bias and to use such a correction in order to improve on the estimation of Σ by means of (A.31). For this purpose, we reinterpret the matrix (A.28) so that it now consists of sample variances and covariances, which means that (A.30) yields sample rather than population canonical correlation coefficients. If (A.28) refers to the specification (A.3), it is a matrix of order $2n \times 2n$, or 16×16 for $n = 8$. Since there are only 15 observations, (A.28) is then a singular matrix and the largest canonical correlation coefficient is 1, which implies singularity of the associated Σ in view of (A.31). But the true Σ is positive definite by assumption, which suggests that the largest sample canonical correlation coefficient should be corrected in the direction of zero. However, this is more easily said than done when this largest coefficient is 1: if we consider the special case in which the largest sample canonical correlation coefficient is a multiple correlation coefficient R and apply the correction (A.32), we find that $R = 1$ implies $R = 1$, which amounts to no correction at all.

Why is the matrix (A.28) singular when it is interpreted as consisting of sample variances and covariances? The answer is that these are the second-order moments of the sample distribution, and this distribution is always discrete because it assigns a mass $1/N$ (N = sample size) to each data point. For $N = 15$, the matrix (A.28) is then unavoidably singular given that its order is 16×16. But the dependent and independent variables of the demand model (A.3) are *continuous*, not discrete. This raises the question of whether we can use a sample of observations on such variables in order to obtain a continuous multivariate distribution (with nonsingular covariance matrix) as an estimator of the parent distribution of these variables. We shall pursue this matter of density estimation in a univariate context in Appendix B and in a multivariate context in Appendix C, using the maximum entropy distribution proposed by Theil and Laitinen (1980). Next, in Appendix D, we shall return to canonical correlation theory, after which we shall provide further evidence on homogeneity and symmetry testing in Appendix E.

Appendix B

THE UNIVARIATE MAXIMUM ENTROPY DISTRIBUTION

The Maximum Entropy Principle

Maximum entropy is a general principle for estimating the distribution function of one or several random variables. The basic idea is that the statistician knows something (but not everything) about this distribution, and that it is rational to estimate this distribution by a fitted distribution which is as uninformative as possible subject to the constraint of what he knows. To show that this is rational, assume that our statistician selects any other distribution. By construction, this distribution is more informative and, hence, contains more information than the constraint implies. This is indeed irrational, because the constraint is supposed to contain all prior information which the statistician has about the parent distribution.

To apply this principle, we must specify a measure of the degree of "uninformativeness." For a discrete distribution with probabilities $p_1, ...,$ p_k, the measure used in statistical information theory is minus the expectation of the logarithm of the probability,

$$H = -\sum_{i=1}^{k} p_i \log p_i \tag{B.1}$$

which is known as the *entropy* of the distribution with probabilities $p_1, ..., p_k$. Thus, the criterion of maximum uninformativeness subject to the constraint of what the statistician knows about the parent distribution amounts to constrained entropy maximization. A justification of the use of the entropy follows in the next subsection.

To illustrate how this method works, assume that the statistician's prior knowledge is confined to the fact that there are k possible outcomes. He should then maximize (B.1) by varying the p_i's subject to the constraint that they add up to 1. So we construct the Lagrangean function

$$-\sum_{i=1}^{k} p_i \log p_i - \mu \left(\sum_{i=1}^{k} p_i - 1\right) \tag{B.2}$$

which we differentiate with respect to p_i. With log interpreted as natural log, this yields $-1 - \log p_i - \mu$. When we set this equal to zero, p_i becomes independent of i and, hence, equals $1/k$. Thus, when the statistician's prior knowledge is confined to the fact that there are k possible outcomes, the maximum entropy principle yields a distribution with equal probabilities.

The Information Concept

The introduction of the entropy in statistical information theory is from Shannon (1948), although the concept played a role in thermodynamics in the nineteenth century. The paragraphs which follow serve to provide an intuitive justification of the definition (B.1).

Consider an arbitrary event E with probability p; the nature of E is completely irrelevant. At some point in time we receive a reliable message stating that E has in fact occurred. The question is: How much information is contained in this message? To answer this question, consider first the case in which p is close to 1, say, $p = .95$. It is then quite likely that E will take place even before the message arrives, which means that this message is not very informative. Next, suppose that p is close to 0, say, $p = .01$. Then, if a message arrives stating that E occurred in spite of this low p value (remember that the message is reliable by assumption), we are greatly surprised and the message is quite informative.

These numerical exercises suggest that if we want to measure the information content of such a message in terms of the probability p of the event that prevailed prior to the arrival of the message, we should select a decreasing function: the more unlikely the event was before the message arrived, the more informative this message is. The function used in statistical information theory is

$$h(p) = -\log p \tag{B.3}$$

which decreases from ∞ at $p = 0$ to 0 at $p = 1$. The reason for this specific choice is its additivity for stochastically independent events. To clarify this, let E and E' be two events with probabilities p and p', respectively, and let them be stochastically independent so that the probability of their joint occurrence is pp'. Using (B.3), we find that the information of the message stating that both E and E' occurred is equal to $h(pp') = -\log pp' = -\log p - \log p' = h(p) + h(p')$, i.e., this information is equal to that of the message on E only plus that of the message on E' only. The additivity of the information definition (B.3) is very convenient in applications. In fact, it is not difficult to derive (B.3) as the unique solution of certain axioms (unique up to the choice of the logarithmic base), the main axiom being that of additivity; see, e.g., Theil (1967, Sec. 1.3).

Next consider a complete system of mutually exclusive events $E_1, \ldots E_k$ with probabilities $p_1, \ldots, p_k$. If a message arrives stating that E_i occurred, the information received is $h(p_i) = -\log p_i$. Before the message arrives, we do not know which E_i will occur, but we do know that its probability is p_i. Therefore, the expected information computed prior to the arrival of the message equals

$$\sum_{i=1}^{k} p_i h(p_i) = -\sum_{i=1}^{k} p_i \log p_i$$

and a comparison with (B.1) shows that this equals the entropy. In other words, the entropy (B.1) is nothing but the expected information of the message that states which of the events $E_1, \ldots, E_k$ will take place given that their probabilities are $p_1, \ldots, p_k$.

The expected information interpretation is also useful in relation to the result obtained in the discussion following (B.2). We found there that the entropy is maximized at $p_1 = \ldots = p_k = 1/k$. By substituting this into (B.1) we obtain

$$H = \log k \tag{B.4}$$

which is the maximum entropy value given that there are k possible outcomes. Thus, for $k = 3$, the entropy of the distribution with probabilities $(\frac{1}{3}, \frac{1}{3}, \frac{1}{3})$ is log 3 and it is larger than that of the distribution with probabilities (.98, .01, .01). This reflects the fact that in the latter case there is less *uncertainty* as to which outcome will be realized. When there are $k = 100$ possible outcomes, each having probability .01, $\log k$ becomes log 100, which exceeds log 3, thus showing that this distribution is characterized by even more uncertainty than $(\frac{1}{3}, \frac{1}{3}, \frac{1}{3})$. Indeed, expected information and uncertainty should be viewed as two sides of the same coin. When more information is expected from the message on which outcome occurred, there is more uncertainty prior to the arrival of the message, and vice versa. Thus, the entropy is similar to the variance of a distribution in that both are uncertainty or dispersion measures. The major difference between the two is that (B.1) involves only probabilities, not the values taken by the random variable, so that the entropy (in contrast to the variance) can also be used for nonnumerical variables. However, we shall not go further into this matter, since our interest in what follows is confined to continuous distributions.

The Entropy of a Continuous Distribution

Recall that the entropy definition (B.1) amounts to minus the expectation of the logarithm of the probability. The extension to a continuous distribution with density function $f(\cdot)$ is minus the expectation of the logarithm of the density:

$$H = -\int_{-\infty}^{\infty} f(x) \log f(x)\, dx \tag{B.5}$$

It is customary to use natural logarithms for the entropy of a continuous distribution. For example, if the distribution is normal, with mean μ and variance σ^2, the entropy (B.5) is easily verified to be

$$H = \tfrac{1}{2} \log 2\pi e \sigma^2 \tag{B.6}$$

where $\log e = 1$. Thus, the normal entropy depends only on the variance, not on the mean, which reflects the fact that the variance is the exclusive

Table B.1
Distributions with maximum entropy

Range	Restriction on expectation of	Density function with maximum entropy
(0, 1)	–	$f(x) = 1$ (Uniform)
(0, 1)	$\log X$ $\log(1 - X)$	$f(x) = \dfrac{x^{m-1}(1-x)^{n-1}}{B(m,n)}$ (Beta)
$(0, \infty)$	X	$f(x) = ae^{-ax}$ (Exponential)
$(0, \infty)$	X $\log X$	$f(x) = \dfrac{a^p}{\Gamma(p)} x^{p-1} e^{-ax}$ (Gamma)
$(-\infty, \infty)$	X X^2	$f(x) = \dfrac{1}{\sigma\sqrt{2\pi}} e^{-(x-\mu)^2/2\sigma^2}$ (Normal)
$(-\infty, \infty)$	$\|X\|$	$f(x) = \tfrac{1}{2} ae^{-a\|x\|}$ (Laplace)

source of uncertainty as to the value of a random outcome from a normal distribution.

There are numerous situations in which a statistician wants to select a continuous distribution which is as uninformative as possible subject to certain constraints. For example, when Bayesian statisticians face the problem of formulating a prior distribution of a parameter which varies continuously, they may select the distribution with maximum entropy as defined in (B.5) subject to the constraint of what they know about the parameter a priori. The basic rule is the following: use *all* the information on the parameter which you have, but avoid using *any* information which you do not have. The entropy definition (B.5) provides a tool to make this rule operational. Table B.1, from Kagan et al. (1973), provides another tool; it lists six well-known distributions, each of which maximizes the entropy (B.5) subject to certain constraints. For proofs of the statements which follow, we refer to Kagan et al. (1973, Sec. 13.2).

The first line of Table B.1 should be read as follows. Suppose that a random variable X has range $(0, 1)$. Suppose that is all we know; then the distribution which maximizes the entropy (B.5), the integration limits being $(0, 1)$ rather than $(-\infty, \infty)$, is the uniform distribution over this range. In the second line we have the same range, but the expectations of $\log X$ and $\log(1 - X)$ are known, or, equivalently, the geometric means of X and $1 - X$ are known (both positive). The distribution which maximizes the entropy (B.5) subject to these constraints is the beta distribution with these means.

In the third and fourth lines, the range of X is $(0, \infty)$ and the mean of X is known. If that is all which is known, the distribution with maximum entropy is the exponential distribution with this mean. If the geometric mean is also known (and positive), the distribution with maximum entropy is the gamma distribution with this mean and geometric mean. These two results can be used as a justification of the use of Koyck's distributed lag and the gamma distributed lag; see Theil and Fiebig (1981). Similarly, the maximum entropy properties of the uniform and the exponential distributions can be used to justify two well-known methods of depreciation of assets; see Lev and Theil (1978).

The last two lines of the table concern distributions with unrestricted range. When the mean and the variance are given, the maximum entropy (ME) distribution is the normal with this mean and variance. When the expectation of the absolute value of the random variable is given, the ME distribution is the Laplace distribution with this expected absolute value.

The ME Distribution of a Sample from a Continuous Population

Let $(x_1, ..., x_N)$ be a sample of observations from an unknown continuous population with range $(-\infty, \infty)$. Our objective is to estimate the density function of this population by maximizing the entropy subject to the knowledge provided by the sample. This requires that our knowledge be organized in a particular way. The account which follows is largely based on Theil and Laitinen (1980).

Let $f(\cdot)$ be the estimated density function (which is to be derived), so that H of (B.5) is the associated entropy. Our criterion for $f(\cdot)$ is that of maximum H subject to certain constraints which represent the knowledge about the parent distribution that is provided by the sample, and we formulate these constraints in terms of moments of order zero and one after the sample values have been rearranged in the form of order statistics. We indicate these order statistics by means of superscripts:

$$x^1 < x^2 < ... < x^N \tag{B.7}$$

We define intermediate points between successive order statistics,

$$\xi_i = \xi(x^i, x^{i+1}) \qquad i = 1, ..., N-1 \tag{B.8}$$

where $\xi(\cdot)$ is a symmetric differentiable function of its two arguments whose value is not outside the range defined by these arguments. Each pair of successive ξ_i's defines an interval, $I_2 = (\xi_1, \xi_2)$, ... $I_{N-1} = (\xi_{N-2}, \xi_{N-1})$, while there are two open-ended intervals, $I_1 = (-\infty, \xi_1)$ and $I_N = (\xi_{N-1}, \infty)$. Therefore, there are N intervals, $I_1, ..., I_N$, each containing one order statistic x^i and, hence, a fraction $1/N$ of the mass of the sample distribution. We impose on the density estimator $f(\cdot)$ that it preserves these fractions,

$$\int_{I_i} f(x) = \frac{1}{N} \qquad i = 1, ..., N \tag{B.9}$$

which is a *mass-preserving constraint* (a constraint on moments of order zero).

The order constraint is a *mean-preserving constraint*, which refers both to the overall mean,

$$\bar{x} = \frac{1}{N} \sum_{k=1}^{N} x_k = \frac{1}{N} \sum_{i=1}^{N} x^i \tag{B.10}$$

and also to the mean of each interval I_i separately, in the same way that the mass-preserving constraint (B.9) is imposed on each interval. We implement this constraint by means of the order statistics associated with each I_i, i.e., those which determine the end points of I_i. These end points are ξ_1 and ξ_{N-1} for the open-ended intervals I_1 and I_N, respectively, so that x^1 and x^2 are the order statistics associated with I_1 in view of (B.8), while x^{N-1} and x^N are associated with I_N. Similarly, x^{i-1}, x^i and x^{i+1} are associated with I_i for $1 < i < N$. Since the set of all order statistics is nothing but a rearranged form of the sample distribution, a natural way of imposing the mean-preserving constraint on each I_i is by requiring its mean to be some weighted average of the associated order statistics. This yields N constraints in addition to the preservation constraint on the overall mean (B.10).

Thus, subject to this mean-preserving constraint and to the mass-preserving constraint (B.9), we seek the density estimator $f(\cdot)$ which maximizes the entropy (B.5). The solution, which will be referred to as the ME distribution from now on, is derived in the next subsection and it can be summarized as follows. The $N - 1$ intermediate points of (B.8) become midpoints between successive order statistics,

(B.11) $$\xi_i = \tfrac{1}{2}\,(x^i + x^{i+1})$$

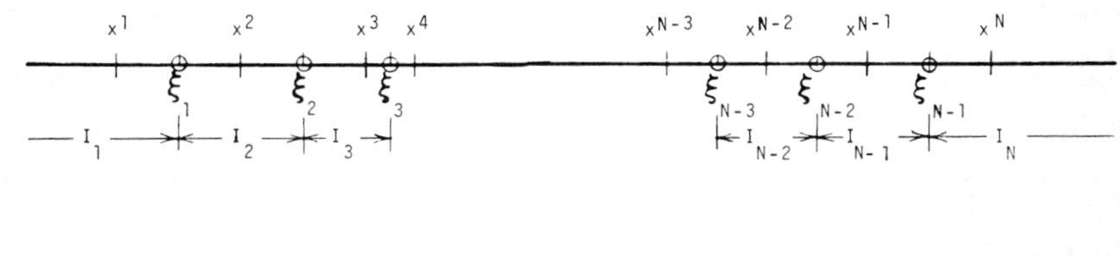

Figure B.1. The density function of the univariate ME distribution

which is illustrated in the upper part of Figure B.1. The ME distribution is uniform in each closed interval $I_2, \ldots, I_{N-1}$ and exponential in the open-ended intervals I_1 and I_N as illustrated in the lower part of the figure. Integration of this density picture yields a cumulated ME distribution function which is continuous and monotone increasing everywhere, piecewise linear around each of the order statistics $x^2, \ldots, x^{N-1}$, and exponential around the extreme order statistics x^1 and x^N.

In addition, the interval means of the ME distribution are

$$\bar{x}^i = \tfrac{1}{2}(\xi_{i-1} + \xi_i) \qquad i = 1, \ldots, N \tag{B.12}$$

where ξ_0 and ξ_N are defined as x^1 and x^N, respectively. The simplest way of visualizing these interval means is by enlarging the set of N order statistics shown in (B.7) by two values equal to the extremes:

$$x^0 \equiv x^1 < x^2 < \ldots < x^{N-1} < x^N \equiv x^{N+1} \tag{B.13}$$

Then there are $N + 1$ *primary midpoints* between successive order statistics, defined in (B.11) for $i = 0, 1, \ldots, N$, which includes $\xi_0 = x^1$ and $\xi_N = x^N$. The N interval means of (B.12) are now *secondary midpoints*, i.e., midpoints between successive primary midpoints. The secondary midpoints are shown at the bottom of Figure B.1.

It will be shown in Appendix C that the variance of the ME distribution (the ME variance for short) can be written as the sum of three terms:

$$\frac{1}{N}\sum_{k=1}^{N}(x_k - \bar{x})^2 - \frac{1}{4N}\sum_{i=1}^{N-1}(x^{i+1} - x^i)^2 - \frac{1}{24N}\sum_{i=2}^{N-1}(x^{i+1} - x^{i-1})^2 \tag{B.14}$$

The first term is the sample variance and the next two terms are both negative. Therefore, the ME variance is subject to *shrinkage* relative to the sample variance.

Derivations

We write $\mathscr{E}(X \mid X \in I_i)$ for the conditional mean of the ME distribution given that the variable is confined to interval I_i. The mean-preserving constraint on these intervals as described in the discussion following (B.10) amounts to

$$\text{(B.15)} \quad \mathscr{E}(X \mid X \in I_i) = \begin{cases} ax^1 + (1-a)x^2 & \text{if } i = 1 \\ b_i x^{i-1} + (1 - b_i - c_i)x^i + c_i x^{i+1} & \text{if } 1 < i < N \\ dx^N + (1-d)x^{N-1} & \text{if } i = N \end{cases}$$

where a, d, the b_i's and the c_i's are constants which must be determined.

Since each interval I_i is assigned mass $1/N$, the conditional ME density function given $X \in I_i$ equals $f_i(x) = Nf(x)$, $x \in I_i$. It thus follows from (B.5) that the entropy to be maximized can be written as

$$\text{(B.16)} \qquad H = \text{constant} + \frac{1}{N} \sum_{i=1}^{N} H(X \mid X \in I_i)$$

where $H(X \mid X \in I_i)$ is the conditional entropy given $X \in I_i$:

$$H(X \mid X \in I_i) = -\int_{I_i} f_i(x) \log f_i(x)\, dx$$

We conclude from (B.16) that maximizing H can be performed for each interval separately. Note that this convenient property ultimately results from the additivity of the information concept.

For the intervals I_i with $1 < i < N$, we know that they are bounded above and below. It may seem from (B.15) that we also know something about the mean given $X \in I_i$, but this knowledge is empty as long as b_i and c_i are unspecified. Therefore, the ME criterion yields a uniform distribution for each $I_i = (\xi_{i-1}, \xi_i)$ with $1 < i < N$, and the mean of this distribution is $\frac{1}{2}(\xi_{i-1} + \xi_i)$, where ξ_i is defined in (B.8). On combining this mean with that in (B.15) for $1 < i < N$, we obtain

$$\text{(B.17)} \qquad \tfrac{1}{2}\,\xi(x^{i-1}, x^i) + \tfrac{1}{2}\,\xi(x^i, x^{i+1}) = b_i x^{i-1} + (1 - b_i - c_i)x^i + c_i x^{i+1}$$

for $i = 2, \ldots, N-1$. Recall that $\xi(\cdot)$ is assumed to be a symmetric differentiable function of its two arguments. This means that the derivatives of the left side with respect to x^{i-1} and x^{i+1} must be equal; hence, $b_i = c_i$ is implied by the right side. It also means that the derivative of the left side with respect to x^i must be twice as large; hence, $1 - b_i -$

$c_i = 1 - 2b_i$ must be $2b_i$, so that $b_i = c_i = \frac{1}{4}$. Therefore, we can write the right side of (B.17) as

$$\frac{1}{2}\left(\frac{x^{i-1}+x^i}{2}+\frac{x^i+x^{i+1}}{2}\right)$$

which shows that $\xi(\cdot)$ of (B.8) becomes the arithmetic mean of its two arguments in agreement with (B.11).

The mean-preserving constraint also requires the preservation of the overall mean (B.10). Given that each interval is assigned mass $1/N$, this amounts to

$$\frac{1}{N}\sum_{i=1}^{N} \mathscr{E}(X \mid X \in I_i) = \bar{x}$$

and, hence, to

$$\sum_{i=1}^{N} \mathscr{E}(X \mid X \in I_i) = \sum_{i=1}^{N} x^i \tag{B.18}$$

This means that the sum of the weights attached to each of the order statistics $x^1, ..., x^N$ in (B.15) must be equal to 1. For $x^2, ..., x^{N-1}$, this is satisfied because $b_i = c_i = \frac{1}{4}$. For x^1 and x^N the implications are $a + b_2 = 1$ and $c_{N-1} + d = 1$, and hence, $a = d = \frac{3}{4}$. A comparison of $d = \frac{3}{4}$ with (B.15) for $i = N$ shows that this specifies the conditional mean given $X \in I_n$; the distribution with this mean which maximizes the entropy is the exponential. For $X \in I_1$ we obtain an analogous distribution with a tail in the direction of $-\infty$. The corresponding variances are

$$\text{var}(X \mid X \in I_1) = \tfrac{1}{4}(\xi_1 - \xi_0)^2 \tag{B.19}$$

$$\text{var}(X \mid X \in I_N) = \tfrac{1}{4}(\xi_N - \xi_{N-1})^2 \tag{B.20}$$

which may be verified from the property that the exponential distribution has a variance equal to the squared difference between the mean and the (lower or upper) bound of the distribution, and from (B.11) for $i = 0, 1, N-1$ and N.

The ME Median and Quartiles

We continue the discussion of the univariate ME distribution by presenting some evidence on its merits. Since the distribution is formulated in terms of order statistics, it is natural to consider related characteristics of the ME distribution such as its median and quartiles. The ME quartiles should be viewed as alternatives to sample quartiles in that both are estimators of the population quartiles. The account which follows is based on O'Brien (1980) and Theil and O'Brien (1980).

Let N be even and write $r = \frac{1}{2} N$. Since the ME distribution assigns probability $1/N$ to each of its N component distributions, the ME median is the median ξ_r of the primary midpoints or, equivalently, the arithmetic average of the two middle order statistics x^r and x^{r+1} (see Figure B.2 for $N = 2$ and $N = 4$). For even N, the sample median is any number between x^r and x^{r+1}, and is thus not unique. The conventional choice is the arithmetic average of x^r and x^{r+1}. This particular choice can therefore be justified as being the median of the ME distribution.

Let N be odd and write $m = \frac{1}{2}(N + 1)$ so that the sample median is x^m. The ME median is now the median of the mth component distribution, which equals

$$\bar{x}^m = \tfrac{1}{2}(\xi_{m-1} + \xi_m) = \tfrac{1}{4} x^{m-1} + \tfrac{1}{2} x^m + \tfrac{1}{4} x^{m+1} \tag{B.21}$$

because the mth component distribution is uniform so that its mean and median are identical (see Figures B.3 and B.4 for $N = 3$ and $N = 7$). Thus, for odd N, the ME median is the median of the secondary rather than the primary mid-points, and it differs from the sample median x^m.

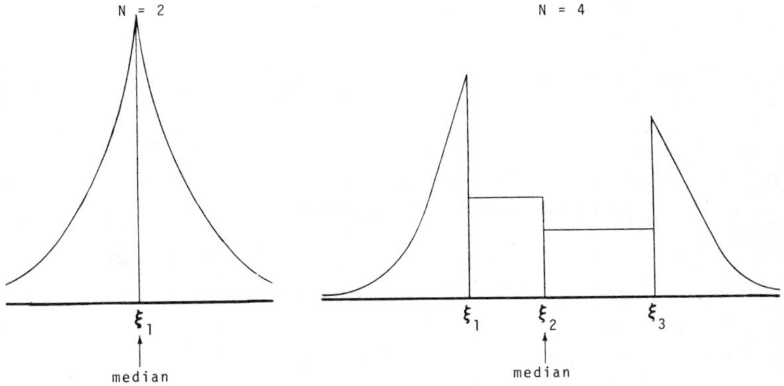

Figure B.2. The ME median for $N = 2$ and $N = 4$

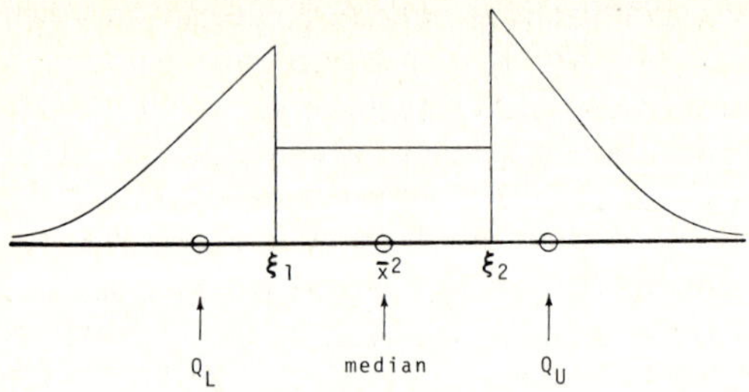

Figure B.3. The ME median and quartiles for $N = 3$

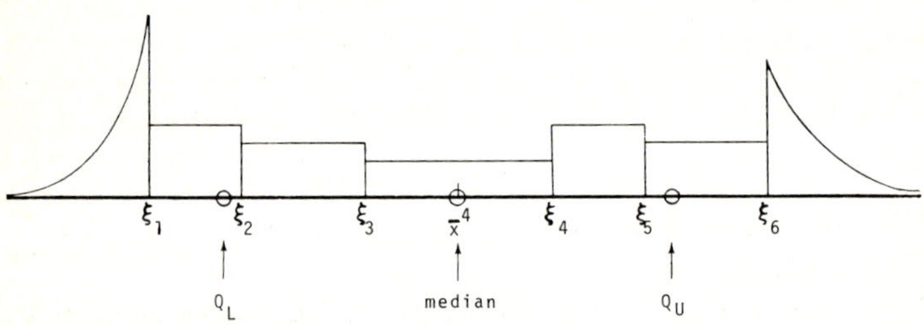

Figure B.4. The ME quartiles for $N = 7$

Let $N + 1$ be a multiple of 4 and write $q = \frac{1}{4}(N + 1)$ so that the sample lower and upper quartiles are x^q and x^{3q}, respectively. We write Q_L and Q_U for the ME lower and upper quartiles. For $q = 1$ (or $N = 3$; see Figure B.3), Q_L equals the upper quartile of the exponential distribution on the left, while Q_U equals the lower quartile of the exponential distribution on the right. The exponential distribution with range $I_N = (\xi_{N-1}, \infty)$ and variance σ^2 has a lower quartile equal to $\xi_{N-1} + \sigma \log_e \frac{4}{3}$. Using (B.20) for σ^2 and proceeding similarly for $I_1 = (-\infty, \xi_1)$, we find that

$$\text{(B.22)}\; Q_L = .57192x^1 + .42808x^2, \quad Q_U = .42808x^2 + .57192x^3$$

holds for $q = 1$ (or $N = 3$), where $.57192 = \frac{1}{2} + \frac{1}{4}\log_e \frac{4}{3}$ and $.42808 = 1 - .57192$. For $q \geq 2$, $Q_L = \frac{1}{4}\xi_{q-1} + \frac{3}{4}\xi_q$ and $Q_U = \frac{3}{4}\xi_{3q-1} + \frac{1}{4}\xi_{3q}$ (see Figure B.4 for $N = 7$ or $q = 2$), so that

$$Q_L = \tfrac{1}{8}\, x^{q-1} + \tfrac{1}{2}\, x^{q} + \tfrac{3}{8}\, x^{q+1}, \quad Q_U = \tfrac{3}{8}\, x^{3q-1} + \tfrac{1}{2}\, x^{3q} + \tfrac{1}{8}\, x^{3q+1} \tag{B.23}$$

The ME quartiles (including the ME median) discussed in the previous paragraphs are all linear functions of order statistics. Since the expectations, variances and covariances of normal order statistics have been tabulated, we can use these to tabulate the expectations and expected squared errors of the ME and sample quartiles for random samples from a standard normal distribution. Table B.2 provides the expected squared errors of the ME and sample medians for odd N. (Their expectations are obviously zero.) The numbers shown indicate how much the ME distribution gains for small N by exploiting the knowledge that the parent distribution is continuous. The last column of the table contains the relative difference, defined as the excess of the expected squared error of the sample median over that of the ME median measured as a fraction of the former expected squared error. As $N \to \infty$, this relative difference converges to zero, which agrees with the asymptotic equivalence of the ME and sample medians.

Table B.3 concerns the upper quartile of the standard normal distribution, the true value of which is .6745. The sample size N is such that $N + 1$ is a multiple of 4; hence, the sample upper quartile is x^{3q} with $q = \frac{1}{4}(N + 1)$ and the ME upper quartile is Q_U as shown in (B.22) for $q = 1$ and in (B.23) for $q \geq 2$. The first two columns of Table B.3 contain the expectations of Q_L and x^{3q}, with those of x^{3q} all exceeding the true value .6745. Therefore, the sample upper quartiles are upwardly biased. Recall from the discussion following (B.14) that the ME distribution involves shrinkage. Evidently, such a shrinkage is precisely what is needed in the case of the upper quartile of a normal distribution. The figure in the upper left of Table B.3 shows that at $N = 3$ there is too much shrinkage as far as bias is concerned, the bias of Q_U being $.4840 - .6745 = -.1905$, which exceeds the bias $.8463 - .6745 = .1718$ of the sample quartile in absolute value, but for $N \geq 7$ the bias of Q_U becomes quite small. (Actually, the bias is virtually eliminated at $N = 4$ because Q_U then equals $\xi_3 = \frac{1}{2}x^3 + \frac{1}{2}x^4$ with expectation .6632; see Figure B.2 for $N = 4$.) The next three columns of the table concern the expected squared errors of Q_U and x^{3q} around the true value .6745. Those of x^{3q} exceed their ME counterparts even at $N = 3$, for which the bias of the ME quartile exceeds that of the sample quartile in absolute value. The relative differences are larger than those of the medians shown in the last column of Table B.2.

It follows from the symmetry and the zero mean of the standard normal distribution that the interquartile distances $Q_U - Q_L$ and $x^{3q} - x^q$ have expectations equal to twice the expectations of Q_U and x^{3q}, respectively. The last three columns of Table B.3 concern the expected squared errors of the ME and sample interquartile distances around the true value 2 x .6745 = 1.3490. Note that their relative differences are even larger than those of the upper quartiles.

Table B.2
Expected squared sampling errors of ME and sample medians under normality

N	ME median	Sample median	Relative difference
3	.3405	.4487	.241
5	.2336	.2868	.186
7	.1791	.2104	.149
9	.1454	.1661	.124
11	.1225	.1372	.107
13	.1059	.1168	.093
15	.0932	.1017	.083
17	.0833	.0900	.075
19	.0753	.0808	.068

Table B.3
Expectations and expected squared sampling errors of ME and sample quartiles under normality

	Upper quartile					Interquartile distance		
	Expectations		Expected squared errors			Expected squared errors		
N	ME[a]	Sa[b]	ME[a]	Sa[b]	RD[c]	ME[a]	Sa[b]	RD[c]
3	.4840	.8463	.4365	.5890	.259	.4033	.9073	.555
7	.6800	.7574	.2036	.2636	.228	.2236	.3810	.413
11	.6704	.7288	.1407	.1687	.166	.1662	.2378	.301
15	.6693	.7149	.1077	.1239	.130	.1316	.1723	.236
19	.6694	.7066	.0873	.0978	.107	.1087	.1350	.194

[a] Computed from the ME distribution.
[b] Computed from the sample distribution.
[c] Relative difference.

The Nature of the Gain Obtained from the ME Distribution

Tables B.2 and B.3 clearly indicate that the ME distribution gains relative to the discrete sample distribution by exploiting the knowledge that the parent distribution is continuous, but they also show that this gain disappears as $N \to \infty$. Asymptotically, the ME approach is equivalent to the sample distribution approach. However, there are situations in which the ME principle can be used to exploit *more* prior knowledge about the parent distribution than just continuity, in which case we may gain for both small and large samples. Since this is an important issue, we shall present an example here even though we shall not use the result for the issues raised in Appendix A. The account which follows is based on Theil (1980b, 1981).

Suppose that we know that the sample is drawn from a population with a symmetric density function. One way of exploiting this knowledge is by symmetrizing the order statistics $x^1, ..., x^N$. If the parent density function is symmetric, the difference $x^i - \bar{x}$ has a sampling distribution identical to that of $\bar{x} - x^{N+1-i}$ for each i, where $\bar{x}$ is the sample mean (B.10). We define $\tilde{x}^i - \bar{x}$ as the average of these two differences, which amounts to

$$\tilde{x}^i = \bar{x} + \tfrac{1}{2}\,(x^i - x^{N+1-i}) \qquad i = 1, ..., N \tag{B.24}$$

It is easily verified that $\tilde{x}^1, ..., \tilde{x}^N$ are symmetrized order statistics located symmetrically around $\bar{x}$. An alternative justification of the definition (B.24) is by means of least squares: construct adjusted order statistics $\tilde{x}^1, ..., \tilde{x}^N$ so that the sum of their squared differences from the original order statistics is minimized,

$$\min \sum_{i=1}^{N} (\tilde{x}^i - x^i)^2 \tag{B.25}$$

subject to the constraint that $\tilde{x}^1, ..., \tilde{x}^N$ are located symmetrically around $\bar{x}$:

$$\tilde{x}^i + \tilde{x}^{N+1-i} = 2\bar{x} \qquad i = 1, ..., N \tag{B.26}$$

It is easily verified that this constrained minimization yields the solution (B.24).

The symmetric ME distribution (the SYME distribution) is obtained from the symmetrized order statistics (B.24) in exactly the same way that the ordinary ME distribution is obtained from the x^i's. The SYME median is obviously identical to the sample mean. We indicate the SYME lower and upper quartiles by $\widetilde{Q}_L$ and $\widetilde{Q}_U$. When $N + 1$ is a multiple of 4, we obtain these quartiles from (B.22) and (B.23) by adding a tilde to each x. It is then easily verified from (B.24) that

$$\text{(B.27)} \qquad \widetilde{Q}_L = \bar{x} - \tfrac{1}{2}(Q_U - Q_L), \quad \widetilde{Q}_U = \bar{x} + \tfrac{1}{2}(Q_U - Q_L)$$

which implies $\widetilde{Q}_U - \widetilde{Q}_L = Q_U - Q_L$, i.e., the interquartile distances of the ME and SYME distributions are identical. However, the quartiles themselves are different.

If the parent density function is symmetric, we have

$$\text{(B.28)} \qquad \operatorname{cov}(x^i, x^j) = \operatorname{cov}(x^{N+1-i}, x^{N+1-j})$$

for each (i, j), which implies $\operatorname{cov}(\bar{x}, x^t) = \operatorname{cov}(\bar{x}, x^{N+1-t})$ for $t = 1, \ldots, N$. When we apply this to $t = q - 1$, q and $q + 1$, we find that the sampling covariance of $\bar{x}$ and Q_L of (B.23) equals that of $\bar{x}$ and Q_U, so that $\bar{x}$ and $Q_U - Q_L$ are uncorrelated and (B.27) implies

$$\text{(B.29)} \qquad \operatorname{var}\widetilde{Q}_L = \operatorname{var}\widetilde{Q}_U = \operatorname{var}\bar{x} + \tfrac{1}{4}\operatorname{var}(Q_U - Q_L)$$

It is now not difficult to derive the asymptotic efficiency gain from symmetrizing with respect to the quartiles of a standard normal population. Using Kendall and Stuart (1963, pp. 238–243), we find that Q_U, Q_L, x^{3q} and x^q all have asymptotic variance $1.857/N$ and that the asymptotic variance of $Q_U - Q_L$ is $2.476/N$. By substituting the latter variance into (B.29), we find that the asymptotic variances of $\widetilde{Q}_U$ and $\widetilde{Q}_L$ are equal to $1.619/N$, which amounts to a reduction of almost 13 percent below the asymptotic variance $1.857/N$ of Q_U and Q_L, thus illustrating that the gain obtained from the SYME distribution is not confined to small samples.

Appendix C

THE MULTIVARIATE MAXIMUM ENTROPY DISTRIBUTION

The Bivariate ME Distribution

Let (x_k, y_k) for $k = 1, ..., N$ be a sample from a continuous bivariate distribution with range $(-\infty, \infty)$ for both variables. Our objective is now to find the joint density function $f(x, y)$ which maximizes the bivariate entropy subject to mass- and mean-preserving constraints. This bivariate entropy is defined as a direct extension of the univariate entropy (B.5):

(C.1) $$H = -\int_{-\infty}^{\infty}\int_{-\infty}^{\infty} f(x, y) \log f(x, y)\, dx\, dy$$

We write $(x_k, y_k) = (x^i, y^j)$, which means that the kth observation contains the ith order statistic of the first and the jth of the second variable. Figure C.1 provides an example for $N = 7$. The ξ's at the bottom are the intermediate points (B.8) and the I's on top are the associated intervals; the η's on the left and the J's on the right are the analogous intermediate points and intervals, respectively, of the second variable. The figure con-

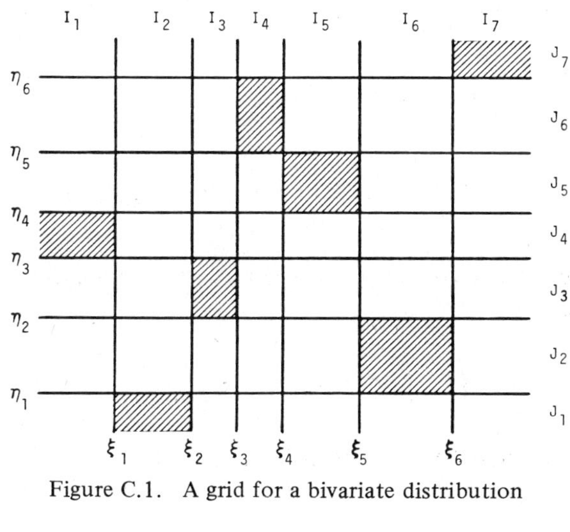

Figure C.1. A grid for a bivariate distribution

tains $N^2 = 49$ cells. Out of these, $N = 7$ cells (shaded) contain one observation each and $N^2 - N = 42$ cells contain no observation. So we extend (B.9) by assigning mass $1/N$ to each shaded cell and zero mass to all others.

It is shown in the next paragraph that, within each shaded cell, the entropy is at its maximum when stochastic independence is imposed. Four shaded cells in Figure C.1 are bounded on all sides; their ME distribution is the bivariate uniform distribution. Two shaded cells are open-ended on one side, with an ME distribution equal to the exponential (for the open-ended variable) multiplied by the uniform (for the other variable). The shaded cell upper right is open-ended on two sides; its ME distribution is the product of two exponentials. We conclude that the cumulated distribution function (cdf) of the bivariate ME distribution is a continuous function of its two arguments, and that it is piecewise linear except for exponential tails. The cdf of the bivariate ME distribution differs from its univariate counterpart in that the former is a nondecreasing function of its two arguments, whereas the latter is strictly increasing.

The proposition that the bivariate entropy is maximized under stochastic independence (given the univariate marginal entropies) holds generally. Consider two random variables, X and Y, and let $f(x, y)$ be the joint density function and $f_1(x)$, $f_2(y)$ the marginal density functions. It is then easily verified that

$$H(X, Y) = H(X) + H(Y) - M \tag{C.2}$$

where $H(X, Y)$ is the joint entropy (C.1), $H(X)$ and $H(Y)$ are the marginal entropies,

$$H(X) = -\int_{-\infty}^{\infty} f_1(x) \log f_1(x)\,dx$$

$$H(Y) = -\int_{-\infty}^{\infty} f_2(y) \log f_2(y)\,dy$$

while M is the expected mutual information of the bivariate distribution, which is defined as

$$M = \int_{-\infty}^{\infty}\int_{-\infty}^{\infty} f(x, y) \log \frac{f(x, y)}{f_1(x) f_2(y)}\,dx\,dy \tag{C.3}$$

The proposition then follows from (C.2) and $M \geq 0$ with the equal sign holding if and only if there is stochastic independence. We note that the discrete version of (C.3) can be viewed as a measure of the dependence of a discrete bivariate distribution comparable to the product-moment correlation, in the same way that the entropy (B.1) is a dispersion measure comparable to the variance; see the discussion following (B.4).

The ME Cross-Moment

We now return to the interpretation of $f(x, y)$ as the density function of the bivariate ME distribution. The ME cross-moment of the two variables can then be written as

$$\mathscr{E}(XY) = \int_{-\infty}^{\infty} \int_{-\infty}^{\infty} xyf(x, y)\, \mathrm{d}x\, \mathrm{d}y \tag{C.4}$$

Since $f(x, y)$ is nonzero only in the N shaded cells of Figure C.1, the integral in (C.4) equals the sum of N terms, one for each shaded cell. If $(x_k, y_k) = (x^i, y^j)$, this term for the kth shaded cell takes the form

$$\int_{I_i} \int_{J_j} xyf(x, y)\, \mathrm{d}x\, \mathrm{d}y = \frac{\overline{x}^i \overline{y}^j}{N} \tag{C.5}$$

To verify this result, note that the left side equals

$$\frac{1}{N} \int_{I_i} \int_{J_j} xy\,[Nf(x, y)]\, \mathrm{d}x\, \mathrm{d}y \tag{C.6}$$

where $Nf(x, y)$ is the density function of the conditional ME distribution given that the variables are confined to the cell (I_i, J_j). Since these variables are stochastically independent within the cell, the integral in (C.6) equals the product of the two conditional expectations. The proof of (C.5) is completed by noting that these expectations are the secondary midpoints $\overline{x}^i$ and $\overline{y}^j$, where $\overline{y}^j = \frac{1}{2}(\eta_{j-1} + \eta_j)$ with $\eta_j = \frac{1}{2}(y^j + y^{j+1})$ as primary midpoint; compare with (B.11) and (B.12).

Therefore, to obtain $\mathscr{E}(XY)$ we must sum (C.5) over the N shaded cells. For this purpose we note that each secondary midpoint is always uniquely associated with a coordinate of one observation. For example, if $x_7 = x^1$ in the upper part of Figure B.1 (i.e., if the seventh observation has the lowest x value), then $\overline{x}^1$ in the lower part is associated with x_7 because both are in the interval I_1. Similarly, if $y_7 = y^4$, then $\overline{y}^4$ is associated with y_7 because both are in J_4. The observation pair is in this case $(x_7, y_7) = (x^1,$

y^4), and associated with this observation is the secondary midpoint pair $(\overline{x}^1, \overline{y}^4)$, which may thus be written as $(\overline{x}_7, \overline{y}_7)$. Replacing the observation point $P_7 = (x_7, y_7)$ by $\overline{P}_7 = (\overline{x}_7, \overline{y}_7)$ amounts to a displacement within the cell (I_1, J_4), as is illustrated in Figure C.2. It will be noted that P_7 and $\overline{P}_7$ are both located in the left-most shaded cell of Figure C.1.

More generally, since for each $k = 1, ..., N$ the observation point $P_k = (x_k, y_k)$ equals (x^i, y^j) for some (i, j), there is an associated point $\overline{P}_k = (\overline{x}_k, \overline{y}_k) = (\overline{x}^i, \overline{y}^j)$ whose coordinates are equal to the corresponding secondary midpoints. Therefore, $\overline{x}^i \overline{y}^j/N$ in (C.5) equals $\overline{x}_k \overline{y}_k/N$. Recall from the beginning of the previous paragraph that this must be summed over k to yield $\mathscr{E}(XY)$. We conclude that

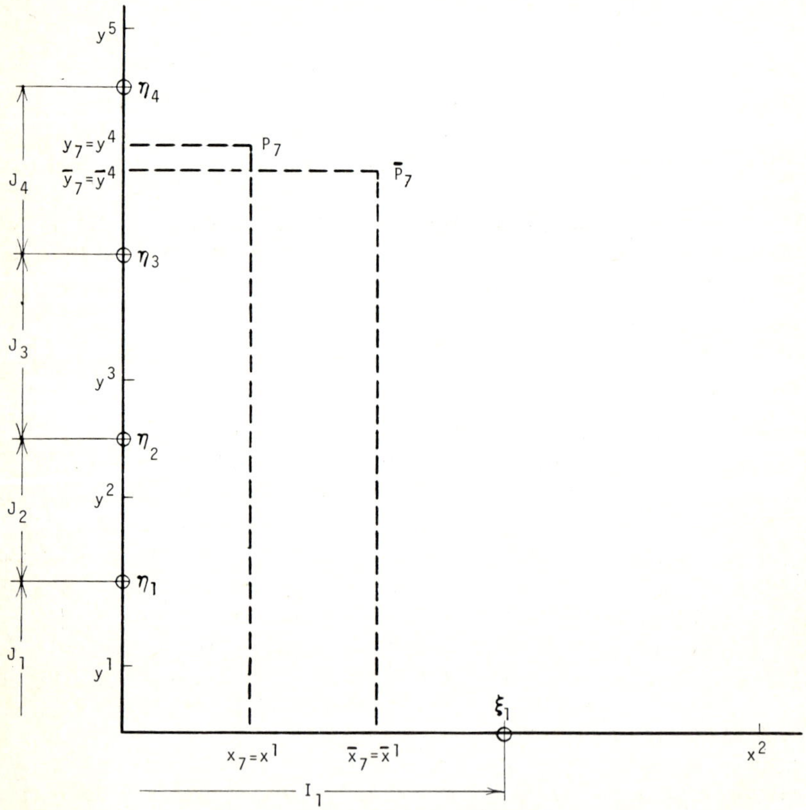

Figure C.2. An observation pair and the associated secondary midpoints

(C.7) $$\mathscr{E}(XY) = \frac{1}{N} \sum_{k=1}^{N} \bar{x}_k \bar{y}_k$$

or, in words, that the ME cross-moment is equal to the cross-moment of the secondary midpoints which are associated with the N observation pairs on the two variables.

The ME Covariance Matrix

The overall sample means of the two variables are $\bar{x}$ and $\bar{y}$. The mean-preserving constraint implies that these are also the means of the ME distribution. Thus, by subtracting the product of these means from both sides of (C.7), we obtain

(C.8) $$\mathscr{E}[(X - \bar{x})(Y - \bar{y})] = \frac{1}{N} \sum_{k=1}^{N} (\bar{x}_k - \bar{x})(\bar{y}_k - \bar{y})$$

so that the ME covariance equals the covariance of the secondary midpoints.

The result (C.8) does not apply to $X \equiv Y$ because the ME variance $\mathscr{E}(X - \bar{x})^2$ exceeds the variance of the secondary midpoints. In fact, we have

(C.9) $$\mathscr{E}(X - \bar{x})^2 = \frac{1}{N} \sum_{k=1}^{N} (\bar{x}_k - \bar{x})^2 + \frac{1}{12N} \sum_{i=2}^{N-1} (\xi_i - \xi_{i-1})^2 + \frac{(\xi_1 - \xi_0)^2 + (\xi_N - \xi_{N-1})^2}{4N}$$

which is nothing but the variance decomposition between and within intervals. To clarify this proposition, recall that the secondary midpoints are the means of the conditional ME distributions within the intervals $I_1, ..., I_N$. Thus, the first term on the right in (C.9) is the variance between intervals. The sum of the next two terms is the average variance within intervals; i.e., the arithmetic mean (all intervals being equally weighted because each has mass $1/N$) of the conditional variance given $X \in I_i$ over $i = 1, ..., N$. For $i = 2, ..., N - 1$, the conditional distribution is uniform over (ξ_{i-1}, ξ_i) with variance $(\xi_i - \xi_{i-1})^2/12$; for $i = 1$ and $i = N$, the conditional variance is shown in (B.19) and (B.20).

We conclude from (C.8) and (C.9) that the 2×2 ME covariance matrix can be written in the form $\boldsymbol{C}+\boldsymbol{D}$, where $\boldsymbol{C}$ is the covariance matrix of the secondary midpoints and $\boldsymbol{D}$ is a diagonal matrix whose typical diagonal element takes the form of the sum of the last two terms in (C.9). These terms are both positive so that $\boldsymbol{D}$ can be viewed as the *ridge* of the ME covariance matrix relative to the covariance matrix of the secondary midpoints. Since the covariance matrix is a bivariate concept, the formulation $\boldsymbol{C}+\boldsymbol{D}$ holds for the ME covariance matrix of any number of variables. It is the ridge $\boldsymbol{D}$ which prevents the ME covariance matrix from becoming singular even when the number of variables equals or exceeds the number of observations N.

Recall from (B.14) that the ME variance is smaller than the sample variance. We reproduce this result in the form

$$\text{(C.10)} \qquad \mathscr{E}(X-\bar{x})^2 = \frac{1}{N}\sum_{k=1}^{N}(x_k-\bar{x})^2 - \frac{1}{4N}\sum_{i=1}^{N-1}(x^{i+1}-x^i)^2 - \frac{1}{24N}\sum_{i=2}^{N-1}(x^{i+1}-x^{i-1})^2$$

which we shall derive from (C.9) in the next subsection. We conclude from (C.9) and (C.10) that the ME variance has a ridge (relative to the variance of the secondary midpoints) and that it is also subject to shrinkage (relative to the sample variance). Evidence on these two different features will be presented in the two subsections immediately following the next.

The ME Variance and the Sample Variance

By adding the square of $\bar{x}$ to both sides of (C.9) we obtain

$$\text{(C.11)} \qquad \mathscr{E}(X^2) = \frac{1}{N}\sum_{k=1}^{N}\bar{x}_k^2 + \frac{1}{12N}\sum_{i=2}^{N-1}(\xi_i-\xi_{i-1})^2 + \frac{(\xi_1-\xi_0)^2+(\xi_N-\xi_{N-1})^2}{4N}$$

Next we square $2\bar{x}^i = \xi_{i-1}+\xi_i$,

$$4(\bar{x}^i)^2 = \xi_{i-1}^2+\xi_i^2+2\xi_{i-1}\xi_i$$

and we use $2\xi_{i-1}\xi_i = \xi_{i-1}^2 + \xi_i^2 - (\xi_i - \xi_{i-1})^2$ to write this as

$$4(\bar{x}^i)^2 = 2\xi_{i-1}^2 + 2\xi_i^2 - (\xi_i - \xi_{i-1})^2 \tag{C.12}$$

Similarly, by squaring $2\xi_{i-1} = x^{i-1} + x^i$ and $2\xi_i = x^i + x^{i+1}$ we obtain

$$2\xi_{i-1}^2 = (x^{i-1})^2 + (x^i)^2 - \tfrac{1}{2}(x^i - x^{i-1})^2$$

$$2\xi_i^2 = (x^i)^2 + (x^{i+1})^2 - \tfrac{1}{2}(x^{i+1} - x^i)^2$$

Hence, using $\xi_i - \xi_{i-1} = \frac{1}{2}(x^{i+1} - x^{i-1})$ also, we conclude from (C.12) that $4(\bar{x}^i)^2$ can be written as a weighted sum of six squares:

$$(x^{i-1})^2 + 2(x^i)^2 + (x^{i+1})^2 - \tfrac{1}{2}(x^i - x^{i-1})^2 - \tfrac{1}{2}(x^{i+1} - x^i)^2 - \\ - \tfrac{1}{4}(x^{i+1} - x^{i-1})^2$$

It then follows from $x^0 = x^1$ and $x^{N+1} = x^N$ that

$$\frac{1}{N}\sum_{i=1}^{N}(\bar{x}^i)^2 = \frac{1}{N}\sum_{i=1}^{N}(x^i)^2 - \frac{1}{4N}\sum_{i=1}^{N-1}(x^{i+1} - x^i)^2 - \frac{1}{16N}\sum_{i=2}^{N-1}(x^{i+1} - x^{i-1})^2 - \frac{(x^2 - x^1)^2 + (x^N - x^{N-1})^2}{16N} \tag{C.13}$$

The left side is identical to the first term on the right in (C.11), while the first term on the right in (C.13) equals the sample variance plus the squared sample mean. Substitution from (C.13) into (C.11) followed by minor rearrangements will then yield (C.10).

Discussion of a Numerical Example

Table C.1, from Theil and Laitinen (1980), concerns price log-changes, multiplied by 100, of 14 goods. (A price log-change is the annual change in the natural log of a price.) The matrix on top is the sample covariance matrix of the price log-changes, and that at the bottom is the ME covariance matrix. The diagonal elements of the latter matrix are all smaller

Table C.1
Covariance matrices of 14 price log-changes

1	2	3	4	5	6	7
					Sample covariance matrix	
5.49	2.68	3.03	2.08	.18	4.37	1.56
	6.48	2.62	− 3.53	− .12	3.83	6.43
		9.18	− 3.78	2.77	− .16	3.22
			52.12	8.98	15.15	− .89
				12.36	1.47	− .68
					9.51	4.28
						10.80
					ME covariance matrix	
5.06	2.59	2.59	1.61	.41	3.83	1.25
	5.94	1.83	− 3.54	− .36	3.05	5.22
		8.49	− 5.08	2.94	− .54	1.53
			46.98	7.89	14.29	− 2.28
				11.32	1.64	− 1.41
					8.72	2.71
						8.61

8	9	10	11	12	13	14	
1.32	.63	4.58	−1.47	−2.06	1.70	1.15	1
5.57	3.04	5.57	.02	−5.65	2.34	1.93	2
1.90	− .26	3.40	.71	−3.16	5.23	− .29	3
−1.02	−6.31	−3.45	−1.90	5.47	3.84	−2.94	4
− .51	−2.17	−3.17	−1.20	2.74	1.86	−3.01	5
3.51	.21	4.52	−1.01	−2.57	2.31	1.18	6
9.00	2.96	5.32	− .52	−6.52	6.08	3.15	7
8.02	3.07	3.87	−1.20	−5.06	4.94	2.97	8
	2.80	2.54	− .76	−3.02	.02	1.58	9
		8.26	.13	−6.66	1.64	1.99	10
			2.74	− .59	− .67	− .66	11
				6.87	−2.23	−1.82	12
					6.71	1.30	13
						2.20	14
1.41	.87	4.60	−1.16	−1.31	1.58	1.16	1
4.88	2.95	4.42	− .10	−4.26	1.18	2.03	2
.97	.05	3.33	1.11	−2.57	4.31	− .27	3
−1.40	−4.71	−2.08	−3.00	3.73	3.49	−2.95	4
− .94	−1.44	−1.63	−1.59	.79	1.33	−2.84	5
2.68	.09	3.84	−1.12	−1.31	2.03	.97	6
7.09	3.03	2.96	− .53	−4.21	3.90	2.96	7
6.92	3.04	2.30	−1.07	−3.49	3.40	2.71	8
	2.49	1.58	− .65	−2.28	.12	1.43	9
		7.21	.61	−4.00	1.07	1.64	10
			2.40	− .77	− .47	− .33	11
				5.21	−1.16	−1.08	12
					6.07	.98	13
						2.04	14

Table C.1
Covariance matrices of 14 price log-changes

1	2	3	4	5	6	7
					Inverse of the ME covariance matrix	
3.62	− .22	−1.67	.07	.30	− 1.37	.66
	3.49	− .51	.26	− .63	− 1.47	− .13
		2.64	.29	− .43	.89	.09
			.44	.16	− .88	.02
				.80	− .43	− .19
					3.14	− .10
						1.25

than the corresponding elements of the former, thus illustrating the shrinkage of the ME variances relative to the sample variances. The off-diagonal elements are also pairwise different. This reflects the displacements caused by the use of secondary midpoints in the ME covariances.

The number of observations on which Table C.1 is based is $N = 9$, which implies that the sample covariance matrix is singular. This singularity is confirmed by the latent roots of the matrix, of which six are zero and the others are

$$61.5, \quad 42.1, \quad 15.6, \quad 10.2, \quad 7.12, \quad 4.77, \quad 1.51, \quad .833$$

The eight largest latent roots of the ME covariance matrix are

$$55.7, \quad 32.3, \quad 14.5, \quad 9.89, \quad 6.91, \quad 4.43, \quad 1.64, \quad .867$$

A comparison of these two sets of roots indicates that the largest roots of the ME covariance matrix are smaller than the corresponding roots of the sample covariance matrix, whereas the opposite holds for the smaller

8	9	10	11	12	13	14	
.76	−.53	−1.16	2.50	−.49	.36	−1.57	1
−.83	−2.60	.11	−1.50	.17	.84	−.76	2
.06	.16	−.34	−1.47	.19	−2.15	2.07	3
−.04	.01	.10	.22	.08	−.45	1.24	4
−.18	.99	.19	1.17	−.13	.20	1.63	5
−.23	1.25	−.52	−.94	−.10	−.08	−1.18	6
−.40	−.09	−.28	.13	.28	−.45	−1.02	7
2.63	−1.08	.17	.46	.21	−.84	−1.52	8
	5.92	.37	2.36	.81	.48	1.43	9
		1.74	−.38	.80	.52	−.20	10
			4.06	.10	.53	.59	11
				1.38	−.04	−1.02	12
					2.67	−1.88	13
						10.19	14

roots. This is probably the typical picture. The six smallest roots of the ME covariance matrix are .386, .304, .188, .131, .103, .0765; hence, the ratio of the largest to the smallest root is $55.7/(.0765) \approx 7 \times 10^2$, which is not particularly large. The inverse of the ME covariance matrix is shown above.

Figure C.3 provides a picture of the sample and ME correlation coefficients of the 14 price log-changes. It consists of a scatter of $\binom{14}{2} = 91$ points, each representing the sample correlation coefficient r_{ij} and the ME correlation coefficient $\hat{\rho}_{ij}$ for some pair (i, j) of price log-changes (obtained by dividing each of the off-diagonal elements of the first two matrices in Table C.1 by the square root of the product of the corresponding diagonal elements). Most of the 91 points are close to the straight line through the origin with unit slope, thus indicating that the ME and sample correlation coefficients tend to be pairwise close to each other in spite of the fact that they are computed from only nine observations. For further evidence on ME correlation coefficients, see Meisner (1980a).

The Ridge and the Shrinkage under Normality

Recall from the paragraph preceding (C.10) that the ME covariance matrix takes the form $\boldsymbol{C} + \boldsymbol{D}$ and that the ridge $\boldsymbol{D}$ is responsible for its nonsingularity. The behavior of this ridge is an important matter, as is that of the shrinkage of the ME variance below the sample variance. The account which follows is based on Haque and Meisner (1980) and further work done by Meisner.

The shrinkage of the ME variance below the sample variance is equal to the sum of the last two terms in (C.10), apart from sign. This sum is a quadratic form in order statistics. The typical element of the ridge $\boldsymbol{D}$ equals the sum of the last two terms in (C.9), which is also a quadratic

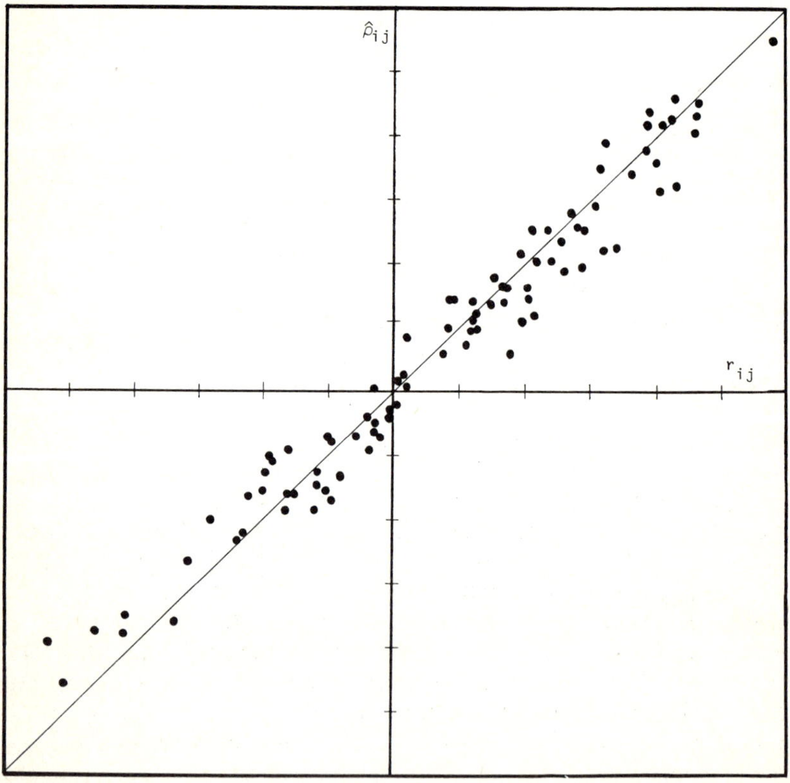

Figure C.3. Sample and ME correlation coefficients of 14 price log-changes

form in order statistics in view of (B.11). Therefore, if the sample is randomly drawn from a standard normal population, we can use the tables of the expectations, variances and covariances of normal order statistics to tabulate the expectations of the ridge and the shrinkage. These expectations are shown in Table C.2 along with the estimated standard deviations. For $N \geq 40$, the expectations are approximated by arithmetic averages of 10,000 simulations each, based on independent standard pseudo-normal variates. The standard deviations are estimated as square roots of

$$\frac{1}{9999}\left(\sum_{t=1}^{10000} u_t^2 - 10000\bar{u}^2\right)$$

Table C.2
The ridge and shrinkage of the ME variance

N	Ridge		Shrinkage	
	Expectation	Estimated standard deviation	Expectation	Estimated standard deviation
2	.12500	.178	.25000	.356
3	.07425	.0749	.24625	.250
4	.05195	.0461	.19761	.168
5	.03927	.0314	.15901	.118
6	.03155	.0229	.13069	.0869
7	.02556	.0191	.10968	.0724
8	.02152	.0149	.09373	.0567
9	.01846	.0131	.08132	.0492
10	.01609	.0113	.07147	.0423
11	.01421	.00962	.06349	.0364
12	.01268	.00864	.05692	.0325
13	.01141	.00773	.05144	.0289
14	.01035	.00679	.04682	.0253
15	.00945	.00628	.04286	.0236
16	.00868	.00576	.03945	.0215
17	.00802	.00521	.03649	.0194
18	.00744	.00511	.03389	.0190
19	.00692	.00448	.03160	.0167
20	.00647	.00439	.02956	.0164
40	.00258	.00173	.01187	.00634
60	.00154	.00106	.00704	.00388
80	.00106	.00075	.00487	.00274
100	.00081	.00056	.00365	.00206

where u_t is the ridge or shrinkage of trial t and $\bar{u}$ is the arithmetic mean of $u_1, ..., u_{10000}$.

Table C.2 clearly shows that the expectation and the standard deviation of both the ridge and the shrinkage decrease toward zero as $N \to \infty$; hence, under normality the ridge and the shrinkage both have zero probability limit as $N \to \infty$. The expected ridge is smaller than the expected shrinkage for each N. The ratio of the latter expectation to the former increases with N until it stabilizes at a value just below 4.6. Figure C.4 provides a picture of each of the four columns of Table C.2 on a double-log scale. It shows that for large values of N, the four expectations and standard deviations are approximately proportional to $N^{-\alpha}$ with $\alpha \approx 1.3$ in all four cases.

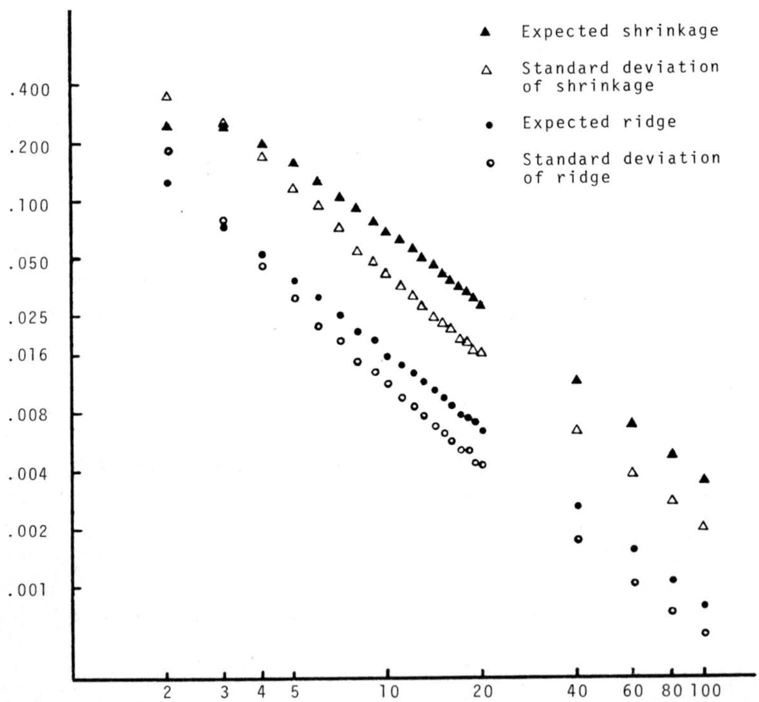

Figure C.4. Expectations and standard deviations of the ME ridge and shrinkage under normality

A Risk Evaluation of the ME Covariance Matrix

Let Σ be some nonsingular $p \times p$ covariance matrix and let $\hat{\Sigma}$ be an estimator of Σ. One way of evaluating the merits of $\hat{\Sigma}$ as an estimator of Σ is by formulating a loss function, such as

$$l(\hat{\Sigma}, \Sigma) = \frac{1}{p} \operatorname{tr} \Sigma^{-1} \hat{\Sigma} - \frac{1}{p} \log_e |\Sigma^{-1} \hat{\Sigma}| - 1 \tag{C.14}$$

and then taking the expectation in order to obtain the corresponding risk function. This particular loss function imposes an infinite penalty on singular estimators because the determinant in (C.14) vanishes when $\hat{\Sigma}$ is singular. A simple way of analyzing this loss function is by means of the product matrix $\boldsymbol{K} = \Sigma^{-1/2} \hat{\Sigma} \Sigma^{-1/2}$, where $\Sigma^{-1/2}$ is a symmetric positive definite matrix such that $(\Sigma^{-1/2})^2 = \Sigma^{-1}$. Let $\mu_1, ..., \mu_p$ be the latent roots of $\boldsymbol{K}$; then the right side of (C.14) can be written as

$$\frac{1}{p} \sum_{i=1}^{p} (\mu_i - 1 - \log_e \mu_i)$$

which vanishes when each μ_i equals 1 and which is positive otherwise. This shows that the loss (C.14) vanishes if and only if $\boldsymbol{K} = \boldsymbol{I}$ or, equivalently, $\hat{\Sigma} = \Sigma$.

Here and in the next subsection we report on a simulation study by Fiebig (1981a) which uses (C.14) as one of two specifications of the loss function. His experiment is based on independent pseudo-normal vectors consisting of p elements with zero expectation and a covariance matrix of the equicorrelated form

$$\Sigma = (1 - \rho)\boldsymbol{I} + \rho \iota \iota' \tag{C.15}$$

where ι is a column of p unit elements. Let $\boldsymbol{X}$ be an $N \times p$ matrix whose N rows are independent pseudo-normal vectors with these first- and second-order moments. Then the maximum likelihood (ML) estimator of Σ is $\hat{\Sigma}_{\mathrm{ML}} = N^{-1} \boldsymbol{X}'(\boldsymbol{I} - N^{-1} \iota\iota')\boldsymbol{X}$, which yields an infinite loss (C.14) for $p \geq N$ because the determinant then vanishes, whereas the ME estimator $\hat{\Sigma}_{\mathrm{ME}} = \boldsymbol{C} + \boldsymbol{D}$ always has a finite loss (C.14).

Table C.3 shows the average loss (C.14) over 100 trials for $N = 21$, five values of ρ, and seven values of p. Evidently, there is not much difference between the performance of ML and that of ME as long as p and ρ both take modest values, but when p increases the ME estimator tends to dominate the ML estimator, whereas the opposite holds for $\rho = .99$ and

Table C.3
Average loss (C.14) over 100 trials[a]

	$\rho = 0$		$\rho = .3$		$\rho = .6$		$\rho = .9$		$\rho = .99$	
p	ML	ME	ML	ME	ML	ME	ML	ME	ML	ME
2	78	78	77	78	78	78	74	74	82	150
4	132	133	128	129	137	135	133	125	154	247
6	200	199	205	203	197	194	186	168	219	306
8	266	263	269	265	262	255	266	235	275	346
12	427	419	425	414	434	413	436	363	443	415
20	1087	898	1087	880	1101	836	1063	664	1085	545
30	b	1775	b	1659	b	1468	b	1031	b	642

[a] All entries are to be divided by 1000.
[b] Infinite.

modest values of p. The superior performance of the ME estimator for large p is due to the ridge $\boldsymbol{D}$, which prevents the estimator from becoming singular. The less satisfactory performance for large ρ is also due to the ridge: the matrix to be estimated is close to singularity when $\rho = .99$, but the ME estimator is kept away from being so close to singularity because of the ridge.

Further Discussion of the ME Covariance Matrix

Fiebig (1981a) found that insofar as the ME estimator of the covariance matrix (C.15) is superior to the ML estimator in terms of the loss function (C.14), this is due to the ridge $\boldsymbol{D}$, not to the use of the secondary midpoints in the matrix $\boldsymbol{C}$. He considered the covariance matrix of the SYME distribution as a third estimator (see the end of Appendix B), but it appears that exploiting the symmetry of the marginal distributions yields little or no gain. He also used a second loss function equal to the mean square of the p^2 elements of the matrix $\Sigma^{-1}\hat{\Sigma} - \boldsymbol{I}$. The average losses based on this function are also smaller for the ME than for the ML estimator (except when p is small and ρ is large), but there is a difference in that the superiority of the ME estimator in terms of this loss function is due to the use of the secondary midpoints in $\boldsymbol{C}$, not to the ridge $\boldsymbol{D}$. Thus, a risk evaluation of the ME versus the ML estimator of the covariance matrix depends on the loss function chosen, and the selection of this function should be carefully done depending on which problem is to be solved.

The problem discussed in Appendix A concerns the disturbance covariance matrix of a demand system. The estimators of this matrix defined in (A.13) and (A.18) become ill-conditioned and even singular when the number of goods n is not sufficiently small relative to the number of observations N. For such a problem it is important to use a loss function which implies a large penalty for singular estimation. This is satisfied by (C.14), not by the mean square of the elements of $\boldsymbol{\Sigma}^{-1}\hat{\boldsymbol{\Sigma}} - \boldsymbol{I}$. We should add here that Theil and Laitinen's original objective with the ME approach was to solve another problem involving a singular sample covariance matrix, viz., in the context of simultaneous equation estimation. All standard methods of estimating such equations involve the inverse of the sample covariance matrix of the predetermined variables, but this matrix is singular when the number of these variables exceeds the number of observations (as is typically the case). See Meisner (1980b), Theil (1981), and Theil and Meisner (1980) for simulation experiments which show how this problem can be solved by means of the ME distribution.

We mentioned at the end of Appendix B how the ME principle can be used to exploit more prior knowledge about the parent distribution than just continuity, such as the symmetry of the population density function. In that case the theoretical model is more informative than the standard ME approach assumes it to be. Here we proceed in the opposite direction by considering the case of *missing values* for some variables; the data are then less informative than would be the case if there were no missing values. Conway and Theil (1980) derived the ME covariance matrix under the condition that these missing values are distributed randomly. A brief summary of their results follows here.

Let there be N observation pairs; let there be $N_1 \leq N$ known values for the first variable, and $N_2 \leq N$ for the second. The grid of Figure C.1 will now consist of $N_1 N_2$ rather than N^2 cells. The mass-preserving constraint implies that a mass $1/N$ be allocated to each cell which contains an observation, but this can be applied only to observations without missing values. If a value is missing, all we can do is exploit the knowledge that it was randomly drawn from the same distribution as that of the (N_1 or N_2) values which are not missing. Accordingly, if an observation has a missing value, we apply the marginal ME distribution (computed from the available data) to the missing component. When this approach is diligently pursued, it appears that the ME covariance takes the form (C.8), reproduced here,

Table C.4
Average loss (C.14) over 100 trials with missing values[a]

	$\rho = .3$			$\rho = .6$			$\rho = .9$			$\rho = .99$		
	Incomplete observations deleted			Incomplete observations deleted			Incomplete observations deleted			Incomplete observations deleted		
p	ML	ME	MVME	ML	ME	MVME	ML	ME	MVME	ML	ME	MVME
One missing value												
2	77	78	75	79	80	71	74	70	94	72	189	1863
4	131	132	123	149	146	133	133	124	144	134	303	1639
6	198	197	183	208	202	184	201	184	194	213	348	1337
8	268	266	248	286	278	253	274	250	246	289	394	1160
12	449	437	403	459	434	396	463	386	362	468	466	990
20	b	948	853	b	881	792	b	683	636	b	576	934
30	b	1734	1608	b	1551	1437	b	1053	1002	b	677	912
Four missing values												
2	104	106	86	107	107	90	99	95	432	102	242	8039
4	175	172	127	160	161	125	165	152	436	165	338	6369
6	255	249	181	239	236	181	244	208	405	253	393	4851
8	356	347	250	341	329	246	339	283	408	344	439	3928
12	612	580	404	594	543	389	583	443	472	599	516	2921
20	b	1217	813	b	1113	783	b	795	702	b	632	2129
30	b	1992	1582	b	1749	1416	b	1170	1065	b	730	1712
Seven missing values												
2	125	127	92	130	132	122	118	110	804	130	318	14664
4	210	210	127	214	210	166	218	191	740	220	528	11412
6	329	321	188	328	312	215	327	267	641	338	585	8591
8	463	443	244	452	418	261	447	351	596	457	643	6875
12	867	740	380	858	682	389	883	532	598	887	718	4984
20	b	1529	803	b	1358	775	b	879	779	b	763	3233
30	b	2204	1572	b	1921	1413	b	1206	1106	b	852	2471

a All entries to be divided by 1000.

$$\text{(C.16)} \qquad \frac{1}{N} \sum_{k=1}^{N} (\overline{x}_k - \overline{x})(\overline{y}_k - \overline{y})$$

with the understanding that $\overline{x}_k$ is interpreted as the sample mean $\overline{x}$ when x_k is missing (similarly for $\overline{y}_k$). Note that this does not imply that we act as if the missing x_k takes some particular value. No such value is assumed; the only thing needed for the ME covariance is a specification of the secondary midpoint $\overline{x}_k$ for missing x_k, and this specification is $\overline{x}_k = \overline{x}$, which follows directly (as can be shown) from the ME principle subject to mass- and mean-preserving constraints.

When N_1 observations are available on the first variable, the ME variance formula (C.9) is changed into

$$\text{(C.17)} \quad \frac{1}{N} \sum_{k=1}^{N} (\overline{x}_k - \overline{x})^2 + \frac{N - N_1}{NN_1} \sum_{k=1}^{N} (\overline{x}_k - \overline{x})^2 + \frac{1}{12N_1} \sum_{i=2}^{N_1 - 1} (\xi_i - \xi_{i-1})^2 + \frac{(\xi_1 - \xi_0)^2 + (\xi_{N_1} - \xi_{N_1 - 1})^2}{4N_1}$$

which in conjunction with (C.16) shows that the ME covariance matrix with missing values has a second ridge along the diagonal, consisting of the second term in (C.17) plus an analogous term for the other variable.

Fiebig (1981a) included this missing value case in his experiment based on independent pseudo-normal vectors with zero mean and covariance matrix (C.15). His results are shown in Table C.4 for $N = 21$ and selected values of p and ρ. The first variable has missing values: one, four or seven, and all other variables have no missing values. The figures shown are the average losses (C.14) over 100 trials for three estimators of the covariance matrix: the ML and ME estimators obtained when the incomplete observations are simply deleted, and the ME estimator based on the missing value results (C.16) and (C.17), abbreviated as the MVME estimator. For $\rho = .3$ and $.6$ the MVME estimator clearly dominates the two others. For $\rho = .9$ this holds only if the number of variables p is sufficiently large, and for $\rho = .99$ it does not hold at all. The extra ridge of the MVME estimator works at its disadvantage when the true covariance matrix is nearly singular, but otherwise the estimator performs satisfactorily, particularly for large p. When both p and ρ are large, the ME covariance matrix which ignores the incomplete observations appears to be preferable. Whether or not these observations are used, the ME approach has the advantage of yielding an easily computable positive definitive estimate of the covariance matrix, which is in contrast to several other proposals made to handle the missing value problem; see, e.g., Srivastava and Zaatar (1973) and the references quoted in that article.

Appendix D

MAXIMUM ENTROPY CANONICAL CORRELATIONS

Comparison of Sample and ME Canonical Correlations

Let nine variables $X_1, ..., X_9$ be generated as independent standard pseudo-normal variates. Let $v_1, ..., v_9$ be another set of independent standard pseudo-normal variates (also independent of the X_i's) and consider

$$Y_i = \rho_i X_i + (1 - \rho_i^2)^{1/2} v_i \qquad i = 1, ..., 9 \tag{D.1}$$

Then $Y_1, ..., Y_9$ are also independent standard pseudo-normal, while X_i and Y_j are uncorrelated for $i \neq j$ and the correlation of X_i and Y_i equals ρ_i, $i = 1, ..., 9$. This means that $\rho_1, ..., \rho_9$ are the canonical correlation coefficients of the two sets of random variables, $X_1, ..., X_9$ and $Y_1, ..., Y_9$. The joint covariance matrix of all variables can then be written in partitioned form as

$$\begin{bmatrix} \Sigma_{11} & \Sigma_{12} \\ \Sigma_{12}' & \Sigma_{22} \end{bmatrix} \tag{D.2}$$

where $\Sigma_{11} = \Sigma_{22} = I$ of order 9 x 9, while Σ_{12} is a diagonal matrix with $\rho_1, ..., \rho_9$ on the diagonal.

Fiebig (1980) conducted a simulation experiment based on the design of the previous paragraph for sample sizes varying from $N = 10$ to $N = 100$. The true values of the canonical correlations are specified as

$$\rho_1 = .9, \quad \rho_2 = .8, ..., \quad \rho_8 = .2, \quad \rho_9 = .1 \tag{D.3}$$

By specifying the matrix (D.2) as consisting of either ME or sample variances and covariances, and then solving the associated determinantal equation (A.30), we obtain the nine ME or sample canonical correlation coefficients for a sample of size N. This experiment was replicated 100 times and the results are summarized in Table D.1 in terms of means and RMSEs (root-mean-square errors) around the true value. The upper part of the table concerns the largest canonical correlation coefficient, the true value of which is $\rho_1 = .9$. The first two columns contain the two sets of means over 100 trials and the next two show the excesses of these means over $\rho_1 = .9$, which are estimates of the bias. The figures indicate that both the largest sample canonical correlation coefficient and the largest ME canonical correlation coefficient are upwardly biased, that the bias slowly converges to zero as $N \to \infty$, and that the bias is larger for the sample than for the ME canonical correlation. The last two columns show

Table D.1
ME and sample canonical correlation coefficients

	Mean		Estimated bias		RMSE	
N	ME	Sample	ME	Sample	ME	Sample
			Largest canonical correlation coefficient			
10	.991	a	.091	a	.091	a
15	.992	a	.092	a	.092	a
20	.986	.994	.086	.094	.087	.094
25	.973	.978	.073	.078	.073	.079
30	.963	.967	.063	.067	.064	.068
40	.945	.949	.045	.049	.050	.052
50	.936	.939	.036	.039	.040	.042
100	.919	.920	.019	.020	.026	.028
			Average canonical correlation coefficient			
10	.826	a	.326	a	.328	a
15	.733	a	.233	a	.235	a
20	.678	.685	.178	.185	.181	.188
25	.635	.640	.135	.140	.139	.144
30	.613	.618	.113	.118	.118	.122
40	.583	.586	.083	.086	.088	.091
50	.562	.563	.062	.063	.068	.069
100	.530	.531	.030	.031	.037	.039
			Sum of squared canonical correlation coefficients			
10	6.74	a	3.89	a	3.91	a
15	5.67	a	2.82	a	2.84	a
20	4.95	5.06	2.10	2.21	2.14	2.23
25	4.46	4.52	1.61	1.67	1.63	1.69
30	4.19	4.25	1.34	1.40	1.38	1.43
40	3.83	3.86	.98	1.01	1.00	1.04
50	3.60	3.62	.75	.77	.79	.81
100	3.23	3.23	.38	.38	.41	.42

[a] Not computed.

that the RMSE around the true value $\rho_1 = .9$ is also larger for the sample than for the ME canonical correlation. The sample results for $N = 10$ and $N = 15$ are not shown, because the largest sample canonical correlation coefficient is then identically equal to 1.

The middle part of Table D.1 deals with the arithmetic average canonical correlation coefficient, with true value $(\rho_1 + ... + \rho_9)/9 = .5$, and the lower part with the sum of the squared canonical correlations, the true value of which is $\rho_1^2 + ... + \rho_9^2 = 2.85$. This sum of squares plays a role in Hooper's (1959) trace correlation coefficient. The results shown in these parts are similar to those in the upper part: there is an upward bias which slowly decreases as N increases, and both the bias and the RMSE are larger when sample moments are used than when ME moments are used.

Correcting ME Canonical Correlations for Bias

Although the results of Table D.1 are encouraging for the ME approach relative to the sample moment approach, it should be admitted that the upward bias of the former approach (although smaller than that of the latter) is quite substantial. In fact, in most lines of the table the bias is close to the corresponding RMSE, which is easily verified from the last four columns of the table. A correction for bias is therefore in order.

Recall from the second-last paragraph of Appendix A that such a correction is difficult when a sample canonical correlation coefficient equals 1. Fortunately, this cannot occur for ME canonical correlation coefficients because such coefficients are smaller than 1 even when the number of observations is smaller than the total number of variables in the two sets for which canonical correlations are estimated. Let us add hats to the matrix (D.2) in order to indicate that it consists of ME variances and covariances:

$$\text{(D.4)} \qquad \begin{bmatrix} \hat{\Sigma}_{11} & \hat{\Sigma}_{12} \\ \hat{\Sigma}'_{12} & \hat{\Sigma}_{22} \end{bmatrix}$$

Let there be p variables in one set and $q \geq p$ variables in the other so that there are p canonical correlations, to be written $r_1, ..., r_p$ when they are obtained from the ME covariance matrix (D.4). It follows from (A.30) that their squares are obtained from the determinantal equation

(D.5) $$|\hat{\Sigma}_{12}\hat{\Sigma}_{22}^{-1}\hat{\Sigma}_{12}' - r_i^2\hat{\Sigma}_{11}| = 0$$

We proceed to consider corrected ME canonical correlation coefficients $\bar{r}_1, ..., \bar{r}_p$, defined as

(D.6) $$1 - \bar{r}_i^2 = (1 - r_i^2)^{N/(N+p+q+2)}$$

which is a correction in exponential form rather than a multiplicative correction such as (A.32). Since there are p variables in one set and q in the other, and since each canonical correlation equals the correlation coefficient of some linear combination of one set and some linear combination of the other, the numbers of coefficients adjusted in the two sets are $p + 1$ and $q + 1$ (including a constant term in each combination). Therefore, $p + q + 2$ in the exponent of (D.6) should be viewed as the total number of adjusted coefficients. Fiebig (1981b) applied the correction (D.6) for $p = q = 9$, with the same experimental design as that underlying the simulation results of Table D.1 and the same true values of the canonical

Table D.2
Corrected and uncorrected ME canonical correlation coefficients

	True value of squared canonical correlation								
	.81	.64	.49	.36	.25	.16	.09	.04	.01
	Mean of uncorrected squared ME canonical correlations								
$N =$ 10	.98	.97	.96	.94	.90	.83	.69	.43	.08
15	.98	.97	.95	.89	.77	.57	.36	.13	.02
20	.97	.93	.87	.76	.61	.43	.24	.09	.01
25	.95	.88	.79	.67	.52	.37	.21	.08	.01
30	.92	.84	.74	.62	.47	.33	.18	.07	.01
40	.90	.80	.67	.54	.40	.26	.14	.06	.01
50	.88	.76	.64	.50	.36	.24	.14	.06	.01
100	.84	.71	.56	.43	.31	.20	.11	.05	.01
	Mean of corrected squared ME canonical correlations								
$N =$ 10	.74	.70	.66	.61	.54	.45	.33	.18	.03
15	.83	.79	.73	.61	.47	.31	.18	.06	.01
20	.84	.75	.64	.51	.38	.25	.13	.05	.01
25	.81	.70	.59	.46	.34	.22	.12	.05	.01
30	.78	.68	.56	.44	.32	.21	.11	.04	.01
40	.78	.66	.53	.40	.29	.18	.10	.04	.00
50	.78	.65	.52	.39	.28	.18	.10	.04	.01
100	.79	.64	.50	.38	.26	.17	.09	.04	.01

correlations given in (D.3). The squares of these values are shown at the top of Table D.2. The next eight lines of this table contain the means over 100 trials of the uncorrected squared ME canonical correlation coefficients $r_{1t}^2 > r_{2t}^2 > \ldots > r_{9t}^2$, where the subscript t refers to trial t. The upward bias appears to be substantial even at $N = 100$, except for the smallest coefficients.

The last eight lines of Table D.2 contain the means over the same 100 trials of the corrected squared ME canonical correlations, obtained from (D.6) with $p + q + 2 = 20$ in this experiment. The correction appears to be nearly perfect for $N = 100$, quite satisfactory for the largest canonical correlation when $N \geq 15$, but not so satisfactory for the next several correlations when $N \leq 30$. In the last case, the corrections should have been larger.

Further Discussion of the Correction

An adequate appraisal of the correction (D.6) requires a description of its use. Recall that the problem discussed in Appendix A is that the F statistics (A.15) and (A.23) involve the inverse of the disturbance covariance matrix Σ. This Σ occurs in the determinantal equation (A.31). When we add hats to indicate that we use ME rather than population covariance matrices, ρ_i in (A.31) becomes r_i in agreement with (D.5):

$$|\hat{\Sigma} - (1 - r_i^2)\hat{\Sigma}_{11}| = 0 \tag{D.7}$$

Associated with each root is a characteristic vector z_i, $i = 1, \ldots, p$, which we normalize so that $z_i'\hat{\Sigma}_{11} z_j = \delta_{ij}$ (Kronecker delta). Therefore,

$$[\hat{\Sigma} - (1 - r_i^2)\hat{\Sigma}_{11}]z_i = 0$$

for $i = 1, \ldots, p$ or, more compactly,

$$\hat{\Sigma} Z = \hat{\Sigma}_{11} Z \Lambda \tag{D.8}$$

where $Z = [z_1 \ldots z_p]$ and Λ is the diagonal $p \times p$ matrix whose ith diagonal element equals $1 - r_i^2$. Premultiplication of (D.8) by Z' yields $Z'\hat{\Sigma}Z = Z'\hat{\Sigma}_{11} Z\Lambda$, which can be simplified to

$$Z'\hat{\Sigma}Z = \Lambda \tag{D.9}$$

because $Z'\hat{\Sigma}_{11}Z = I$ is implied by $z_i'\hat{\Sigma}_{11}z_j = \delta_{ij}$. From (D.9), $\hat{\Sigma} = (Z')^{-1}\Lambda Z^{-1}$ and hence $\hat{\Sigma}^{-1} = Z\Lambda^{-1}Z'$, which we write as

$$\hat{\Sigma}^{-1} = \sum_{i=1}^{p} (1 - r_i^2)^{-1} z_i z_i' \tag{D.10}$$

In Appendix E we shall use this $\hat{\Sigma}^{-1}$ as one estimator of Σ^{-1} in the F statistics (A.15) and (A.23). As a second estimator we shall use

$$\hat{\Sigma}_C^{-1} = \sum_{i=1}^{p} (1 - \overline{r}_i^2)^{-1} z_i z_i' \tag{D.11}$$

where $\overline{r}_i$ is the corrected ME canonical correlation coefficient obtained from (D.6). By subtracting (D.11) from (D.10) we obtain

$$\hat{\Sigma}^{-1} - \hat{\Sigma}_C^{-1} = \sum_{i=1}^{p} [(1 - r_i^2)^{-1} - (1 - \overline{r}_i^2)^{-1}] z_i z_i' \tag{D.12}$$

It follows from (D.6) that the expression in brackets is nonnegative for each i. Therefore, the difference on the left in (D.12) is a positive semidefinite matrix.

The most important correction in (D.11) is the coefficient of $z_1 z_1'$. The first column of Table D.2 shows that, for $N = 15$, $(1 - r_1^2)^{-1}$ is of the order of 50, whereas the true value is $(1 - .81)^{-1} \approx 5$, which means that the coefficient of $z_1 z_1'$ is overstated by a factor of the order of 10 if no correction is made. The correction (D.6) reduces this overstatement substantially. It is true that Table D.2 has shown that (D.6) is less successful with respect to the smaller canonical correlations, but these are less crucial for the estimation of Σ^{-1}. It is also true that the characteristic vectors $z_1, \ldots, z_p$ are imperfect estimates and that no attempt is made to correct these. We do not pretend that (D.6) is an ideal correction. Nor is (A.32) ideal, since it may yield a negative $\overline{R}^2$. By contrast, (D.6) ensures that $0 \leq \overline{r}_i^2 < 1$ for $i = 1, \ldots, p$.

Appendix E

THE TESTS AND THE CONSTRAINED ESTIMATORS FURTHER CONSIDERED

The Design of the Experiment

We proceed to apply the results of Appendix D to the F tests discussed in Appendix A. Thus, going back to the covariance matrix (A.28) of the dependent and the independent variables of the demand systems (A.3) and (A.16), we note that p becomes $n - 1$ so that (D.10) and (D.11) become

$$\hat{\Sigma}^{-1} = \sum_{i=1}^{n-1} (1 - r_i^2)^{-1} z_i z_i' \tag{E.1}$$

$$\hat{\Sigma}_C^{-1} = \sum_{i=1}^{n-1} (1 - \bar{r}_i^2)^{-1} z_i z_i' \tag{E.2}$$

As in Section 3.4, we shall present simulation evidence on the performance of homogeneity and symmetry tests, but the tests will now be F rather than χ^2 tests with the ME estimator $\hat{\Sigma}$ or the corrected ME estimator $\hat{\Sigma}_C$ substituted for the true value of the disturbance covariance matrix. Such an experiment requires a numerical specification of the coefficients of the system (A.3) for the $n = 8$ goods. The constant terms (the α_i's) can be left unspecified when we measure all dependent and independent variables as deviations from their means. The β_i's are specified as the ML estimates discussed in Section 3.5. For the Slutsky coefficients we use the preference independent form,

$$\pi_{ij} = \phi(\theta_i \delta_{ij} - \theta_i \theta_j) \tag{E.3}$$

where ϕ is specified as $-.61837$ (the ML estimate of Section 3.5) and the marginal share θ_i as $\bar{w}_i + \beta_i$ with $\bar{w}_i$ defined as the arithmetic average budget share of good i across the 15 countries. The values of β_i, $\bar{w}_i$ and θ_i are shown in Table E.1.

Note that the specification (E.3) satisfies both homogeneity and symmetry. Also note that (E.3) does not coincide with the preference independence specification of Sections 3.5 and 3.6. The reason is that $\theta_i = \bar{w}_i + \beta_i$ implies that the marginal shares do not vary across the 15 countries, whereas it is assumed in Sections 3.5 and 3.6 that the marginal share

Table E.1
Parameter specification of the simulation experiment

	β_i	$\bar{w}_i$	θ_i
Food	−.15262	.37272	.22010
Clothing	.00416	.08489	.08905
Rent	.02607	.12307	.14914
Furniture	.02665	.07126	.09791
Medical care	.02583	.06141	.08724
Transport	.02104	.08365	.10469
Recreation	.02431	.10865	.13296
Other expenditure	.02456	.09435	.11891

of good i in country c equals $w_{ic} + \beta_i$. The latter assumption is undoubtedly more attractive, but it has not been used in the simulation experiment because substitution of $w_{ic} + \beta_i$ for θ_i in (E.3) yields Slutsky coefficients that are not constant across countries. The numerical values of the Slutsky coefficients obtained from (E.3) are shown in the upper part of Table E.2.

The values taken by the independent variables in the 15 countries are treated as constant in the successive trials of the experiment. The disturbance vectors $[\epsilon_{1c} \; ... \; \epsilon_{nc}]$ of (A.3) are generated as independent pseudonormal vectors with zero mean and a covariance matrix equal to the ML estimate obtained in Section 3.6. This matrix is shown in the middle part of Table E.2; the leading 7 x 7 submatrix of this matrix is thus the true Σ of the simulation experiment. The lower part of the table contains Σ^{-1}. Given the values of the independent variables and the coefficients, it is thus possible to compute the y_{ic}'s of (A.3) and hence the F ratios (A.15) and (A.23) once the disturbances are generated.

The simulation experiments described in Section 3.4 clearly show how much the performance of a test can depend on the size of the demand system. Therefore, the eight goods are not only considered separately, but are also combined into four groups. The first two goods (Food and Clothing) serve as the first two groups. The third group is Housing, consisting of the third and fourth goods (Rent and Furniture), while the fourth group is the Rest, consisting of the four other goods (Medical care, Transport, Recreation, and Other expenditure). The simplest way to obtain the results for $n = 4$ from those of $n = 8$ is by means of the 4 x 8 aggregation matrix

(E.4) $$A = \begin{bmatrix} 1 & 0 & 0 & 0 & 0 & 0 & 0 & 0 \\ 0 & 1 & 0 & 0 & 0 & 0 & 0 & 0 \\ 0 & 0 & 1 & 1 & 0 & 0 & 0 & 0 \\ 0 & 0 & 0 & 0 & 1 & 1 & 1 & 1 \end{bmatrix}$$

The vectors of β_i's, $\bar{w}_i$'s and θ_i's for $n = 4$ are then obtained from the corresponding vectors for $n = 8$ by premultiplication by $\boldsymbol{A}$, while the Slutsky and disturbance covariance matrices for $n = 4$ are similarly obtained by pre- and postmultiplication by $\boldsymbol{A}$ and $\boldsymbol{A}'$, respectively. The prices and quantities of Housing and the Rest are straightforwardly derived from Summary Multilateral Tables 4.1 and 4.5 of Kravis et al. (1978).

Discussion of the Test Results

Recall from (A.28) that the demand model (A.3) contains $n - 1$ dependent and $n + 1$ independent variables. Therefore, $p + q = 2n$ in (D.6) and hence, given that there are $N = 15$ observations,

(E.5) $$1 - \bar{r}_i^2 = (1 - r_i^2)^{15/(17+2n)}$$

For $n = 8$ the $n - 1 = 7$ uncorrected squared ME canonical correlations are

(E.6) .965, .719, .544, .347, .258, .103, .039

and the corrected values based on (E.5) are

(E.7) .781, .438, .300, .176, .127, .048, .018

For $n = 4$ the three corrected and uncorrected squared ME canonical correlations are as follows:

uncorrected: .932, .331, .235
corrected: .801, .214, .148

When we use (A.16) to test for symmetry given homogeneity, the number of dependent variables remains $n - 1$, but that of the independent variables is reduced to n. Therefore, (D.6) now takes the form

Table E.2
The Slutsky and disturbance covariance matrices of the simulation experiment

	Food	Clothing	Rent	Furniture	Medical care	Transport	Recreation	Other expenditure
				Slutsky matrix[a]				
Food	−10615							
Clothing	1212	− 5016						
Rent	2030	821	−7847					
Furniture	1333	539	903	−5462				
Medical care	1187	480	805	528	− 4924			
Transport	1425	576	965	634	565	−5796		
Recreation	1810	732	1226	805	717	861	− 7129	
Other expenditure	1618	655	1097	720	642	770	978	−6479
				Disturbance covariance matrix[b]				
Food	9975							
Clothing	− 612	2088						
Rent	− 992	− 946	7305					
Furniture	− 2828	398	−1504	3235				
Medical care	− 1015	465	− 106	482	1079			
Transport	− 2743	− 1940	− 46	−1163	− 788	8580		
Recreation	160	− 272	−2004	268	− 754	774	2075	
Other expenditure	− 1946	820	−1707	1111	636	−2674	− 248	4008
				Inverse[c]				
Food	3943							
Clothing	3573	10304						
Rent	2776	3808	4486					
Furniture	4401	4320	3693	8781				
Medical care	4552	2916	4982	3068	21684			
Transport	2839	4007	2270	3659	3556	3637		
Recreation	2870	3760	5104	2407	10998	1961	12974	

[a] All entries to be multiplied by 10^{-5}.
[b] All entries to be multiplied by 10^{-7}.
[c] Inverse of the leading 7 x 7 submatrix of the disturbance covariance matrix.

(E.8) $$1 - \bar{r}_i^2 = (1 - r_i^2)^{15/(16+2n)}$$

For $n = 8$ the uncorrected squared ME canonical correlations are

(E.9) .975, .951, .926, .863, .603, .441, .079

while the corrected values based on (E.8) are

(E.10) .822, .756, .705, .607, .351, .239, .038

For $n = 4$ we have the following corrected and uncorrected squared ME canonical correlations for the symmetry test:

uncorrected: .929, .698, .287
corrected: .808, .527, .191

The figures presented in the two previous paragraphs are those obtained from the observed values of the dependent variables of the demand systems (A.3) and (A.16). When the latter values are obtained from pseudonormal disturbances, as is the case in the simulation experiment, the ME canonical correlations and their corrected values will vary from sample to sample. The results of the experiment are shown in Table E.3 in the form of percentages (rounded to the nearest percentage point) of rejections out of 500 samples of size $N = 15$. The test statistics used are the F ratios (A.15) and (A.23) for homogeneity and for symmetry given ho-

Table E.3
Rejection percentages out of 500 artificial samples

Significance level	$n = 4$			$n = 8$		
	$\hat{\Sigma}$	$\hat{\Sigma}_C$	Σ	$\hat{\Sigma}$	$\hat{\Sigma}_C$	Σ
			Homogeneity			
5%	10	8	7	22	13	5
1%	4	2	1	13	3	1
			Symmetry			
5%	7	5	6	42	16	4
1%	1	1	1	22	5	1

mogeneity, respectively, with either the true Σ or the ME estimator $\hat{\Sigma}$ or the corrected ME estimator $\hat{\Sigma}_C$. The last estimator is obtained from (E.2) with $\bar{r}_i$ defined as shown in (E.5) for homogeneity and in (E.8) for symmetry given homogeneity.

Table E.3 shows that when the true Σ is used, the rejection percentages are in approximate agreement with the significance levels chosen (either five percent or one percent). When $\hat{\Sigma}$ is used instead, the rejection percentages tend to increase, particularly for $n = 8$. This increase is substantially, but not completely, reduced when $\hat{\Sigma}_C$ is used. Perhaps we should have expected this result given our knowledge (see Appendix D) that the correction underlying $\hat{\Sigma}_C$ does not go far enough with respect to the canonical correlations smaller than the largest.

To obtain further insight into this result we recall that the F statistic equals the ratio of a numerator to a denominator, each divided by its degrees of freedom. Table E.4 concerns both the F statistic and its numerator and denominator. For each of these and for both the homogeneity

Table E.4
Quantiles of the homogeneity and symmetry test statistics[a]

	Numerator				Denominator			F ratio		
	S	$\hat{\Sigma}$	$\hat{\Sigma}_C$	Σ	$\hat{\Sigma}$	$\hat{\Sigma}_C$	Σ	$\hat{\Sigma}$	$\hat{\Sigma}_C$	Σ
					Homogeneity, n = 4					
25	50	44	28	37	1821	1189	1601	14	12	13
50	80	77	50	67	1974	1347	1807	25	24	20
125	178	149	98	138	2242	1540	2177	50	46	46
250	381	279	182	256	2591	1814	2586	97	94	91
375	730	520	328	418	2942	2067	3127	188	172	162
450	1262	845	531	670	3317	2376	3613	292	278	250
475	1759	1024	677	848	3595	2537	4032	400	364	311
					Homogeneity, n = 8					
25	b	282	164	191	2965	2070	2170	32	28	27
50	b	371	225	271	3240	2215	2418	45	39	38
125	b	664	388	416	3602	2447	2895	78	65	60
250	b	1057	630	621	4042	2816	3450	132	108	92
375	b	1680	933	907	4532	3212	4150	215	166	131
450	b	2706	1285	1199	4989	3576	4594	348	248	184
475	b	3199	1495	1386	5368	3739	4922	420	290	234

[a] All entries to be divided by 100.
[b] Not applicable due to the singularity of $\boldsymbol{S}$.

and the symmetry test as well as for both $n = 4$ and $n = 8$, the table contains quartiles: the 125th, 250th, and 375th values in ascending order, to which the 25th and 50th (both from the bottom and from the top) are added in order to capture the tails in more detail. As in Table E.3, the specifications of the disturbance covariance matrix are $\hat{\Sigma}$, $\hat{\Sigma}_C$ and the true Σ, but the least-squares residual moment matrix S is added in the case of the numerator. The highlights of Table E.4 can be summarized in three points:

(1) A comparison of the quantiles in the last three columns shows that the use of $\hat{\Sigma}_C$ rather than $\hat{\Sigma}$ tends to push the distribution of the F ratio in the direction of that of the ratio based on the true Σ. The case of the symmetry test for $n = 4$ does not quite conform to this rule, but the three distributions are rather close to each other in this case.

(2) The quantiles of the numerator based on $\hat{\Sigma}_C$ are all below those of

	Numerator				Denominator			F ratio		
	S	$\hat{\Sigma}$	$\hat{\Sigma}_C$	Σ	$\hat{\Sigma}$	$\hat{\Sigma}_C$	Σ	$\hat{\Sigma}$	$\hat{\Sigma}_C$	Σ
					Symmetry, $n = 4$					
25	38	47	26	35	3245	2006	1834	12	11	11
50	67	82	45	59	3315	2121	2049	20	18	19
125	138	156	93	125	3570	2299	2461	40	35	41
250	255	304	182	224	3907	2545	2912	80	71	79
375	463	584	323	392	4204	2755	3483	143	127	136
450	815	1005	554	638	4562	2965	4022	247	219	239
475	1071	1236	700	831	4736	3104	4416	323	296	302
					Symmetry, $n = 8$					
25	2544	2889	1287	1136	6125	3083	2738	76	59	49
50	3261	3664	1458	1291	6370	3305	2947	95	68	58
125	4965	4739	1841	1593	6848	3555	3554	128	91	73
250	8256	6256	2343	2001	7432	3997	4191	166	118	96
375	17468	8050	2978	2441	7950	4364	4792	223	157	127
450	45677	10509	3667	2882	8528	4683	5487	297	200	155
475	73403	12145	4152	3254	8924	4933	5772	355	232	174

the numerator based on $\hat{\Sigma}$. This also holds for the quantiles of the denominators based on $\hat{\Sigma}_C$ and $\hat{\Sigma}$. Obviously, this results from the positive semi-definiteness of the matrix on the left in (D.12), and it implies that the F ratio based on $\hat{\Sigma}_C$ is obtained from that based on $\hat{\Sigma}$ by shrinking both the numerator and the denominator. Note that the numerator and the denominator of the F ratio based on $\hat{\Sigma}_C$ do not have the standard χ^2 distributions. The only reason why the F test based on $\hat{\Sigma}_C$ performs as well as it does is that the F ratio involves Σ only up to a multiplicative scalar.

(3) The first column confirms the problems with the asymptotic χ^2 test based on $\boldsymbol{S}$. The quantiles of the symmetry test statistic for $n = 4$ are not excessive, but those for $n = 8$ are, which agrees with Meisner's (1979a) result described in Section 3.4.

In (E.6) to (E.8) we presented corrected and uncorrected squared ME canonical correlation coefficients for the observed data. When these values are used in the F test of homogeneity for $n = 8$, we obtain a ratio of .84 using $\hat{\Sigma}$ and .58 using $\hat{\Sigma}_C$, neither of which suggests that homogeneity should be rejected. [Recall from the discussion following (A.26) that the test based on $\boldsymbol{S}$ could not be performed.] For $n = 4$, the F ratio of the homogeneity test equals 1.56 based on $\hat{\Sigma}$ and 1.83 based on $\hat{\Sigma}_C$, and that of the symmetry test given homogeneity is 1.22 based on $\hat{\Sigma}$ and 1.06 based on $\hat{\Sigma}_C$; none of these four ratios is significant. Also for $n = 4$, the numerator test based on $\boldsymbol{S}$ yields 5.25 for homogeneity and 3.74 for symmetry given homogeneity, neither of which is significant for $\chi^2(3)$ at conventional standards. The F test for symmetry (given homogeneity) for $n = 8$ yields a ratio 4.08 based on $\hat{\Sigma}$ and 2.91 based on $\hat{\Sigma}_C$. Since the one percent significance limit of $F(21, 42)$ is 2.33, this suggests that symmetry should be rejected for $n = 8$. (Another argument in favor of this conclusion is that both 4.08 and 2.91 are exceeded by only one of the 500 simulated F ratios based on $\hat{\Sigma}$ and $\hat{\Sigma}_C$, respectively.) Of course, this negative result has no implications for the approach followed in Sections 3.5 and 3.6, since the specification used here involves constant Slutsky coefficients.

Symmetry-Constrained Coefficient Estimates

The best linear unbiased symmetry-constrained coefficient estimator is given in (A.24) and its covariance matrix is shown in (A.25). Both expressions involve the unknown matrix Σ. The standard procedure amounts to replacing Σ by S of (A.18). The coefficient estimator then takes the form

$$\hat{\beta} - C(S)R'[RC(S)R']^{-1}R\hat{\beta} \tag{E.11}$$

and its standard errors are computed by taking square roots of the diagonal elements of the matrix

$$C(S) - C(S)R'[RC(S)R']^{-1}RC(S) \tag{E.12}$$

Obviously, it is also possible to substitute $\hat{\Sigma}$ or $\hat{\Sigma}_C$ for the true Σ. The simulation experiments discussed in the previous subsection include symmetry-constrained estimation based on S, $\hat{\Sigma}$, $\hat{\Sigma}_C$ and the true Σ for both $n = 4$ and $n = 8$. The results are shown in Table E.5. The true values of the coefficients in the first column are reproduced from Tables E.1 and E.2. The columns under Bias provide the estimated bias, computed as the average of the estimates (E.11) over 500 trials minus the true value (similarly for $\hat{\Sigma}$, $\hat{\Sigma}_C$, Σ). The bias columns are followed by RMSE columns; these contain root-mean-square errors around the true value over the 500 trials. It is evident from Table E.5 that bias is not much of a problem in this case, the estimated bias values being small in absolute value relative to the corresponding RMSE, which should be contrasted with the results shown in Table D.1 for canonical correlation coefficients. However, there is a problem with respect to the RMSEs of the estimates based on S, because they tend to be larger than the corresponding RMSEs based on Σ, particularly for $n = 8$. This matter is pursued for $n = 8$ in the first column of Table E.6, which contains the ratio of the RMSE based on Σ to the RMSE based on S for each of the 35 coefficients, followed by analogous ratios for $\hat{\Sigma}$ and $\hat{\Sigma}_C$ (rather than S) in the next two columns. The ratios in these three columns clearly indicate that the efficiency of the symmetry-constrained estimation procedure increases when we use $\hat{\Sigma}$ rather than S, and again when we use $\hat{\Sigma}_C$ rather than Σ.

Another matter of interest is whether the standard errors of the symmetry-constrained estimates provide an adequate picture of the variability of these estimates around their true values. This question is answered by the RMSSEs of Table E.5: the root-mean-square standard errors, computed by averaging the diagonal elements of the matrices (A.25) and (E.12) over the 500 trials (similarly for $\hat{\Sigma}$ and $\hat{\Sigma}_C$) and taking square roots of these averages. The RMSSEs of the estimates based on S tend to be smaller than the corresponding RMSEs, particularly for $n = 8$, thus suggesting that the standard errors tend to understate the variability

Table E.5
Symmetry-constrained estimation, 500 trials[a]

	True value	S			$\hat{\Sigma}$			$\hat{\Sigma}_C$			Σ		
		Bias	RMSE	RMSSE	Bias	RMSE	RMSSE	Bias	RMSE	RMSSE	Bias	RMSE	RMSSE
Coefficients β_i for n = 4													
$i = 1$	−1526	− 9	183	173	− 7	181	175	− 8	180	264	−10	181	179
$i = 2$	42	− 3	76	72	− 2	76	61	− 3	77	72	− 2	74	74
$i = 3$	527	9	137	127	7	139	111	7	139	151	6	134	134
Diagonal Slutsky coefficients π_{ii} for n = 4													
$i = 1$	−1061	−23	696	628	−14	687	617	−14	680	958	−20	673	664
$i = 2$	− 502	5	193	172	5	188	143	8	181	165	5	179	181
$i = 3$	−1150	− 5	530	466	− 7	525	395	−13	526	526	1	503	498
Off-diagonal Slutsky coefficients π_{ij} for n = 4													
$i = 1,\ j = 2$	121	−13	261	233	−12	259	206	−18	263	260	−11	243	251
$i = 1,\ j = 3$	336	16	487	425	11	483	387	14	494	573	4	470	461
$i = 2,\ j = 3$	136	0	224	196	0	219	164	3	218	200	1	207	212
Coefficients β_i for n = 8													
$i = 1$	−1526	10	284	174	54	236	153	32	235	280	15	209	218
$i = 2$	42	3	121	70	− 6	96	53	− 4	89	76	1	83	86
$i = 3$	261	4	126	118	4	123	81	2	122	118	4	117	124
$i = 4$	266	− 2	232	106	−27	172	87	− 6	162	130	− 5	151	150
$i = 5$	258	− 2	75	48	− 7	59	39	− 6	59	67	− 3	53	58
$i = 6$	210	8	183	130	3	159	93	2	158	132	3	147	147
$i = 7$	243	− 8	157	84	−33	126	70	−24	123	102	− 7	109	112

Diagonal Slutsky coefficients π_{ii} for $n = 8$

$i = 1$	−1061	−10	1069	643	119	893	554	64	864	1097	47	816	823
$i = 2$	− 502	0	241	133	6	210	98	11	185	138	−12	173	174
$i = 3$	− 785	− 2	321	285	9	308	187	−22	302	269	− 1	285	304
$i = 4$	− 546	42	806	305	30	582	257	75	509	376	42	483	480
$i = 5$	− 492	4	100	60	5	89	51	13	86	89	6	77	77
$i = 6$	− 580	13	534	399	10	498	270	−36	474	362	0	458	459
$i = 7$	− 713	2	311	151	45	241	127	37	229	186	3	207	211

Off-diagonal Slutsky coefficients π_{ij} for $n = 8$

$i = 1,\ j = 2$	121	12	386	198	−13	312	161	−17	307	257	− 3	273	270
$i = 1,\ j = 3$	203	14	383	279	18	366	218	23	386	401	3	337	324
$i = 1,\ j = 4$	133	7	785	335	−67	568	282	−27	538	451	−30	509	495
$i = 1,\ j = 5$	119	− 1	250	137	−18	204	119	−12	194	231	−13	176	182
$i = 1,\ j = 6$	142	17	564	359	− 1	499	282	5	518	473	4	441	450
$i = 1,\ j = 7$	181	−18	457	211	−93	352	187	−53	338	298	− 9	303	309
$i = 2,\ j = 3$	82	− 4	177	126	− 5	162	86	− 1	147	118	1	143	145
$i = 2,\ j = 4$	54	− 6	306	132	13	240	105	5	206	152	3	199	196
$i = 2,\ j = 5$	48	− 2	114	60	− 2	99	48	− 7	91	75	1	82	83
$i = 2,\ j = 6$	58	− 8	262	161	− 7	226	113	6	207	155	5	202	201
$i = 2,\ j = 7$	73	0	214	97	16	164	79	11	145	116	− 2	137	138
$i = 3,\ j = 4$	90	−14	245	170	−16	219	116	− 6	202	162	− 4	198	195
$i = 3,\ j = 5$	80	− 2	120	84	− 2	109	63	− 2	106	105	− 1	96	98
$i = 3,\ j = 6$	96	27	284	229	29	270	153	22	260	211	22	260	260
$i = 3,\ j = 7$	123	1	199	139	0	178	96	2	166	134	− 3	161	156
$i = 4,\ j = 5$	53	−11	202	88	0	145	73	0	131	112	1	122	127
$i = 4,\ j = 6$	63	−26	417	222	−19	325	162	4	293	231	− 7	292	293
$i = 4,\ j = 7$	80	− 2	410	149	43	291	134	0	264	199	− 6	244	244
$i = 5,\ j = 6$	56	9	181	109	13	163	84	13	159	132	8	137	141
$i = 5,\ j = 7$	72	3	134	69	11	100	55	9	94	85	2	89	93
$i = 6,\ j = 7$	86	−17	282	162	−13	232	121	− 9	214	173	− 8	205	209

[a] All entries to be divided by 10^4.

of these estimates. The last four columns of Table E.6 contain (for $n = 8$) the ratio of the RMSSE to the corresponding RMSE for each of the four specifications of the disturbance covariance matrix. When the true Σ is used, these ratios are tightly distributed around 1, as they should. When S is used, all ratios are less than 1 and many are substantially less than 1. The use of $\hat{\Sigma}_C$ yields a considerable improvement over that of S and $\hat{\Sigma}$.

The RMSEs of Table E.5 also provide some evidence on the virtues and vices of aggregation over goods. Since the aggregation of the eight goods

Table E.6
Ratios of RMSEs and RMSSEs of symmetry-constrained estimates

	Ratio of RMSE based on true Σ to RMSE based on			Ratio of RMSSE to RMSE			
	S	$\hat{\Sigma}$	$\hat{\Sigma}_c$	S	$\hat{\Sigma}$	$\hat{\Sigma}_c$	Σ
			Coefficients β_i				
$i = 1$	.74	.89	.89	.61	.65	1.19	1.04
$i = 2$	.69	.87	.93	.58	.55	.85	1.04
$i = 3$	.93	.95	.96	.93	.66	.97	1.06
$i = 4$	.65	.88	.93	.46	.51	.80	.99
$i = 5$	.71	.89	.90	.64	.65	1.15	1.09
$i = 6$	.80	.92	.93	.71	.59	.83	1.00
$i = 7$	.70	.86	.88	.54	.55	.83	1.03
			Diagonal Slutsky Coefficients π_{ii}				
$i = 1$	.76	.91	.94	.60	.62	1.27	1.01
$i = 2$	.72	.82	.93	.55	.47	.75	1.01
$i = 3$	.89	.92	.94	.89	.61	.89	1.07
$i = 4$	.60	.83	.95	.38	.44	.74	.99
$i = 5$	.76	.86	.89	.60	.57	1.04	1.00
$i = 6$	.86	.92	.97	.75	.54	.77	1.00
$i = 7$	.66	.86	.90	.49	.53	.81	1.02

to the four groups of goods leaves Food ($i = 1$) and Clothing ($i = 2$) unchanged, the coefficients β_1, β_2, π_{11}, π_{22} and π_{12} have the same interpretation for $n = 4$ as they have under $n = 8$. Table E.7 reproduces the RMSEs of the estimates of these five coefficients under the four specifications of the disturbance covariance matrix. With only one exception out of 20 cases, the RMSEs increase when the coefficients are computed from an eight-equation system rather than a four-equation system, thus suggesting that aggregation over goods is desirable. Clearly, a much more

	Ratio of RMSE based on true Σ to RMSE based on			Ratio of RMSSE to RMSE			
	S	$\hat{\Sigma}$	$\hat{\Sigma}_c$	S	$\hat{\Sigma}$	$\hat{\Sigma}_c$	Σ
	Off-diagonal Slutsky Coefficients π_{ij}						
$i = 1, \quad j = 2$	.71	.88	.89	.51	.52	.84	.99
$i = 1, \quad j = 3$	.88	.92	.87	.73	.60	1.04	.96
$i = 1, \quad j = 4$	.65	.90	.95	.43	.50	.84	.97
$i = 1, \quad j = 5$	.70	.86	.90	.55	.59	1.19	1.04
$i = 1, \quad j = 6$	.78	.88	.85	.64	.57	.91	1.02
$i = 1, \quad j = 7$	.66	.86	.89	.46	.53	.88	1.02
$i = 2, \quad j = 3$	.81	.89	.97	.71	.53	.80	1.01
$i = 2, \quad j = 4$	.65	.83	.97	.43	.44	.74	.98
$i = 2, \quad j = 5$	.72	.83	.90	.53	.49	.82	1.02
$i = 2, \quad j = 6$	.77	.89	.98	.62	.50	.75	1.00
$i = 2, \quad j = 7$	.64	.83	.94	.45	.48	.80	1.01
$i = 3, \quad j = 4$	.81	.91	.98	.69	.53	.80	.98
$i = 3, \quad j = 5$	.80	.88	.91	.70	.57	1.00	1.02
$i = 3, \quad j = 6$	.92	.96	1.00	.80	.56	.81	1.00
$i = 3, \quad j = 7$	.81	.90	.97	.70	.54	.80	.98
$i = 4, \quad j = 5$	.60	.84	.93	.43	.50	.86	1.04
$i = 4, \quad j = 6$	.70	.90	1.00	.53	.50	.79	1.00
$i = 4, \quad j = 7$	.60	.84	.92	.36	.46	.75	1.00
$i = 5, \quad j = 6$	.76	.84	.87	.60	.52	.83	1.03
$i = 5, \quad j = 7$	.66	.88	.94	.52	.55	.90	1.05
$i = 6, \quad j = 7$	.72	.88	.96	.57	.52	.81	1.02
	Quartiles						
Lower	.66	.86	.90	.49	.50	.80	.99
Median	.72	.88	.93	.58	.53	.83	1.01
Upper	.80	.90	.96	.70	.57	.91	1.03

extensive analysis is needed before this conclusion can be firmly made, but the results summarized in Table E.7 are sufficiently suggestive to indicate that such an analysis is worthwhile.

Conclusions

Simulation experiments cannot be conclusive, but they can be quite valuable in guiding our intuition. The F test for homogeneity and symmetry based on $\hat{\Sigma}_C$ is not perfect, nor have we presented evidence on its power. Yet, the test has several appealing virtues, especially that $\hat{\Sigma}_C$ is derived from a sound principle of density estimation, viz., that of maximizing our ignorance subject to the constraint of what we know (the maximum entropy principle).

Table E.7
RMSEs at different levels of aggregation[a]

Level of aggregation	S	$\hat{\Sigma}$	$\hat{\Sigma}_C$	Σ
		Coefficient β_1		
$n = 4$	183	181	180	181
$n = 8$	284	236	235	209
		Coefficient β_2		
$n = 4$	76	76	77	74
$n = 8$	121	96	89	83
		Diagonal Slutsky coefficient π_{11}		
$n = 4$	696	687	680	673
$n = 8$	1069	893	864	816
		Diagonal Slutsky coefficient π_{22}		
$n = 4$	193	188	181	179
$n = 8$	241	210	185	173
		Off-diagonal Slutsky coefficient π_{12}		
$n = 4$	261	259	263	243
$n = 8$	386	312	307	273

[a] All entries to be divided by 10^4.

The evidence shown in Table E.3 suggests that when the number of equations is on the order of one-half the number of observations, the best way to test at the 5 percent significance level is to use the 1 percent significance point of the relevant F distribution. This discrepancy illustrates the imperfection of the test based on $\hat{\Sigma}_C$, but it is conceivable that the discrepancy can be reduced by a better correction of the maximum entropy canonical correlation coefficients than that which is described in Appendix D. Before passing a negative verdict on the test because of this imperfection, it is appropriate to recognize that the procedure works even when the conventional test statistic (based on $\boldsymbol{S}$ as an estimate of Σ) fails to exist due to the singularity of a matrix whose inverse is needed.

Our conclusions with respect to symmetry-constrained estimation are similar. When the number of equations is about one-half the number of observations, the root-mean-square errors (RMSEs) of the constrained estimates based on $\boldsymbol{S}$ are substantially larger than those based on the true Σ, whereas the discrepancies between the RMSEs of the estimates based on $\hat{\Sigma}_C$ and those based on Σ are much smaller. Equally importantly, the standard errors of the estimates based on $\boldsymbol{S}$ underestimate their RMSEs substantially, whereas the standard errors of the estimates based on $\hat{\Sigma}_C$ are in much better agreement with the corresponding RMSEs. This does not mean that the symmetry-constrained estimation procedure based on $\hat{\Sigma}_C$ is perfect. The simulation experiment clearly indicates that it is better to use the true Σ if this matrix is known. In particular, the standard errors of the estimates based on $\hat{\Sigma}_C$ are on the average still too low relative to the corresponding RMSEs, and correcting these standard errors by raising them by about 20 percent would yield a better agreement with the RMSEs. Such an upward correction implies that the estimates are less accurate than they appear to be, which is entirely in agreement with the use of 1 percent points for a 5 percent significance level that was suggested in the previous paragraph. Again, it is conceivable that the size of such a correction can be reduced when we have a better correction of the maximum entropy canonical correlation coefficients.

Bibliography

Anderson, T.W. (1958). *An Introduction to Multivariate Statistical Analysis.* New York: John Wiley and Sons.

Balassa, B. (1964). "The Purchasing Power Parity Doctrine: A Reappraisal." *Journal of Political Economy*, 72, pp. 584–596.

Barnett, W.A. (1979). "Theoretical Foundations for the Rotterdam Model." *Review of Economic Studies*, 46, pp. 109–130.

Barnett, W.A. (1981). *Consumer Demand and Labor Supply.* Amsterdam: North-Holland Publishing Company.

Barten, A.P. (1964). "Consumer Demand Functions under Conditions of Almost Additive Preferences." *Econometrica*, 32, pp. 1–38.

Barten, A.P. (1969). "Maximum Likelihood Estimation of a Complete System of Demand Equations." *European Economic Review*, 1, pp. 7–73.

Bortkiewicz, L. von (1923). "Zweck und Struktur einer Preisindexzahl (Erster Artikel)." *Nordisk Statistisk Tidskrift*, 2, pp. 369–408.

Byron, R.P. (1970). "The Restricted Aitken Estimation of Sets of Demand Equations." *Econometrica*, 39, pp. 816–830.

Christensen, L.R., Jorgenson, D.W., and Lau, L.J. (1975). "Transcendental Logarithmic Utility Functions." *American Economic Review*, 65, pp. 367–383.

Clements, K.W., and Izan, H.Y. (1981). "A Note on Estimating Divisia Index Numbers." *International Economic Review*, forthcoming.

Clements, K.W., and Johnson, L.W. (1980). "Disparities in Income Elasticities by Ethnic Origin." Discussion Paper, Department of Economics, Macquarie University.

Clements, K.W., and Meisner, J.F. (1979). "Measurement Error and the Demand for Money in Australia." *Economics Letters*, 4, pp. 337–340.

Clements, K.W., and Nguyen, P. (1980a). "Money Demand, Consumer Demand and Relative Prices in Australia." *Economic Record*, 56, pp. 338–346.

Clements, K.W., and Nguyen, P. (1980b). "Inflation and Relative Prices: The Australian Experience." Research Discussion Paper 8007, Reserve Bank of Australia, Sydney.

Clements, K.W., Suhm, F.E., and Theil, H. (1979). "A Cross-Country Tabulation of Income Elasticities of Demand." *Economics Letters*, 3, pp. 199–202.

Clements, K.W., and Theil, H. (1979). "A Cross-Country Analysis of Consumption Patterns." Report 7924 of the Center for Mathematical Studies in Business and Economics, The University of Chicago.

Conway, D., and Theil, H. (1980). "The Maximum Entropy Moment Matrix with Missing Values." *Economics Letters*, 5, pp. 319–322.

Cramer, J.S. (1973). "The Interaction of Income and Price in Consumer Demand." *International Economic Review*, 14, pp. 351–363.

Deaton, A.S. (1974). "The Analysis of Consumer Demand in the United Kingdom." *Econometrica*, 42, pp. 341–367.

Deaton, A.S. (1975). *Models and Projections of Demand in Post-war Britain.* London: Chapman and Hall.

Deaton, A.S. (1981, ed.). *Essays in the Theory and Measurement of Consumer Behaviour.* Cambridge, England: Cambridge University Press.

Deaton, A.S., and Muellbauer, J. (1980a). *Economics and Consumer Behavior.* Cambridge, England: Cambridge University Press.

Deaton, A.S., and Muellbauer, J. (1980b). "An Almost Ideal Demand System." *American Economic Review*, 70, pp. 312–326.

Divisia, F. (1925). "L'Indice Monétaire et la Théorie de la Monnaie." *Revue d'Economie Politique*, 39, pp. 980–1008.

Fellner, W. (1967). "Operational Utility: The Theoretical Background and a Measurement." In *Ten Economic Studies in the Tradition of Irving Fisher*, pp. 39–74. New York: John Wiley and Sons.

Fiebig, D.G. (1980). "Maximum Entropy Canonical Coefficients." *Economics Letters*, 6, pp. 345–348.

Fiebig, D.G. (1981a). "Evidence on the Maximum Entropy Covariance Matrix." Modelling Research Group Working Paper, Department of Economics, University of Southern California.

Fiebig, D.G. (1981b). Personal communication.

Frisch, R. (1932). *New Methods of Measuring Marginal Utility.* Tübingen: J.C.B. Mohr.

Frisch, R. (1959). "A Complete Scheme for Computing All Direct and Cross Demand Elasticities in a Model with Many Sectors." *Econometrica*, 27, pp. 177–196.

Griliches, Z. (1971, ed.). *Price Indexes and Quality Change.* Cambridge, Mass.: Harvard University Press.

Haavelmo, T. (1943). "The Statistical Implications of a System of Simultaneous Equations." *Econometrica*, 11, pp. 1–12.

Haavelmo, T. (1944). "The Probability Approach in Econometrics." Supplement to *Econometrica*, 12.

Haque, N. ul, and Meisner, J.F. (1980). "The Expected Ridge and Shrinkage of the Maximum Entropy Variance under Normality." *Economics Letters*, 5, pp. 241–244.

Hicks, J.R., and Allen, R.G.D. (1934). "A Reconsideration of the Theory of Value." *Economica*, New Series, 1, pp. 52–76, 196–219.

Hooper, J.W. (1959). "Simultaneous Equations and Canonical Correlation Theory." *Econometrica*, 27, pp. 245–256.

Houthakker, H.S. (1953). "Compensated Changes in Quantities and Qualities Consumed." *Review of Economic Studies*, 19, pp. 155–164.

Houthakker, H.S. (1957). "An International Comparison of Household Expenditure Patterns, Commemorating the Centenary of Engel's Law." *Econometrica*, 25, pp. 532–551.

Houthakker, H.S. (1960a). "The Influence of Prices and Incomes on Household Expenditures." *Bulletin de l'Institut International de Statistique*, 37, pp. 9–22.

Houthakker, H.S. (1960b). "Additive Preferences." *Econometrica*, 28, pp. 244–257; errata, 30, (1962), p. 633.

Houthakker, H.S. (1961). "An International Comparison of Personal Savings." *Bulletin de l'Institut International de Statistique*, 38/2, pp. 55–69.

Houthakker, H.S. (1963). "Some Problems in the International Comparison of Consumption Patterns." In *Le Rôle et l'Evaluation des Besoins de Biens de Consommation* (R. Mossé, ed.), pp. 89–102. Paris: Centre National de Recherche Scientifique.

Houthakker, H.S. (1965). "New Evidence on Demand Elasticities." *Econometrica*, 33, pp. 277–288.

Isenman, P. (1979). "Inter-country Comparison of 'Real' (PPP) Incomes: Revised Estimates and Unresolved Questions." World Bank Staff Working Paper No. 358.

Izan, H.Y., and Clements, K.W. (1979). "A Cross-Cross-Section Analysis of Consumption Patterns." *Economics Letters*, 4, pp. 83–86.

Judge, G.G., Griffiths, W.E., Hill, R.C., and Lee, T.–C. (1980). *The Theory and Practice of Econometrics.* New York: John Wiley and Sons.

Kagan, A.M., Linnik, Y.V., and Rao, C.R. (1973). *Characterization Problems in Mathematical Statistics.* New York: John Wiley and Sons.

Kendall, M.G., and Stuart, A. (1963). *The Advanced Theory of Statistics.* Vol. 1, second edition. London: Charles Griffin and Co.

Klein, L.R., and Rubin, H. (1948). "A Constant-Utility Index of the Cost of Living." *Review of Economic Studies*, 15, pp. 84–87.

Klevmarken, A. (1975). "On the Small-Sample Properties of Aitken-Type Estimators and Test Statistics Applied to Seemingly Unrelated Regressions." *The 1975 Business and Economic Statistics Session Proceedings of the American Statistical Association*, pp. 362–367.

Kravis, I.B., Heston, A.W., and Summers, R. (1978). *International Comparisons of Real Product and Purchasing Power.* Baltimore, Md.: The Johns Hopkins University Press.

Kravis, I.B., Kenessey, Z., Heston, A.W., and Summers, R. (1975). *A System of International Comparisons of Gross Product and Purchasing Power.* Baltimore, Md.: The Johns Hopkins University Press.

Laitinen, K. (1978). "Why Is Demand Homogeneity So Often Rejected?" *Economics Letters*, 1, pp. 187–191.

Laitinen, K. (1980). *A Theory of the Multiproduct Firm.* Amsterdam: North-Holland Publishing Company.

Lev, B., and Theil, H. (1978). "A Maximum Entropy Approach to the Choice of Asset Depreciation." *Journal of Accounting Research*, 16, pp. 286–293.

Lluch, C. (1971). "Consumer Demand Functions, Spain, 1958–1964." *European Economic Review*, 2, pp. 277–302.

Lluch, C., Powell, A.A., and Williams, R.A. (1977). *Patterns in Household Demand and Saving.* Oxford: Oxford University Press.

Meisner, J.F. (1979a). "The Sad Fate of the Asymptotic Slutsky Symmetry Test for Large Systems." *Economics Letters*, 2, pp. 231–233.

Meisner, J.F. (1979b). "Alternative Demand Models for Close Substitutes." *Economics Letters*, 3, pp. 77–80.

Meisner, J.F. (1979c). "Divisia Moments of U.S. Industry, 1947–1978." *Economics Letters*, 4, 239–242.

Meisner, J.F. (1980a). "A Risk Evaluation of the Maximum Entropy Correlation Coefficients." *Economics Letters*, 5, pp. 335–338.

Meisner, J.F. (1980b). "Further Evidence on LIML/ME Estimates." *Economics Letters*, 6, pp. 23–27.

Meisner, J.F., and Clements, K.W. (1979). "Specific Complements and the Demand for Money in Australia." *Economics Letters*, 3, pp. 207–210.

Muellbauer, J. (1975). "Aggregation, Income Distribution and Consumer Demand." *Review of Economic Studies*, 42, pp. 525–543.

O'Brien, P.C. (1980). "The Quartiles of the Maximum Entropy Distribution." *Economics Letters*, 6, pp. 49–52.

Phlips, L. (1974). *Applied Consumption Analysis.* Amsterdam: North-Holland Publishing Company.

Powell, A.A. (1974). *Empirical Analytics of Demand Systems.* Lexington, Mass.: D.C. Heath and Company.

Russell, R.R. (1967). "International Disparities in Income Elasticities." *Review of Economics and Statistics*, 49, pp. 579–582.

Shannon, C.E. (1948). "A Mathematical Theory of Communication." *Bell System Technical Journal*, 27, pp. 379–423, 623–656.

Solari, L. (1971). *Théorie des Choix et Fonctions de Consommation Semi-agrégées.* Geneva: Librairie Droz.

Srivastava, J.N., and Zaatar, M.K. (1973). "A Monte Carlo Comparison of Four Estimators of the Dispersion Matrix of a Bivariate Normal Population." *Journal of the American Statistical Association*, 68, pp. 180–183.

Stern, N. (1977). "The Marginal Valuation of Income." In *Studies in Modern Economic Analysis* (M.J. Artis and A.R. Nobay, eds.), pp. 209–257. Oxford: Basil Blackwell.

Stone, R. (1954). "Linear Expenditure Systems and Demand Analysis: An Application to the Pattern of British Demand." *Economic Journal*, 64, pp. 511–527.

Suhm, F.E. (1979a). "A Cross-Country Consumption Comparison Based on Divisia Variances and Covariances." *Economics Letters*, 3, pp. 89–96.

Suhm, F.E. (1979b). "A Cross-Country Analysis of Divisia Covariances of Prices and Quantities Consumed." *Economics Letters*, 3, pp. 287–291.

Suhm, F.E. (1979c). "A Cross-Country Analysis of Divisia Variances of Quantities and Budget Shares." *Economics Letters*, 3, pp. 293–298.

Suhm, F.E. (1979d). "Determinants of Cross-Country Consumption Differences Other than the Real Income Difference." *Economics Letters*, 4, pp. 87–91.

Suhm, F.E., and Theil, H. (1979). "Cross-Country Variation in the Quality of Consumption." *Economics Letters*, 3, pp. 391–395.

Theil, H. (1953). "Qualities, Prices and Budget Enquiries." *Review of Economic Studies*, 19, 129–147.

Theil, H. (1967). *Economics and Information Theory.* Amsterdam: North-Holland Publishing Company.

Theil, H. (1971). *Principles of Econometrics.* New York: John Wiley and Sons.

Theil, H. (1975–76). *Theory and Measurement of Consumer Demand.* Two volumes. Amsterdam: North-Holland Publishing Company.

Theil, H. (1979a). "Equicorrelated Substitutes and Nasse's Extension of the Linear Expenditure System." *Economics Letters*, 3, pp. 81–84.

Theil, H. (1979b). "The Effect of Measurement Errors on the Estimation of Demand Systems." *Economics Letters*, 3, pp. 373–376.

Theil, H. (1980a). *The System-Wide Approach to Microeconomics.* Chicago: University of Chicago Press.

Theil, H. (1980b). "The Symmetric Maximum Entropy Distribution." *Economics Letters*, 6, pp. 53–57.

Theil, H. (1981). "The Maximum Entropy Distribution: Second Progress Report." Report 8120 of the Center for Mathematical Studies in Business and Economics, The University of Chicago. [A revised version will appear in the Discussion Paper series of the Center for Econometrics and Decision Sciences (CEDS) of the University of Florida.]

Theil, H., and Brooks, R.B. (1970–71). "How Does the Marginal Utility of Income Change When Real Income Changes?" *European Economic Review*, 2, pp. 218–240.

Theil, H., and Fiebig, D.G. (1981). "A Maximum Entropy Approach to the Specification of Distributed Lags." *Economics Letters*, forthcoming.

Theil, H., and Laitinen, K. (1980). "Singular Moment Matrices in Applied Econometrics." In *Multivariate Analysis-V* (P.R. Krishnaiah, ed.), pp. 629–649. Amsterdam: North-Holland Publishing Company.

Theil, H., and Laitinen, K. (1981). "The Independence Transformation: A Review and Some Further Explorations." In *Essays in the Theory and Measurement of Consumer Behaviour* (A. Deaton, ed.), pp. 73–112. Cambridge, England: Cambridge University Press.

Theil, H., and Meisner, J.F. (1980). "Simultaneous Equation Estimation Based on Maximum Entropy Moments." *Economics Letters*, 5, pp. 339–344.

Theil, H., and O'Brien, P.C. (1980). "The Median of the Maximum Entropy Distribution." *Economics Letters*, 5, pp. 345–347.

Theil, H., Suhm, F.E., and Meisner, J.F. (1980). "Statistical Inference in Cross-Country Demand Systems." *Economics Letters*, 5, pp. 383–387.

Tinbergen, J. (1939). *Statistical Testing of Business Cycle Theories.* Vol. 1, *A Method and Its Application to Investment Activity.* Vol. 2, *Business Cycles in the United States of America, 1919–1932.* Geneva: League of Nations.

Voltaire, K., and Stack, E.J. (1980). "A Divisia Version of the Country-Product-Dummy Method." *Economics Letters*, 5, pp. 97–99.

Von Neumann, J., and Morgenstern, O. (1947). *Theory of Games and Economic Behavior.* Second edition (first edition, 1944). Princeton: Princeton University Press.

Working, H. (1943). "Statistical Laws of Family Expenditure." *Journal of the American Statistical Association*, 38, pp. 43–56.

INDEX